MW00681978

# Write Your Way to a Higher GPA

# Write Your Way to a Higher GPA

## How to Dramatically Boost Your GPA Simply by Sharpening Your Writing Skills

Randall S. Hansen, Ph.D.
and Katharine Hansen

Ten Speed Press
Berkeley, California

TEN SPEED PRESS
Post Office Box 7123
Berkeley, California 94707

Distributed in Australia by E. J. Dwyer Pty. Ltd., in Canada by Publishers Group West, in New Zealand by Tandem Press, in South Africa by Real Books, in Singapore and Malaysia by Berkeley Books, and in the United Kingdom and Europe by Airlift Books.

Interior design by Tasha Hall
Cover design by Cale Burr
Cover illustration by David Uttal

Library of Congress Cataloging-in-Publication Data:
    Hansen, Randall S.
        Write your way to a higher GPA:how to dramatically boost your GPA simply by sharpening your writing skills/Randall S. Hansen and Katharine Hansen.
            p.    cm.
        Includes bibliographical references and index.
        ISBN 0-89815-903-2
        1. English language—Rhetoric—Self-instruction—Data processing. 2. English language—Grammar—Self-instruction—Data processing. 3. Interdisciplinary approach in education. 4. Internet (Computer network) 5. Academic writing. 6. Study skills. I. Hansen, Katharine. II. Title.
        PE1408.H329   1997
        808'.042'0285—dc20                                    96-44857
                                                              CIP

First printing 1997
Printed in Canada

1 2 3 4 5–01 00 99 98 97

# CONTENTS

## ACKNOWLEDGMENTS

**The authors are deeply grateful** to the many people whose participation, support, and assistance brought this book to life. Specifically, the authors wish to acknowledge the Stetson University faculty who participated in a pretest of our writing survey and the 146 professors worldwide who participated in the final survey. The authors also want to acknowledge Stetson reference librarians David Everett and Sue Ryan for their excellent assistance, as well as the magnificent efforts of all reference librarians. Furthermore, the authors want to thank Stetson professors Jeff Horn and Paul Jerome Croce for sharing their thoughts and writing style handouts, and especially Monique Forte for her support and input in all areas of the book. The authors would also like to thank Jennifer McGrew, Jennifer Speck, and Nancy Kernan for providing superb clerical support, Mike (tink) Barker and the Writers On-Line Discussion Group, all of the students who have persevered through Randall's writing-intensive courses and have survived to tell about it, the staff and crew of Camp Winona, and, finally, the folks at Ten Speed Press.

Special acknowledgment goes to Oxford University Press for allowing us to reprint a portion of Peter Elbow's *Writing With Power,* and to *The Journal of Irreproducible Results* for allowing us to reprint Dr. Jerrold Zar's "An Owed to Spelling Checker."

# Introduction: What This Book Is and Is Not

**IF** YOU'RE READING THESE WORDS, YOU ARE PROBABLY ONE OF THE MANY COLLEGE STUDENTS WHO SHUDDER AT THE IDEA OF WRITING A PAPER. WHEN THE PROFESSOR HANDS OUT THE SYLLABUS, YOU CAN ALMOST HEAR THE COLLECTIVE SIGH OF RELIEF IF IT LISTS ONLY EXAMS AND NO WRITING ASSIGNMENTS. LIKE YOU, MOST COLLEGE STUDENTS WOULD RATHER STUDY FOR AN EXAM THAN WRITE A PAPER ANY DAY OF THE WEEK.

What these students don't know is that writing skills can be the ticket to better grades and greater academic success. This book explains how. It also explains how to overcome the terrible anxiety that grips most students at the thought of researching and writing a paper. We believe it is the most comprehensive and cutting-edge book of its kind in describing how to find and use state-of-the-art research technology, as well as how you can benefit enormously from employing technology in the writing process.

This book is designed to target the most common writing pitfalls that you face as a student. Any number of books are available that address writing style, punctuation, syntax, and grammar; in fact, we list some best examples of such books in chapter 8. *Write Your Way to a Higher GPA*, however, hones in on the mistakes that, according to a survey of college instructors, students make most often and that instructors are most likely to consider in the grading process.

It's no secret that college professors feel that student writing could stand considerable improvement. The anguish they experience as they grade student papers is nothing new. Edward Jenkinson wrote in the *Phi Delta Kappan* that a clay tablet of the early Sumerians—the people who gave the world writing— recorded the agonized complaints of a Sumerian teacher about the sudden drop-off in students' writing ability. What we've attempted to do is zero in on the student writing flaws that trouble your professors the most and most affect the way they grade you.

We surveyed 146 college professors in North America and beyond and across virtually all disciplines to learn what *they* believe students can do to improve grades on written work. This survey was posted on several academic/teaching-oriented Internet discussion lists, as well as on the World Wide Web. The specific advice we received from the professors surveyed appears throughout the book. Because the survey was anonymous, however, we can only identify the professors by their discipline and the college or university where they work by its size and type.

This book is not a textbook. Our aim was to write it in student-friendly language and offer inside tips that you'll rarely hear from your professors. We've also endeavored to provide invaluable information in concise, digestible bites that you can read on the fly. You probably won't read the book straight through but will consult specific sections as needed.

*Write Your Way to a Higher GPA* also teaches tricks for polishing your paper that are so subtle that your instructor won't know what hit him or her.

This book acquaints you with every kind of academic writing, tells the time-starved college student how to revise, and offers suggestions for additional ways to raise grades.

But all this good advice will be lost on you if you don't believe writing skills are important and can help you achieve academic success. Our job is to convince you. To begin with, the overwhelming majority—almost 80 percent—of instructors we surveyed said that writing skills are vitally important to academic success.

And if you're one of those students who says "phew" when the syllabus reveals only exams and no papers, what happens when those exams turn out to be essay tests? This book will teach you how to raise your grades on those exams simply by employing the principles of good writing—even if you study no harder and know the material no better than you do now.

Perhaps you've heard that no one cares about your grades once you leave the halls of academia. While that notion holds *some truth*, it is equally true that most potential employers *do* care about writing skills. They care so much that they bemoan the poor preparation of the entry-level pool of grads. In a labor force full of mediocre writers, someone who writes well is bound to stand out and succeed.

Even professors—three quarters of those we surveyed—believe writing skills are important to career success. Academicians and business people view writing skills as crucial, yet increasing numbers of these professionals note a steady erosion in the writing abilities of graduates. The summary of a study published in *Personnel Update* states: "Writing skills...of executives are shockingly low, indicating that schools and colleges dismally fail with at least two-thirds of the people who pass through the education pipeline coming out unable to write a simple letter."

In 1988 Lin Grensing reported in *Management World* magazine that 79 percent of surveyed executives cited writing as one of the most neglected skills in the business world, yet one of the most important to productivity. More recently, a 1992 survey of 402 companies reported by the Associated Press noted that executives identified writing as the most valued skill but said 80 percent of their employees at all levels need to improve. The number of workers needing improvement in writing skills was up 20 percent from results of the same survey in 1991. Results of a 1993 study by Olsten Corp., a placement agency, were almost identical: 80 percent of 443 employers surveyed said their workers needed training in writing skills.

The need for workers with writing skills will only increase. A 1991 report by the United States Labor Department noted that most future jobs will require writing skills.

OK, so we may have convinced you that you need writing skills to succeed in school and in your career...but why should you believe what we tell you about how to improve your writing? Randall Hansen is a professor of marketing whose courses are writing intensive. His students always groan when they see how much writing he requires in his classes, but they always thank him at the end of the semester because their writing has improved and they're less terrified of future writing assignments. Dr. Hansen has also conducted considerable research into Writing Across the Curriculum (an academic movement begun a few years ago that stresses the importance of writing in all disciplines) and using e-mail for writing assignments. Katharine Hansen's experience comes from the trenches of recently having been a student. Returning to college as an older student, she wrote dozens of A papers, won a full scholarship based on a writing portfolio, and graduated with a GPA of 3.87, which she attributes to her writing skills. And did we mention her twenty years as a successful writer and editor before returning to school?

Yes, you can raise your grades in other ways, such as learning better study, note-taking, test-taking, and time management skills. We truly believe, however, that this book can help you improve your grades even if you do nothing else but follow our advice for writing better papers.

"**Employers** say [writing] is the least developed skill they see in graduates. No matter what the field, [students] must learn to communicate effectively."

—a professor of natural resources conservation and management at Virginia Tech

**"While employed by NCR and IBM, I observed a strong correlation between writing skills and success. Technical knowledge matters for a first job, but promotions seem to be tied to written communication skills. I saw engineers canned because they couldn't write. MBAs had the least clear writing because they were too [verbose] and used too much meaningless jargon."**

—a professor of social studies at Michigan Technological University

**"The people from industry that I talked to said their greatest complaint in hiring new personnel was that they did not know how to write—even the Ph.Ds."**

—a professor of ecology at Virginia Tech

**"Students entering the business world today will not grow without written and verbal communications skills. They are primary requirements in the job market today."**

—a professor of marketing at a large public university

# 1 Fear and Loathing and the College Paper

▲ It's 11:30 Thursday night. You have a paper due Friday, and you've done virtually nothing toward writing it. You've known for two weeks that the paper was due, but the idea of writing papers is just so agonizing that you kept procrastinating. Once again, you find yourself getting ready to throw together a slapdash effort at the last minute. And once again, you can expect to end up with a C– or a D+ on your paper.

▲ You've known all semester long that you have a major research paper due at the end of the term. It's now two weeks before the due date—and for the life of you, you can't think of a topic. Assuming you come up with a topic soon, you'll have to cram all the research and writing into the last two weeks—on top of studying for finals.

▲ Your instructor assigned your topic, but you're so bored by it that you can't rouse yourself to research it, much less write about it. Meanwhile, the days approaching the due date are slipping away….

▲ You've got your topic, you've done your research, but you find yourself staring at a blank computer screen. You're paralyzed by your fear of writing. Seems like no matter how hard you try, you earn no better than a C, so you're terrified to put words on paper.

▲ You've done tons of research—so much in fact that you're baffled about where to begin and how to organize your paper. You give it your best shot, but you're not really surprised when the paper comes back with a grade of C– and the comment "poorly organized."

▲ You've written your paper out in longhand, but now you're down to the wire and still have to type it. You type it in such a rush that you don't

▼ 1

have time to proof your paper carefully, and it's filled with typos, misspellings, and grammatical errors—and virtually assured of a mediocre-to-poor grade.

We have designed this chapter to address all these scenarios and more. The chapter details twenty-five techniques for getting past the obstacles that stall the progress and jeopardize the success of countless college papers. You won't need all these techniques, and some may not work for you at all. But if you can identify one or more techniques that help you overcome your anxieties, you'll be on your way to better papers—and better grades.

What you shouldn't do when you get a writing assignment is panic. Let's face it; you're hardly alone. Ask your dorm buddies and other friends; you'll find that most of them hate and fear writing papers just as much as you do. If you can convince yourself to relax and not get rattled by the ordeal, you might just find yourself profiting from the writing process. How?

▲   You will likely receive better grades.
▲   You'll be better prepared for graduate school and professional school, especially law school.
▲   You'll have a competitive edge in your chosen career.
▲   You might even come to enjoy the writing process and learn something.

Several techniques in this chapter (Techniques 13, 14, 17, and 18) are inspired by or adapted from Peter Elbow's *Writing with Power: Techniques for Mastering the Writing Process*. We recommend Elbow's book highly to those who would like to delve even further into ways to stimulate better writing.

A word about the sequence of techniques.... Since we don't expect students to use every technique, and since the purposes of many of the techniques overlap, the order in which we've presented them is not crucial. Still, we've tried to organize them roughly in this sequence:

| | |
|---|---|
| **Techniques 1–3** | *Preliminaries* |
| **Techniques 4–7** | *Developing a topic* |
| **Techniques 8–12** | *Organizing and planning* |
| **Techniques 13–18** | *Getting warmed up to write* |
| **Techniques 19–25** | *Writing and polishing* |

Most of these techniques will be most productive and effective if you use a computer to do your planning, warming up, and writing. Technique 3 addresses the need to compose on the computer.

# Technique 1: Creating a conducive atmosphere

**An important preparatory step** to producing successful college writing assignments is creating the right atmosphere for planning and writing. Once you, as a relative of ours used to say, "commence to begin to start to get ready to write," you'll want to set the right scene. Some students won't need to create a special environment until they actually sit down to write. Others will benefit from conducting planning and organizing exercises under optimal circumstances.

Even as a high school student, you probably began to realize what kind of environment worked best to foster your personal writing process. Some students need an atmosphere so quiet that even their own gum-chewing can be distracting. Others can't write unless the CD player is blasting (and perhaps the TV's on, too).

For the most part, you can recreate at college the same writing atmosphere that worked for you in high school. College does present new difficulties, however. If you're the type that needs total quiet, you'll have a problem if you have noisy room- and dorm-mates. On the flip side, if your quiet roomie can't handle the loud music that gets your creative juices flowing, you may be in trouble.

The trick is to develop a strategy for creating the atmosphere you need in the face of the realities of college life. You may also want to consider the possibility that the environment in which you've written before might not be the one that truly lends itself to your best writing. Less-than-stellar grades may be the result of papers written under less-than-ideal conditions. You may want to experiment until you hit on the setting that works for you. Among the possibilities:

▲    A campus computer lab could be the ideal spot, especially if you don't have your own computer. Some labs tend to be noisy; one solution is to bring a portable stereo and headphones, thus blocking out the talking with your sounds of preference.

▲    Writing in longhand in the library, where resources are close at hand, might work for you. (See, however, Technique 3.)

▲    Can't you just picture yourself sitting under a tree on a sunny day tapping away on a laptop/notebook computer?

▲    If you can't find a quiet enough place for writing on campus, and you live close enough to school to travel home on some weekends and breaks, you may want to plan your writing timetable so that you can work in a quiet place at home. If you don't live close to school, can you cultivate a friend who lives off campus and will let you write in his or her apartment?

▲    Food and drink rituals may be crucial to your writing process. If you can't imagine writing without a bag of chips at your side, by all means, indulge yourself. Perhaps caffeine helps you get your brain in gear. Treat yourself to an espresso or cappuccino before writing, but take caution not to get too wired on caffeinated drinks or you won't be able to write. Peter Elbow cites a famous writer who always drank a beer and went on a walk before writing. Fine, as long as you're of legal drinking age and you don't convince yourself you can't possibly write on less than a six-pack.

▲    For some, taking a nap before writing might be refreshing; for others, slumber may produce only grogginess. There's always the danger, too, that what you planned as a quick snooze could turn into eight hours of heavy Zs.

▲    A better way to charge up body and brain may be to swim, run, walk, bicycle, play tennis, do aerobics, or otherwise work out before writing.

**HINT**

Once you get going, you'll probably want to pace yourself. Plan regular breaks as incentives for getting words down on paper. For example, tell yourself you'll write for another ninety minutes, after which you'll have a snack, swim some laps, watch your favorite TV show, call home, or socialize with your dorm-mates for a while.

# Technique 2: Devising a timetable

**One of the most sinister** enemies of the college paper is procrastination. After all, you can put off researching and writing a paper in a way that you can't put off studying for an exam, especially if you have an entire quarter or semester before the paper is due.

Some instructors recognize the prevalence of procrastination and assign preliminary projects, such as an abstract (or other statement of topic), outline, bibliography, and rough draft to keep you on task. Burdensome as it may seem to have all those extra assignments piled on you on top of the paper, the instructor is doing you a favor. By setting up a series of deadlines for preliminary work on the paper, he or she is ensuring that you won't put everything off until the last minute. (The advice "Start early" was one of the most prominent caveats offered by the professors we surveyed.)

Your professor probably recognizes that students are much less likely to procrastinate if they frame their tasks as manageable chunks. Students are much more likely to procrastinate after saying, "I'm going to write my paper today," than they are if their goal is a smaller, more specific component of the paper: "I'm going to develop my outline today."

Even if the instructor does not give preliminary paper assignments, you can avoid procrastination and keep yourself on task by creating your own timetable—and sticking to it. As you develop your timetable, however, keep in mind that you'll have other classes, assignments, exams, and, yes, even other papers. Be sure that the deadlines you set for yourself for each paper don't conflict impossibly with other responsibilities.

## SAMPLE TIMETABLES

Let's say your semester begins September 1, and you receive a syllabus detailing an assignment for a major research paper due December 1. Here's how you might set up your timetable:

| | |
|---|---|
| SEPT. 1 | *Receive assignment* |
| SEPT. 1 TO SEPT. 15 | *Develop and finalize topic (Techniques 4–7)* |
| SEPT. 15 TO OCT. 15 | *Conduct research (chapter 2 shows you how)* |

| Oct. 15 to Oct. 30 | *Do preliminary bibliography (see Technique 19 for why the bibliography should be one of the first elements of the paper you complete. Chapter 2 further tells how to use your bibliography in your research, while chapter 8 describes software that can help organize your notes and bibliography)* |
| Oct. 30 to Nov. 5 | *Do outline (Techniques 9–10)* |
| Nov. 5 to Nov. 15 | *First draft* |
| Nov. 15 to Dec. 1 | *Edit, revise, proofread, and polish final draft; finalize bibliography (chapter 6 guides you through the revision process)* |

If you anticipate that you'll be excruciatingly busy at the end of the term, or you predict that you will procrastinate no matter what, set the deadline for the final draft of your paper for two weeks to a month before the actual due date. That way, you'll have a built-in cushion if you're not able to meet all your self-imposed deadlines along the way.

Even a short-term writing assignment can benefit from a timetable. Let's say you have a five-page English paper on a specific piece of literature due in two weeks. Here's how your timetable might look:

| Jan. 15 | *Receive assignment* |
| Jan. 15–17 | *Develop and finalize topic/thesis* |
| Jan. 17–20 | *Conduct reading, research* |
| Jan. 20–23 | *Plan organization of paper; do outline, if necessary* |
| Jan. 23–25 | *Rough draft* |
| Jan. 25–30 | *Edit, revise, proofread, and polish final draft; do bibliography, if necessary* |

A good software tool to help get and keep you organized is *Project KickStart* for Windows. (See chapter 8 for details.)

HINT

Any one of the steps you've created for yourself can benefit from consultation with the instructor. Most instructors will be only too happy to discuss your selection of topic, make research suggestions, check your bibliography, go over your outline, and even look over your rough draft. Discussing the progress of your paper with the instructor serves two purposes:

1) It helps you to write a better paper, one that targets what the instructor is looking for (see also Technique 23). If you've developed your topic

with your instructor's assistance, she or he is bound to find it a more interesting paper and view it more favorably in the grading process.

2) It shows the instructor that you care about doing a good job. Even if your paper ends up being less than he or she hoped for, chances are the instructor will give you at least some benefit of the doubt when it comes to grading simply because he or she knows you tried hard to write a successful paper.

Make sure, however, that your professor *knows* that you're following a reasonable timetable. The prof will be much less inclined to lend a hand if you approach him or her at the eleventh hour having done little or nothing!

"**Give** yourself plenty of time for comprehensive writing: reading, drafting, revision, getting response, editing."

—a composition professor at a medium-sized public university

"**TTT—Things Take Time. No one can write a paper the night before it is due.**"

—a journalism professor at a northwestern state university

"**Set time horizons that are achievable; allow time for collection of information and the process of rewriting/refining ideas.**"

—a business professor at a medium-sized public university

"**Don't wait until the last minute to work on the assignment.**"

—a political science professor at a small private university

# **T**echnique 3: Composing on the computer

**When it comes to writing** the college paper, time is at a premium. Yet, most college students still make the writing process twice as long as it needs to be by first composing their papers in longhand and then typing them. Essentially, they do double the work. Composing a first draft in longhand made sense back in the days of typewriters; papers needed to be as polished as possible before being committed to final form because making changes on a typewritten draft was so difficult.

Computers have changed all that. A computer with a good word-processing program makes it possible to compose and revise as you type. The delete key zaps any text that you would have crossed out on your longhand draft. You don't have to make your word-processed draft perfect because you can always change it. You will likely find, in fact, that the ease with which you can move text around and make changes will free up the writing process for you and make you a better writer.

Old habits die hard. If you've always composed in longhand before typing, you may find it difficult to break out of the routine. For some students, the two-step process will always be the most comfortable way to write. Indeed, some of the world's most successful writers still do their initial drafts in long-hand. If you can learn to cut the two-step process down to one, however, you can save yourself enormous amounts of time. The faster you can write a paper, the less you have to fear and dread about the writing process. You can even allow yourself a little procrastination!

But how to break out of that compose-first, type-later routine? First, you need decent typing skills. You needn't master touch-typing (typing without looking at the keyboard) to be effective, but you won't increase your writing speed dramatically unless you learn to type with more than two fingers. If you've never taken a typing course, you can obtain software that teaches you quickly and efficiently (see chapter 8 for suggested programs). Remember, too, that the more you type, the more you will improve your typing speed.

If you're a technophobe who is terrorized by computer hardware and software, your college or university computer services office can probably help. Your school probably offers credit courses and noncredit workshops in various computer applications. And the wonks in that office can generally answer specific questions or make suggestions in a crisis.

If you've never composed on a computer, you will likely benefit from a road map, such as an outline (Technique 9) or mind map (Technique 12) for your paper. In fact, the more techniques from this chapter that you can do on the computer, the more ahead of the game you'll be. For example, if you do your brainstorming (Technique 6) and/or journal-keeping (Technique 7) on the computer, you'll have notes already stored that you can probably incorporate into your paper. At the very least, you'll want to organize your notes and sources in a coherent fashion so you can compose in an orderly way.

Technique 19 (page 44) also ties in nicely with composing on the computer. It enables you to type certain things you know you will need in your paper before you've actually written it.

To test the brain-to-computer technique, choose a paper with a due date fairly far in the future. It's best also to start with a shorter writing assignment, such as a two- or three-page paper. And then…just do it! If you find the technique simply doesn't work for you, you'll still have time to write your longhand draft and type it before the due date.

**HINT**

Be sure to save your document as soon as you start typing it and continue to save it frequently as you go along (say, after completing each page). Don't suffer the fate of one student we know who finished writing a four-thousand-word book report in the early morning hours of the day it was due. She went to print it out, and her computer gave her a "system error" message. Since she had never saved the document while typing it, her report was completely lost, and she had to rewrite it. Some software programs also have a timed backup option for which you can adjust the timing. You can adjust the program to update a backup copy of your paper as often as every minute. Thus, if a power failure occurs, for example, and you lose your main document, a virtually up-to-date backup copy will still be available. (But the backup won't work if you've failed initially to save and name your document.) If you have easy access to a printer, it doesn't hurt to print out your paper before you've finalized it. That way, if something happens to zap your document off the disk or hard drive, you'll have hard copy from which to retype. You may also find it useful to edit from hard copy. (Chapter 6 expands on editing and revising techniques.)

# Technique 4: Thinking creatively to develop and hone ideas and topics

**The first major obstacle** in the paper-writing process is choosing a topic. Agonizing and wavering over a topic increases your anxiety level and eats up valuable time. You'll feel so much better once you've nailed down what you're going to write about, so why not choose a topic early?

Once you pass the topic selection hurdle, you can breathe a little easier because you know the path toward developing the rest of the paper is pretty well mapped out. The fine art of developing a topic entails striking a balance between the too-broad and the too-narrow. Topic development also requires the ability to hone in on a theme that is appropriate to the assignment, compelling to the instructor, and manageable to research.

The process benefits from a little creativity. Here are some ways to approach topic development creatively:

▲ Consult with your instructor in developing your topic. (See Techniques 2 and 23.) Your teacher should have a wealth of ideas and can also steer you toward resources for research.

▲ Develop a topical topic. Current newspapers, magazines, talk shows, and broadcast news can be among your best sources for paper ideas, as can the new-releases shelf at the library or bookstore, book review sections, and the list of current best-selling books. Keep your eye open for trends, too. Consider the successful "ripped from the headlines" paper ideas these four students developed based on news items and trends.

At least one movie each year deals with ethical issues in business, so Greg decided to compare fact with fiction and wrote a review of three movies of the 1990s (*Disclosure*, *Glengarry Glen Ross*, and *Other People's Money*), comparing the movies to current legal and ethical standards in business.

Newspapers were reporting the release of a new study about low self-esteem in adolescent girls. Sue had a sociology paper due, so she decided to explore the effect of low self-esteem on teenage pregnancy, applying the results of the new study. Sue got an A on the paper.

Following a series of articles on the market for recycled plastics, Brian conducted a survey of local residents about how much plastic they recycle, and whether they were aware of the many new products on the market that were produced from this recycled plastic. Brian received an A on the paper.

For a history class about slavery, Claudia wanted to write about the rape of slave women. To make her paper topical, she focused on the controversial 1991 United States Senate confirmation hearings for Supreme Court Justice Clarence Thomas. She turned her topic from a study of rape under slavery to an exploration of how the same attitudes toward slave women may have carried over to the late-twentieth-century Senate hearings, in which an African-American woman accused Thomas of sexual harassment. Claudia's outline appears under Technique 9, on page 20.

▲   Find out what resources are available to help you research a topic in which you may be interested. (See chapter 2 for research techniques and sources.) If little material exists on your prospective topic, you'll obviously have a hard time coming up with enough research to support your thesis. Conversely, an enormous amount of material could be a sign that your topic is too broad.

At best, a plethora of material could mean you'll have an unmanageable amount of research to wade through when it comes time to organize your paper.

▲   Scan your library's CD-ROM databases (see chapter 2) on general topics that interest you. Seeing the wide variety of research that's been done in your area of interest may suggest ideas for your paper. You probably won't want to duplicate someone else's research exactly, but scanning the database may trigger ideas on how to apply another's approach to your specific interest. For example, Mark was scanning the PsycLIT CD-ROM database (which indexes and abstracts psychology and education articles in some thousand journals worldwide) and found several article abstracts on consumer buying behavior related to cars. He was then able to find the articles in the library and from them develop a study of local car buying behavior.

▲   Take a spin on the information superhighway. Many, if not most, colleges give students free or cheap access to e-mail accounts that hook up to the Internet, the vast network of computer networks that connects with a nearly limitless supply of information and resources. A number of search mechanisms on the Internet (see chapter 2) enable you to conduct quick searches of what info on your topic is available electronically. On campuses where students and faculty are networked, you can brainstorm and consult with friends and teachers electronically. Your e-mail account will also enable you to share ideas with, for instance, your best friend who's halfway across the country or your mentor from high school. The Internet's World Wide Web provides numerous on-line writing labs and centers, including the Writing Center at Texas A&M, which has a section on developing a topic. Find the Texas A&M site at **http: //engserve.tamu.edu/files/ writingcenter/invention.html**.

▲ Sharpen your topic by asking pointed questions. If your topic seems too broad, framing it in terms of a very specific question may narrow it and bring it into sharper focus. The sharper and more specific your topic, the better your paper will be. In his book, *Writing Well*, Donald Hall suggests asking questions that start "What is the most...?" or "What is the best...?"

Let's check in with our friend Sue, who wrote the teen pregnancy paper. Instead of writing a broad paper on teen pregnancy, she asked the question, "What factors most influence teenage girls to become pregnant?" For another paper she wrote about women in leadership, Sue asked, "What characteristics do the most successful women leaders have in common?"

▲ Do your own research study/survey. If you have even a rudimentary grasp of statistical methods, you might want to design and disseminate a survey, writing your paper on the survey results. For a sociology paper, for example, you might want to create a survey on student attitudes about behaviors that prevent infection with the AIDS virus and distribute the surveys on campus. Your paper would report on the results of your survey and suggest implications.

▲ Conduct interviews. A variation on the survey idea is to interview people to answer the question your topic poses. For her paper on women in leadership, our friend Sue interviewed several top women in a Florida state government department to find out the leadership traits they had in common.

▲ Brainstorm with a buddy. If you have a friend in the class, you might want to work together to locate topics (see Technique 6). If your cohorts in the class are writing about *similar* topics but not exactly the same as yours, you may benefit from the similarities. You can agree to steer each other to any appropriate research you may come across (see Technique 25).

**HINT**

You may want to find out what topics your classmates are using. If several plan to write about the same subject, you may find research resources tied up. And, if the class overachiever plans to write on your chosen topic, consider how your paper will stack up next to his or hers. If you feel yours will pale in comparison, you may want to switch to a topic that will give you a better opportunity to shine. Choosing a topic that's off the beaten path (as long as sources are available and your instructor agrees it's not *too* far off) can make your paper stand out from the pack.

# Technique 5: Write about what interests you—and stick with the program

**One of the best ways** you can light a fire under the paper-writing cauldron is to write about what interests you. That advice may seem obvious, but you'd be amazed at how many students settle for a dull topic in which they've invested minimal passion. Choosing a topic that bores you is a virtual guarantee of a less-than-wonderful paper. Research will be tedious, and writing will be unbearable. On the other hand, writing about something that excites you can stimulate the writing process better than almost anything else. Writing about what you care about will lighten your paper-writing burden, and your paper will reflect your passion. Consequently, your instructor will sense your enthusiasm and consider it while grading.

Granted, you will be required to take courses in subjects in which you have almost no interest. If you're creative enough, however, you can usually come up with an interesting idea for a paper even for a class that bores the heck out of you. For example, Mark felt the idea of writing a paper for his basic economics course was one of the most agonizing things he would ever have to do. But, since he was interested in ecology and energy, he managed to transform a boring economics paper into one that was interesting for him by focusing on the economics of energy and alternative forms of fuel. He received an A+ on that "boring" paper.

13

The most successful college writers take this concept a step further. They do what grad students and other advanced academicians do—they develop a "research stream." That means that just about every paper these students write, no matter what the class, will center around a common theme.

Let's revisit our friend Sue from Technique 4, for example. Sue decided at the beginning of her college career that she was interested in women's studies and that, no matter what class she was taking, she wanted to write all her term papers about women and women's issues. Here's how she did it:

| CLASS | PAPER |
| --- | --- |
| MANAGEMENT | *Marilyn Loden's Feminine Leadership Model Among Top-Level Woman Policy-Makers in Florida Public Education* |
| SOCIAL PHILOSOPHY OF EDUCATION | *How the Higher Education of Women in Postwar America Contributed to a Cult of Motherhood* |
| RELIGION | *Black Womanist Theology: Roots and Models in the Civil Rights Movement* |
| SOCIOLOGY | *School Stress, Quashed Aspirations and Low Self-Esteem in Adolescent Girls: Effects on Teenage Pregnancy* |
| GENDER ISSUES IN MEDIA | *Antifeminist Backlash in Television's Portrayal of Single Women* |
| POLITICAL COMMUNICATIONS | *Crafting and Communicating Political Messages for Women Candidates: The Case for Differentiation* |
| ART HISTORY | *The Subject of Rape in Cinquecento Renaissance Art* |
| BIOLOGY (HUMAN NUTRITION) | *Nutrition and Health Issues of Women* |

You get the idea. In the classes in which Sue was assigned to write book reviews rather than full-blown papers, she reviewed books about women. In literature classes, she wrote about gender-related aspects of the literature. Sue reports that for her, the major advantages of establishing a research stream are:

She is always focused on the general topic about which she plans to write. All she has to do for each new class is adapt her umbrella topic to the specifics of the class.

She is always passionately interested in the topics about which she is writing.

Her research builds on itself so that she can often use bits and pieces from previous papers in new papers. Computers especially lend themselves to this process since it's so easy to extract from old papers and electronically paste pieces onto new papers.

When she applies to graduate school, she will have a convincing portfolio of research that conveys her strong interest in an area she wishes to study further.

**HINT**

Just a cautionary note—as helpful as it is to write about what interests you, don't let your interests blind you to the assignment and responding appropriately. Once again, your instructor will be your best guide to whether a topic tailored to your interests will meet the requirements of the paper. And don't abuse your research stream by submitting virtually the same paper to more than one teacher.

# Technique 6: Brainstorming

**Brainstorming is a technique** that can help with both topic development and organizing the paper itself. Brainstorming is a little like word association; you list everything that you associate with the topic you have in mind.

The cardinal rule of brainstorming is that in making your initial list, no idea that you associate with your topic is too silly or far-fetched for consideration. Never censor yourself on the first go-round. Once you've listed twenty or so associations, you can begin to review your list. If you can't come up with twenty, chances are you don't yet know enough about the topic to consider it your final selection. If, however, you still feel good about the topic, you may want to explore it further before ruling it out.

It's often helpful to put your list down after the initial brainstorming and come back to it later. Now, scrutinize all the silly and far-fetched associations; do they trigger any realistic ideas or approaches to the topic? If not, cross them off the list. Your edited list can serve as a starting point for developing the topic further, narrowing the topic down, and organizing the paper. Here's an example of this brainstorming technique as it might be applied to a paper Brad was writing on advertising to children:

- influence of advertising on children
- socialization factor
- cartoon characters versus live actors
- health issues and junk food ads
- are kids' cereals all bad?
- influence of ads on materialism
- how do ads affect literacy?
- are the ads designed just for kids?
- do kids understand advertising disclaimers?
- dealing with the loss of trust
- advertising's effect on growing disillusionment
- believability of advertising
- age/maturity effects on understanding of ads
- advertising effect on family conflict
- what is effect of new educational programming rules?
- Ninja Turtles versus Power Rangers
- Life cereal's classic Mikey commercial…best of all time?
- stereotyping of socioeconomic and lifestyle
- who is watching ads with the children?
- Sesame Street gang goes commercial
- does type of product matter?
- which comes first—television show or toy/cereal/product?

Based on that brainstorming list, Brad decided to narrow his focus of the topic to the effects of advertising on children (materialism, health, trust, conflict). If this topic is too broad, he is willing to narrow the topic by looking at a specific age range or a specific outcome.

In the corporate world, people generally conduct brainstorming in groups—the old "two heads are better than one" notion. You can enlist agreeable friends, roommates, family members, or your instructor in your quest to brainstorm paper ideas. Bounce some ideas off them. Ask for their feedback and contributions. Again, no idea is too ridiculous during the first round of brainstorming. Remember the old adage, "Many a truth is spoken in jest." You never know what gems may be lurking amid ideas that seem truly absurd on first glance.

Logical next steps after brainstorming may be these:

**Technique 8:**                    *Planning*

| Technique 9: | *Outlining* |
| Technique 12: | *Mind Mapping* |

A technique that combines both brainstorming and outlining is Technique 10 (page 25).

**HINT**

Use your computer to assist in brainstorming. Keep lists of brainstorming ideas in your computer's files. Next time you're writing on a similar topic, consult the files to see if they suggest any new ideas. Several software packages are actually designed to assist with brainstorming, including, for the Macintosh: *Three by Five, Genius Handbook, IdeaFisher, Inspiration,* and *MindLink Problem Solver;* and for DOS/Windows: *Axon Idea Processor, Brainstormer, Creative Whack Pack, Creativity Machine, Genius Handbook, IdeaFisher, The Idea Generator Plus, Inspiration, MindLink Problem Solver,* and *Thoughtline.* One of many helpful books is Gerard Nierenberg's *The Art of Creative Thinking.* See chapter 8 for a complete listing of idea-generating books and software.

# "Think first: Brainstorm ideas, make an outline."

—a business professor at a medium-sized public university

**"Spend a great deal of time on brainstorming, free writing, thinking, and concept mapping before you write your drafts."**

—an English composition professor at a Canadian university

# Technique 7: Journal-keeping

**Keeping a journal** can be a truly invaluable tool for the student writer. Like brainstorming, journal-keeping is helpful both for developing your topic and writing your paper.

You may want to keep a notebook or section of a notebook as your journal for each class in which you expect writing assignments. Or you might prefer a general journal in which you write about anything and everything. Keep your journal(s) with you at all times. Whenever a possible topic occurs to you, jot it down, along with your thoughts, ideas, and associations about the topic. Make notes on where you might find further information.

It's not a bad idea to keep or transfer your journals to your computer so they'll be less likely to get lost or thrown away. Computerized journaling also enables you to jump from journal-writing to paper development more easily.

Once your topic is set, jot down notes, thoughts, observations, experiences, quotes, and phrases you feel may be useful in your paper. Every time you read something or hear something in class that might contribute to your paper, write it down. Expand on your jottings as the spirit moves you. The most successful journals are those that are self-motivated.

Not only does journal-keeping help prevent fleeting ideas from slipping your mind, but the practice can get you in the habit of writing regularly. One of the reasons college students find it so painful to sit down and crank out that paper is that they are not accustomed to frequent writing. If you can discipline yourself to write a little bit in your journal every day, your mind will be limbered up for the task of writing the actual paper when the time comes.

Another kind of journal-keeping involves writing letters to friends, whether by good, old-fashioned "snail mail" or via e-mail on your computer and modem. If you have a friend who is willing to discuss writing assignments, writing letters to him or her can be a great way to hash out topics and discuss progress. The real value, though, is that the discipline and practice of regular writing will increase your comfort level with writing your class assignments. If you have a writing assignment that requires you to argue a point, for example, writing a letter to a friend arguing the same point is an excellent way to increase your comfort level with writing the paper. If you can convince your friend of your viewpoint, you might just convince your instructor of your writing skill. If you write your journal-like letters to your friends on a computer, you can keep copies on a disk in case you want to use pieces of your letters in your actual writing assignments. It's not always simple to download e-mail messages, but it can be done; ask your campus systems administrator.

You may also want to visit these two sites on the World Wide Web that have journal-writing tips: *The Journal Writer* at **http://www.rio.com/~wplace/journal. html**, or *Journal and Essay Writing* at **http://www.azstarnet.com/~poewar/ writer/essay.html**.

Never throw away your old journals (or erase your journal disks if you keep your journal on the computer). The possibility always exists that you can find a new paper idea in an old journal. If nothing else, it's fun to look back at your journals years later and reminisce about that time in your life.

# Technique 8: Planning

**Planning is the simplest,** least formal way of organizing your paper. Where mind mapping and outlining (Techniques 9, 10, and 12) may work best for longer papers, planning is generally adequate for most short papers.

Planning is essentially the mental process of picturing your paper in your head. Conjuring a mental image of your paper will reassure you; your paper exists—all you have to do is transfer that mental image to words on paper. You don't have to write anything down in the planning process, but you certainly can do so if it helps you.

Some of the kinds of questions you may want to think about as your paper takes shape in your mind include:

▲  How long should it be? Your instructor's assignment may already answer this question, but you'll want to think about whether writing as much as assigned or confining yourself to the assigned length will be difficult. If you anticipate problems with length, ask your instructor's policy on too-short and too-long papers. (Professors don't consider length one of the more serious problems with student papers, but it's still a consideration.)

▲  What kinds of research are required and how long will the research process take?

▲  Will you cite outside sources in your paper, hence requiring some form of bibliography? Will you want to prepare any charts, tables, graphs, or illustrations? How long will they take? (See Technique 19 on page 44 for a way to get a head start on these peripheral components.)

▲  Think about your audience—generally your instructor. What is he or she looking for? (See Technique 23 on page 51.)

19

▲    What will the paper's title be? If you can conceptualize a title, you'll have an excellent starting point for writing the paper. (Bear in mind that some instructors prefer you not title your papers; if that's the case, title it in your head even though it won't have a title on paper.) Another way to jump-start the planning process is to imagine your paper is a newspaper story. What should its headline be?

▲    How will you begin the paper? How will you state your thesis?

▲    In what order will you express your supporting points?

**HINT**

Planning works best in a conducive environment (see Technique 1, page 3) in which you have a clear mind and a quiet, comfortable situation to nurture the planning process. Don't panic if nothing jumps into your head immediately; if you relax, ideas should start to gel in your mind. If not, you may want to move onto a different approach, such as those that follow.

"**Know** what you are going to do before you begin and then be willing to take the time to do it all over."

—a communications professor at a small private university

"**Think about the topic before you start to write; let it simmer in your brain so that you'll actually have something to say when you really begin to write.**"

—an English professor at a large private university

# Technique 9: Outlining

**You've known about outlining** at least since middle school and probably elementary school. Indeed the very fact that teachers taught you to outline from an early age may predispose you to resist the technique with your college papers. Outlining can be a faithful old friend to college writers, however, and one that will serve you especially well when you write longer papers.

The outline is an organizational framework, the skeleton of your paper—to which you will add the flesh. The outline can help you fight the college writing flaw that instructors cite as their number one pet peeve: poor organization (see chapter 4). A good outline serves as a road map that enables you to visualize where your paper is headed. If a point seems out of place in an outline, chances are it's going to be even more so in your paper, and your instructor will notice immediately. One of our surveyed professors also points out that an outline helps you to see what research materials you have and don't have ready to write your paper.

Since you undoubtedly already know a lot about outlining, we won't spend a great deal of time here discussing the how-to's of the technique. You should know, however, that there's more than one way to outline, and you can adapt the one that works best for you. You may even want to change formats from paper to paper or start with a rough outline and work your way up to the more thorough sentence outline.

The basic types of outlines include the following:

▲ the rough or working outline
▲ the topic outline
▲ the sentence outline

The rough or working outline is an informal blueprint that may not even be in traditional outline form, such as in the following example:

**Getting a Job after Graduation**
—Preliminaries
  -Networking
  -Researching companies
—Preparing correspondence
  -Resume
  -Cover letters
 Sending correspondence
   -Mass mailings
  -Answering ads
—Interviewing
—Follow-up

The topic outline follows traditional outline form but uses topics and subtopics, expressed as simple words or phrases, for each entry. Note this example:

### Godlike Authority in *Elsie Dinsmore* and its Uses
### in Gendered Social and Religious Discourse

I. Introduction/Thesis Statement: The major characters in *Elsie Dinsmore* possess a Godlike authority that results in power shifts between them.

    A. Horace Dinsmore serves as Godlike authority

        1. The evolving Horace as metaphor for "feminization" of Godlike authority

        2. Horace as promulgator of post-Calvinist theology of Bushnellian Christian Nurture, and hence, "secular authority nonpareil," between which and heavenly authority, Elsie must mediate

            a. Health and fitness

            b. Personal finances

    B. Use of Godlike authority in both Horace and Elsie for chastening/incest/patrimatrimony

    C. Elsie Dinsmore as Godlike authority

        1. Elsie as Evangelist—promulgator of Sunday School didacticism

            a. Moral superiority

            b. Access to power as a result

        2. Promulgator of Calvinist faith vs. works theology

        3. Christlike figure who converts through resurrection

II. Conclusion: Who has more power?

The sentence outline, obviously, uses complete sentences for each entry. The sentence outline is the most formal of organizational techniques and the one that will probably bear the closest relationship to your final paper. The sentence outline helps the organizational process by forcing you to think through the structure of your paper. While the topic outline structures *the general concepts* you will write about, the sentence outline organizes *what you will say* about each concept or topic. Here's an example:

### Why Have There Been No Great Women Artists?

I. Feminists might answer the question in one of at least two ways:

    A. They reclaim examples of "great" woman artists.

    B. They assert that greatness is different for women than it is for men.

II. In fact (according to Nochlin), there have been no great women artists: Why?

A. Education and other institutions are at fault.

    1. It is not in the best interests of those who control institutions (men) to grant complete equality to women.

    2. Women are often weakened by the internalized demands of male-dominated institutions.

B. The "Myth of the Great Artist" assumes that artists possess some innate genius but disregards sociological and other influences on the development of artistic talent.

    1. Fathers and other close relatives who were artists were a major influence on the great artists.

    2. Time demands on women (analogous to those on the aristocracy) often precluded them from becoming great artists.

    3. Women artists had virtually no access to nude models of either gender until recently, yet the nude model was essential to the training of the aspiring artist.

    4. Additional institutions that discriminated against women discouraged their development as artists.

There's nothing wrong with combining techniques. Here's an example that combines topic and sentence outline techniques:

**Slavery, Rape, and Anita Hill:**
**How the Treatment of Professor Hill during the**
**Clarence Thomas Senate Confirmation Hearings Has Its**
**Roots in the Rape of Black Women under Slavery**

I. Introduction

II. The Institutionalization of Rape under Slavery

    A. Dual exploitation of slave women as both laborers and reproducers

    B. Treatment of slave women who resisted forcible intercourse

    C. Perversion of the black male role through the rape of slave women

    D. Lack of legal sanction for rape of slave women

    E. Characterization of slave women as promiscuous concubines and prostitutes

    F. The Abolitionist view of the rape of slave women

    G. "Cliometricians" who attempted to downplay the extent of rape under slavery

III. The Race-Gender Discourse in the Lynching Climate of Post-Slavery

    A. Characterization of black women continues to be one of immorality and licentiousness.

        1. Black women thought to be immoral to the extent that syphilis was thought to be spread by diseased genital organs of black women

        2. Seen in "binary opposition" to their "moral" white counterparts

        3. "Moral" white counterparts seen as irresistible to the rapacious black men

    B. Black men thought to be routinely raping white women without the "civilizing" influence of slavery

        1. Ida B. Wells's research shows fallacies of this assumption.

        2. As a result, all black women branded "prostitutes, thieves, and liars."

        3. This criticism spurs formation of regional organizations for black women.

IV. Stonewalled Race-Gender Discourse in the Era of the Black Woman's Organization

    A. Black women prevented from talking about interracial gender relations and sexuality

        1. by Social Darwinism

        2. by blame-the-victim mentality

        3. by statistics that showed higher rate of syphilis and infant mortality among blacks

    B. To protect themselves, black women adopted "behavior and attitudes...that created the appearance of openness and disclosure but actually shielded the truth of their inner lives and selves from their oppressors."

    C. It is from this climate of the hidden inner truths of black women's lives that Anita Hill's testimony was met with such incredulity.

V. Conclusion

A number of the leading word-processing programs and integrated software packages now have outlining tools. These packages include *Microsoft Word*, *WordPerfect*, and *In Control* (for both Macintosh and Windows) *Claris Works*, *InfoDepot*, *MacThink*, and *More* (for Macintosh). For more details, see chapter 8.

Outlining provides a good checkpoint for how well supported your arguments are. Since instructors cite "failure to support thesis" as the second most serious flaw of college papers, it's important to bolster every point carefully. Developing an outline enables you to see whether you can put forth strong supporting points for every facet of your thesis. If during the outlining process you come across a statement you can't back up, you may want to consider omitting that point. Perhaps even more importantly, an outline helps with the student writing flaw that professors cite as their number one pet peeve: poor organization. An effective outline helps you organize your thoughts and shows the professor you've really put time in up-front thinking about your topic before you started writing. A final caution: Don't let your outline become so much of a crutch that it makes you overconfident with your progress. Not matter how great the outline, you still have to write the paper.

# "Start by outlining your thesis, the shape of your argument, supporting evidence and conclusions."

—an adjunct professor at a private university in Virginia

**"Start by understanding your topic. The best way is to write a good outline."**

—an international-relations professor at a medium-sized private university

**"Think and outline before you write."**

—a professor of fisheries and wildlife science at Virginia Tech

**"Organize your thoughts in outline form."**

—a public-relations professor at Kent State University

# Technique 10: Unconscious outlining

**This technique is bit of a** cross between brainstorming and outlining and is designed for students for whom even outlining is a frightening or painful task.

Get a pad of sticky notes (e.g., Post-it Notes). A good size is 3' x 5'.

On the first note, write your topic. Now, pull that note off the pad.

On the next note, write a word or phrase that's related to your topic, and pull that off.

Repeat the process for as many different words/phrases/ideas on the topic you can think of.

Next, take one of the notes headed with a word or phrase, and write down ideas that relate to the one at the top of the note.

Arrange the sticky notes with related ideas in a logical order. The idea is that if you are frozen by the notion of trying to write anything, this technique will trick you into compiling an outline. Pulling off the sticky notes distracts you from the fact that you're actually thinking about writing and putting ideas in order. You can set aside any notes that don't relate to the way the bulk of ideas are going. (You may want to save them in case they might help you with future research and topic development.)

And, voilà, you have an outline without even realizing that you were outlining!

**HINT**

As soon as you have completed this process, you should probably move onto one of the other techniques mentioned in this chapter, such as outlining (Technique 9) or the Just Do It Method (Technique 20), because this technique is simply a method to get you started and should not be considered as a final step. And you never know when a gust of wind or lack of glue might cause your notes to disappear. To avoid those physical limitations altogether, use one of the software programs that simulate this process: *Three by Five* for Macintosh and *Axon Idea Processor* for Windows.

# Technique 11: Abstracting

**Abstracting is a great way** to avoid those old blank-computer-screen blues. Writing an abstract not only enables you to get words down on paper, but it also serves much the same road map function as an outline, guiding you in what to do next.

Just what is an abstract? It's a summary of the major points of your paper all squeezed into one paragraph. Yes, it's OK if it's a *long* paragraph. In a sense, the abstract is an outline in paragraph form. It's simply a lot broader and more general than an outline, and it may not cover every point that an outline would.

One important thing an abstract accomplishes is to describe your purpose for writing the paper (other than the fact that it's a class requirement); in other words, it states your thesis, the problem your paper will explore, or the question your paper will attempt to answer. You may also wish to touch upon the approach you will take to your exploration and the methodology of your research. Once you've articulated that purpose, you will have gone a long way toward launching your paper.

We've provided a sample abstract below, but if you feel the sample doesn't give you enough to go on, never fear. The wonderful thing about abstracts is that gazillions of examples of them are available in your campus library, both electronically and in print. Any CD-ROM or on-line search (see chapter 2) will produce endless examples of abstracts. Abstracts also appear in numerous print sources, such as *Psychological Abstracts* (the CD-ROM version is called PsycLIT), *Current Index to Journals in Education* (CIJE is part of the ERIC database on CD-ROM), and *Sociological Abstracts* (Sociofile on CD-ROM). If you have any doubt about where to locate examples of abstracts, just ask a campus reference librarian. Meanwhile, our example follows. Note how the abstract describes the writer's purpose and how she plans to approach the paper:

> In her unfinished novella, *Diana and Persis*, Louisa May Alcott, accord-
> ing to Whitney Chadwick, "explores the connections between art, poli-
> tics, spinsterhood, and the female community in late nineteenth-century
> Paris" (212). The character Persis represents Alcott's sister May, whom
> Alcott supported as an artist in Paris beginning in 1873—just when
> Berthe Morisot, Mary Cassatt, and other women artists were making
> their mark in the Impressionist movement. Both characters, like the real
> women artists in this milieu, essentially face a choice between their art
> and domesticity—marriage and motherhood. Using the novella, origi-
> nally written in 1879 but first published in 1978, as a framework, this
> paper will explore how the lives of the real women artists of the period,

particularly the Morisot sisters, aligned with Alcott's depiction. Because she based the story on May and herself, Alcott abandoned it when her sister died a month after giving birth to her only child, a daughter, named after Louisa. The paper will examine the question of whether the ending that one scholar believes Alcott intended is plausible in the context of the lives of real women artists in late nineteenth-century Paris.

**HINT**

If you write an abstract to jump-start and guide your writing process, you can frequently use the same abstract as a basis for the introduction to your paper.

# Technique 12: Mind mapping

**The difference between outlining** and mind mapping relates to the variations in the way people think. If you're the kind of person who can easily conceptualize the linear and hierarchical nature of an outline, outlining should work well for organizing your papers. If instead your mind organizes concepts in a more free-form way, mind mapping may be your best bet. Mind mapping lets you rapidly produce an almost infinite number of ideas and simultaneously helps you to organize your thoughts as well. Mind mapping is a very powerful tool especially for creative and report writing, where getting down all your ideas first is important.

Mind mapping usually begins when you write your major topic or thesis in the middle of a piece of paper and encircle it (see illustration, in which improving business ethics is the major topic). Next, concentrate on what's in that circle, and allow those words to suggest other concepts. On average, you should draw five to ten main ideas that relate to the main topic. As each related idea comes to mind, write it down and draw a circle around it. Next, concentrate on each of the new words, and again try to think of five to ten main ideas that relate to each of these words. Don't spend much longer than about five minutes on this phase.

Next, draw lines to express the relationships among your circled items. Finally, prioritize and organize the concepts the way you visualize them in your final paper. Your final product is a type of outline, simply rendered in a more spatial way than the traditional structure.

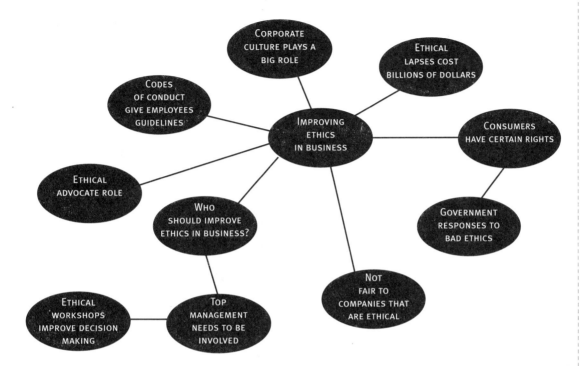

**HINT**

If mind mapping appeals to you, and you'd like to learn more about the process, check out Gabrielle Rico's *Writing the Natural Way: Using Right-Brain Techniques to Release Your Expressive Powers* or Tony Buzan's *The Mind Map Book*. You may also want to check out one of several software programs and Internet resources that are available to help with mind mapping: for the Macintosh, *Inspiration*; for Windows, *Inspiration* and *Mind Mapper*; on the World Wide Web, *Mind Mapping FAQ* (Frequently Asked Questions) at **http://world.std.com/~emagic/mindmap.html**. See chapter 8 for more details.

# Technique 13: Prewriting When You're Stuck with a Topic That Bores You

**All the techniques we've discussed** so far assume that you have the freedom to develop your own topic. But what if your professor has assigned your topic to you and you couldn't be less interested?

A good way to spark your interest is to do a little writing about the topic before you even do any research about it. This prewriting should motivate your research and begin shaping your thinking about the topic. The exercise will help you develop an effective approach to the topic. The prewriting needn't be a major, time-consuming project but as little as a page or so of rough writing and/or notes.

Your prewriting should consist of three components:

▲    what you already know about the topic
▲    how you feel about the topic
▲    your predictions for what you think your research will prove.

Writing what you already know about the topic is very much like brainstorming (Technique 6). Simply list everything you can think of about this terribly dull topic that your professor has saddled you with.

Next, write about your feelings on the topic. Jot down any preconceived notions, biases, or opinions you may have about the subject. Write down any personal memories associated with the topic. Speculate on why you think your professor assigned you this topic.

Finally, make some educated guesses as to the conclusions that your research will lead to. Hypothesize what the arguments will be and which ones will prevail. Predict how your paper will turn out.

We're willing to bet that once you've engaged in this prewriting exercise, you'll feel more gung-ho about plunging into researching this tedious topic than you did before. You will have fooled yourself into believing you are an authority on the subject because you've written about it, and therefore, you'll more actively engage yourself in the research. As you conduct your research from this perspective, you'll be more attuned to material that agrees with or differs from your own brilliant insights. You'll be armed with a vision of the topic that is far less murky than before this exercise. You may even have come up with a truly unique approach to the topic.

**HINT**

If, after conducting your research, you are still stuck because this boring topic fails to inspire you, ask yourself some of the questions under Technique 14 (following), or try some of the tricks listed under Technique 17 (page 42).

# Technique 14: Priming the Pump

**If you're suffering from** writing paralysis, if you just can't get started, if you just don't know how to approach your topic or what to say about it, these questions and exercises, selected and adapted from a wonderful chapter of Peter Elbow's *Writing with Power,* can help. The chapter is chock-full of what the author calls "metaphorical questions that will help you produce more ideas, perceptions, and feelings about a topic." You can simply think about responses to the questions, or you can actually write down your thoughts. Not all these questions apply to every type of writing; they are somewhat geared toward creative writing and writing about literature. But see if you can find several here to spark your creative process. (Used with permission from Oxford University Press.)

For a paper or story about a person (whether real or fictional, such as a character in literature):

1. Describe the person as an ordinary person.
2. Describe the person as a unique and special person.
3. Imagine the person as the opposite sex. Describe the life that he/she would have lived.
4. Describe the life the person would have lived in a very different era.
5. Make up or guess the most important childhood event in the person's life.
6. Describe the person's life if that event hadn't occurred or something entirely different had occurred.
7. Tell a science fiction story with the person in it.

8. Tell a soap opera plot with the person in it.

9. What does this person most need to cry about?

10. Imagine you are very angry and strike the person. How and where do you strike?

11. Give an accurate compliment that the person probably never hears or heard.

12. What's a secret about the person that he/she hasn't told anyone?

13. What's something about the person that even he/she doesn't know?

14. How would the person's mother or father describe him/her?

15. How would the person's child describe him/her?

16. Describe the person as a good president of the United States. A bad president. What would be the important policies and decisions in both cases?

17. Tell a recurring dream that the person has.

18. Describe the person's life and character as essentially unchanging. What may look like changes are really just ways of staying essentially the same.

19. Describe the person's life and character as essentially determined by important changes or turning points (even if it looks to most people as though no such changes or turning points occurred).

20. Imagine you believe people are truly free; they somehow choose or cause everything that happens to them. Describe the person's life or character.

21. Imagine you have the opposite point of view; people are not free and are determined by events they cannot control. Describe the person's life or character.

22. Find as many rhythms or patterns as you can in the person's life: events that repeat or recur whether the scale is in moments or years.

23. What events in the person's life occurred only once?

24. Describe the person as primarily a product of a national, cultural, and ethnic influence.

25. Describe your person as primarily a product of personal and family influences.

26. Describe the person as primarily a product of economic and class influence.

27. Describe the person as essentially the product of conditioning. What behavior was rewarded and what was punished?

28.  Describe the person's character as a solution to past problems.

29.  Describe the person's character as carrying the seeds of future problems.

30.  Think of two or three very unlikely professions or occupations for the person and describe him/her in these professions.

31.  Who would play the person in a movie about his/her life? Who would play the other characters in the person's story?

32.  If the person were the president of a corporation, what corporation would it be—and why?

33.  If this person were your boss, what kind of manager would he/she be?

34.  If this person were a scientist, what would he/she study? What famous discovery would he/she make?

For a paper or story about a place, whether real or fictional (as in a place described in literature):

1.  What is the first thing that comes to your mind that your place makes you think of?

2.  How is your mood affected by being there?

3.  Imagine being there for a whole year. How would that make you better? How worse?

4.  Imagine you have just seen, in only five minutes, the whole history of the place since the beginning of the world. Briefly tell this history.

5.  Imagine you have always been blind. Describe the place briefly.

6.  Let the place describe you.

7.  Your place is an animal. What animal is it?

8.  Your place is a person. Who?

9.  Your place is a corporation. Which?

10.  Your place is a scientific element. Which one?

11.  Name a song, story, and a movie that your place reminds you of.

12.  Imagine your body is the world. Where on your body is this place?

13.  What kind of weather is most typical of your place?

14.  Find as many of your place's rhythms as you can. (For example, find things that happen there at regular intervals—whether they happen every second, every minute, every month, or every thousand years.)

15.  Name as many things as you can that happen there only once.

16.  Think of your place as if it were old and near death. Now tell what place it was when it was only a child.

17.   Think of your place as if it were a young child or young animal. Tell what place it will grow up to be.

18.   Imagine your place was the whole universe and you had always lived there. Tell how you and your neighbors explain the beginning of the universe. How do you folks think the universe is going to end?

19.   Think of your place as carefully planned in every detail. Describe it briefly from this point of view.

20.   Think of your place as if everything happened by accident, chance, and luck. Describe it from this point of view.

21.   Think of your place as haunted. Tell how it became haunted and what it does to people it doesn't like.

22.   Imagine an anti-universe where everything is opposite or backwards from the way we know it. Describe your anti-place in this anti-universe.

23.   Think of your place as a piece of real estate. How would you describe it in a sales pitch, and how much would it cost to buy?

For a paper or story about an object:

1.   Think of a particular moment in which this object was meaningful or important to you. Close your eyes and take yourself back into that moment. Bring back the reality of the object and the scene for a few moments. The time of day. The time of year. The smells. Your feelings.

2.   If you had never seen the object before, what would you notice when you first looked at it?

3.   If you knew it fairly well, what would you notice when you looked at it?

4.   If you knew it better and longer than anyone else—for a whole life-time—what would you see when you looked at it?

5.   Tell two or three different ways you might take it apart.

6.   Tell what it's like to take it apart and then to take apart the parts till you get down to its basic ingredients.

7.   Imagine a different world in which this object was made of completely different materials. What would they be? Tell the advantages and disadvantages of this new configuration.

8.   Tell how this particular object—as opposed to this type of object in general—came to exist.

9.   Pretend it came to exist in a different way and tell what it was like.

10.   Describe how you would develop a marketing plan for this object. What would it cost? Who would buy it? What would the advertising look like?

11.    Tell the history of this particular object since it first existed.

12.    Tell the history of the object for the last five minutes.

13.    Tell how this kind of object came to exist.

14.    Tell another story of how this object came to exist, but this time make it a love story.

15.    Think of as many ways as possible to group or categorize a whole bunch of these objects.

16.    Think of a lot of different ways the object is actually used.

17.    Tell three ways it might be used, but isn't.

18.    Tell a mystery story of how it came to be used in one of those ways.

19.    List three ways it could not possibly be used.

20.    Tell a science fiction story of how the world changes so that it is used in one of the ways you've already said was impossible.

21.    Pretend you were at an auction and you were trying to outbid someone who was bidding for the same object. What would you do?

22.    If the object were an animal, what animal would it be?

23.    If it were a person, whom would it be?

24.    If it were a symbol for a corporation, which would it symbolize?

25.    If it could speak, what would it tell you about yourself that you weren't aware of?

26.    Tell three things it might stand for or remind you of.

27.    Imagine you are much richer than you are and think of something for which it might stand.

28.    What might it stand for if you were much older or younger than you are?

For a paper about a work of art (including painting, sculpture, film, literature, music, etc.):

1.    Pretend you made it. Something important was going on in your life and you poured strong feelings into it. What was going on? What were those feelings?

2.    Pretend you made it, but nothing special was going on in your life and you had no strong feelings. Describe what you liked about this thing you created.

3.    Pretend you made it and are very dissatisfied. Why are you dissatisfied with it?

4.  Pretend you just bought it for a large sum of money, but now you are questioning whether you should have bought it. Why?

5.  You made it as a gift for someone you know. Who? How did he/she feel about your gift?

6.  Imagine this work of art as medicine. What is the disease? What are its symptoms? How does this medicine cure it?

7.  Imagine this work of art as poison. It destroys whoever experiences it. Describe the effects of this poison, the course of deterioration.

8.  Imagine that everyone on the globe owned this work of art or all infants were repeatedly exposed to it. What would be the effects?

9.  What is someone most apt to notice the first time he or she encounters this work of art?

10.  What would you notice about this work of art if you had never encountered any other works in its medium?

11.  What tiny detail in this work says more about it than any other?

12.  Is the work male or female?

13.  What other work of art would it marry?

14.  What works of art are its children?

15.  What if you were trying to sell this piece of art? How would you go about selling it? Who would buy it?

16.  Imagine this work of art as part of an evolutionary process. What work did it evolve from? What work will it evolve into?

17.  This work is the only human artifact transported to Mars, the only evidence Martians have about humans. What guesses or conclusions would they reach about humans based on this work?

18.  Imagine your work of art as evolving into different media. Describe two or three of these new works of art. See what these evolutions tell you about the original work.

19.  Fine art versus craft: Describe the work of art as though it were the opposite category from the one it usually occupies.

20.  Anonymous folk art/signed art made by individual artist: Describe the work of art as though it were the opposite category from the one it usually occupies.

For a paper about an organization or group of people:

1.  What animal is the group?

2.      What are rhythms and patterns in the history of the group? Events or cycles that recur, whether on a scale of decades or days?

3.      What are some of the things that have only happened once to the group?

4.      What are some of the most important moments in the history of the group?

5.      The group is alive, chooses, acts. Describe its behavior as completely conscious, willed, deliberate.

6.      The group has feelings. What does it feel now? What is the history of its feelings?

7.      If there were two groups, where would the second one be? How would they interact?

8.      Imagine the group as a machine, like a car or a pinball machine. Describe how it works.

9.      What is the most important part of the machine? Which part breaks down the most?

10.      If the group were mapped onto your body, where are the head, feet, hands, ears, eyes?

11.      Imagine all organizations had the same structure or mode of operating that your group has. What would be the effect on the world?

12.      What human qualities does it bring out in its members? Which ones does it suppress or fail to use?

13.      Describe the group as a poison; its effects; its antidote.

14.      Describe the group as a weapon. How do you make it go off? What does it do? Who invented it?

15.      Think of the group as a scheme of evolution. What did it evolve from? What is it evolving toward?

16.      What physical shape is the group? Imagine that shape in locomotion: how does it move?

17.      Think about the group as part of an ecological system. On what does it depend? What depends on it? What does it eat? What does it emit? What eats it? What emits it?

For a paper about a problem or dilemma:

1.      The problem has been stated wrong. Find two or three ways of stating it differently.

2.      The problem comes from bad data. Guess what data are wrong and why?

3.  It looks like a problem, but really everything is fine if you only take the right point of view. What is that point of view?
4.  Assume the problem has no solution. What is the sensible course or strategy that follows from this conclusion?
5.  The problem is a color. Which is it and why?
6.  The problem is a scientific element. Which is it and why?

For a paper about an abstract concept:

1.  What color is the concept?
2.  What shape?
3.  Imagine that shape moving around: what is its mode of locomotion?
4.  Give the worst, most biased, distorted definitions of the concept that you can give.
5.  Imagine that the word or phrase for this concept didn't exist. What would people do with no word for it in their language? What would be different because the word did not exist?
6.  Imagine the concept is a place and describe it.
7.  What animal would make a good insignia for the concept?
8.  What people are connected in your mind with the concept?
9.  If the concept fell in love with something else, what would the something else be? What would they have for children?
10. Design a flag for the concept.
11. Think of three or four abstractions that are bigger than your concept or can beat it up, and three or four that are smaller or can be beaten up by your concept.
12. Think of the concept as part of an ecological system. On what does it depend? What depends on it? What does it eat? What does it emit? Who eats it? What emits it?
13. What are the most memorable sounds associated with the concept? Smells?

HINT

If you'd like different sets of questions or approaches to work with to "prime your pump," helpful software includes, for the Macintosh, *IdeaFisher*; and for Windows, *Creative Whack Pack*, *IdeaFisher*, and *Thoughtline*. See chapter 8 for more details.

# Technique 15: Writing by speaking

**Everyone has a different** style of communication. Some students who hate to write and feel they are poor writers perceive that they communicate far more effectively with spoken than written language. If you are one of those students, you can use your ability to express yourself in speech to get past your dread of writing your paper.

The basic tool for this technique is a tape recorder. One of those small, hand-held models that uses microcassettes is ideal because you can carry it around with you and speak into it as ideas come to you. Instead of beginning to write your paper on the computer or in longhand, you will begin to write your paper by speaking it. Imagining that you're giving a speech to a friendly audience will focus your thoughts, but don't worry about being perfect. Indeed, your spoken paper can be very freeform. You can change it as you go along. You can also make notes to yourself about the direction you want to take with your paper and the documentation you will need to support your arguments.

You can also use your tape recorder in much the same way as you would a written journal, speaking ideas and notes into it as they come to you and using those spoken words later to inspire your written paper.

Particularly if you are writing a paper intended to persuade its audience to a certain point of view, you can pretend to have a conversation about your topic into your tape recorder. Imagine you're trying to convince a friend to adopt your viewpoint. What words would you use? How would you make your argument? Argue those points into the tape recorder. Of course, you can also have an actual conversation with a friend—and simply record the conversation.

Even if the words you speak bear only a marginal relationship to those that end up forming your paper, you will have accomplished something major— you will have made your paper exist, whereas it previously consisted of blank pieces of paper and empty computer disks. Yes, you still have to write and/or type it—but your paper exists! Moving from the vast, empty void to tangible spoken words gets you over a major hurdle.

You may want to move to an outline based on your spoken words or use your taped "writing" as an early draft for your paper.

You may also discover that the paper that comes from spoken words will read much more naturally than one that comes directly from writing. Too often, the language students use to write papers sounds stilted and artificial.

**HINT**

Be sure to allot plenty of time for transcribing your spoken words into a written paper. Transcribing is a more time-consuming process than many realize. Because it is so time intensive, writing by speaking is not for everyone. But if you're desperate to bring your paper to life and you feel most comfortable speaking, you could succeed with this technique.

## Technique 16: Jump-starting the writing process: freewriting

**One of the world's most** terrifying sights for a college student with a paper due is a blank piece of paper—or a blank computer screen. While freewriting is not a way to write your actual paper, it is a warm-up exercise to help you get past the paralysis that prevents you from writing your paper. The more you hate and fear writing, the more helpful you will find freewriting. And the more you perform the freewriting exercise, the more comfortable you will be with writing your paper.

Freewriting is a productive activity to replace all the fretting, sweating, and anxiety you're experiencing about writing your paper. It's a way to ease yourself into the writing process even if you feel far from ready to write your paper. If you have a lot on your mind that prevents you from writing your paper, freewriting can be a way of dealing with your concerns and clearing your head of clutter so you can write.

The idea is just to sit down and write for ten minutes straight. Remember that while you are not writing your paper, it's perfectly all right to have your paper in mind as you freewrite. That way, you may likely develop some ideas you can use in your paper.

As you freewrite, you shouldn't worry about the direction your writing is taking or whether it makes any sense. It's fine if the writing is simply your stream of consciousness—a way of talking to yourself on paper. Don't feel constrained by the idea that anyone will read this piece of writing; it's just for you, and it doesn't matter how it looks. Don't worry about spelling, grammar, punctuation, or any rules of writing. Don't go back to correct errors or fix wording. In fact, if you're doing your freewriting on a computer, you may want to cover up or dim the screen so you can't even see what you're writing. Keep writing for the full ten minutes, trying not to pause.

The resulting piece of writing most likely will be a throwaway, but it might contain some good ideas that you can use in your paper.

When should you freewrite? It's definitely worth a try when the due date for your paper is drawing near and you just can't seem to get started. Once you are freewriting, it's always possible that you'll feel energized to start writing your paper. But you may want to do ten minutes of freewriting more frequently, even daily. The more you warm up in the days before your paper is due, the more comfortable you'll be for the big performance. You may also want to try some freewriting sessions before you approach your instructor for direction.

**HINT**

Our friend Mike Barker, who is the administrator of an on-line writers discussion group on the Internet, offers this hint about his mind-set for freewriting: "I usually apply the dictum: 'Plan to throw the first one away.' What does this do? Takes almost all the pressure off. I'm not writing the paper I'm going to turn in; I'm just writing a piece to toss. I can play. I can take digs at the professor's stupid socks. I can do almost anything. If I get stuck because it's a rotten idea, or I can't figure out what to do with it, that's OK because this was just for practice anyway. And now I've got some material. I can organize it, clean out the nasty remarks about how the professor spends his nights, and start to form the piece I'm going to turn in."

"**Use** freewriting to sort out your ideas first."

—a physics professor at Concordia University, Montreal, Canada

# Technique 17: Directed freewriting

**Directed freewriting is a step** closer than freewriting to actually writing your paper. You may wish to employ this technique when time is even more of an issue than it is when you freewrite as a warm-up or when you feel you might be almost ready to start writing your paper.

When you engage in directed freewriting, you should *definitely* have your paper in mind. Where freewriting gets your juices flowing for the writing process in general, directed freewriting gets you in a frame of mind to write *your paper* specifically. In essence, you are writing *about* your paper.

The first step is closely akin to brainstorming (Technique 6). You will write down as many thoughts about your paper topic as you can, but instead of putting them down in a list format, you will write them roughly as sentences and paragraphs. If you've prepared an outline, you might write a paragraph about each point on your outline. You needn't write down the points in order, however; you can skip around as you wish.

As with freewriting, you will pay no attention to writing correctly, and you won't go back to make revisions. You will simply endeavor to get as many words down about your paper topic as possible within a period of about fifteen minutes.

If, at this point, you feel ready to start writing your paper, go for it! Your piece of directed freewriting may have yielded ideas for a starting point or a direction for your paper that will equip you to hop on the true task at hand. Chances are that as you engaged in directed freewriting, a lightbulb flashed on in your head and inspired you to write your paper in a certain way. You can probably use lots of bits and pieces from your directed freewriting exercise in your paper.

If the lightbulb remains dim, and you still don't feel ready to write your paper, you may want to try one or more of the tricks Peter Elbow suggests for expanding on this initial freewriting:

▲    Write a dialogue or argument between two people about your topic.

▲    Write a detailed portrait of a personality connected with your topic.

▲    Write about your topic as though your audience were very different from the one for which it's actually being written. Instead of writing for your instructor, write for a close friend, your mother, or a child, for example.

▲    Pretend that you are a different person, perhaps someone with the opposite point of view about your paper, and write from that point of view.

▲    Write a pack of lies about your topic—ridiculous notions that couldn't possibly be true.

The idea of these approaches is to light a fire under the thought process about your topic and help you get comfortable with writing about it. If the writing gods are smiling on you, you will surely be ready to write your paper after engaging in one or more of these directed freewriting exercises.

**HINT**

Remember not to toss any writing that results from this technique. If you develop a stream of writing that doesn't fit *this* paper, save it in case it works for a future paper.

# Technique 18: Nonstop writing

**Another form of freewriting** that is particularly useful for creative writing (stories and poems), where your topic is wide open, is nonstop writing. Don't worry—it's not literally nonstop; the technique simply continues until you develop your idea and you are ready to write.

Start out as you would for freewriting, writing about anything, but write for a somewhat longer period—twenty to thirty minutes.

Read over what you've written and determine the main focus or theme of this piece of freewriting. Write this focus down in a single sentence and use it as your starting point for your next session of freewriting. Continue this second session for as long as you feel you can. Feel free to wander away from the theme you chose from your first piece.

Repeat this process as often as you need to until it becomes obvious what you should be writing about. The most important aspect of this technique is to do nothing but write (hence the name nonstop writing) until the pathway to your paper or story is clear to you and you feel comfortable with writing it.

You can probably use some of what you've written in your freewriting as part of your assignment, or you may feel the need to start from scratch, perhaps developing an outline (Technique 9).

**HINT**

Remember *not* to use this technique when you're under the gun of a deadline. For those circumstances, Technique 21 (page 47) may be best. When you have the time, however, this technique can be a very rewarding and useful writing tool.

# Technique 19: Committing words to paper, part 1: write everything but the actual paper

**If only you could commit** words to paper, you would feel you'd gotten started, and with any luck, the momentum would build from there, enabling you to finish a good paper on time.

If you are convinced that you are not ready to start writing, you can still get words down on paper and build momentum by typing components you know you will need for your paper. The first part of your paper that we recommend completing under any circumstances is your bibliography. Here's why:

▲ Because a bibliography must be formatted in a prescribed way, it can be a real pain in the posterior to type. If, for example, you've pulled an all-nighter writing a paper, the last thing you're going to feel like doing is typing and formatting a bibliography after you've completed the paper.

▲    If you postpone the bibliography until the end of your paper, you may find that you've forgotten what book you pulled a quotation from, or you may misplace an article you read early in your research. You're not likely to have these problems if you do your bibliography first.

▲    The bibliography can also serve as a guide for your research, as you will see in chapter 2.

You can type the bibliography well ahead of the final paper, and it can be quite preliminary in nature. When you finalize it, you can always delete sources that you didn't end up using and add sources that you did use. If you plan a research stream, as suggested in Technique 5, you can keep a master bibliography on disk and cut/paste for future papers.

You can make the bibliography even easier by using one of several strong bibliographic software programs. These programs not only help keep your references organized but also display them properly in the academic citation style you're using. These useful programs are, for the Macintosh, *Endnote Plus*, *Library Master*, *Perfect Scholar*, *ProCite*, or *Square Note;* and for DOS/Windows, *EndNote Plus*, *Citation 7*, *Bibliography Builder*, *Bookends Pro*, or *ProCite*. See chapter 8 for details.

You can also type any quotations and other material from sources that you are reasonably certain you will use in your paper. Where students have frequently recorded on index cards the bits of research material and quotations that they thought they might use in their papers, computers now allow them to keep a database of such material.

Let's say you keep a computer file of all the quotations and other material from sources that you think you are likely to use in your paper. When the time comes to compose your paper, and you come to a place where you want to use one of the quotes or other material, you can just copy it from the file where you've already typed and stored the material and insert it into your paper instead of having to retype it. Be sure to use the style for citations that your professor requires.

You can also type ahead of time such other peripheral components as cover pages, tables of contents, appendixes, charts, graphs, figures, and tables. Eventually, you'll get to the point where the only thing left to do is actually write the paper! But that won't seem so daunting since you already have so many other words already committed to paper.

If you choose to create a database of quotes and other material from sources, be sure to include only material that you are reasonably certain you will use. If you type a lot of material that you don't end up using, you'll defeat the whole purpose of this technique by making extra work for yourself. If you come across material that you think you *might* use, make a note to yourself to go back and check it as you're actually writing the paper. But if you do end up with quotes you don't use, don't delete them from your computer because you could always use them in future papers.

## Technique 20: Committing words to paper, part 2: the Just Do It method

**So, you've done all the** preliminaries on your paper that you possibly can, and you still don't know how to get started on the actual writing—but time is running out. You may have no other choice but to *Just Do It*.

The Just Do It method is akin to freewriting and directed freewriting but with one important difference. When you Just Do It, you truly are writing your paper. You may or may not be writing your paper when you freewrite. Freewriting, as we've said, is not so much the writing of your paper as an exercise to get you warmed up to write your paper. And directed freewriting is not writing your paper but writing *about* your paper.

Just Do It. Easier said than done, right? Try as you might, you just can't seem to write that opening sentence. There's no rule that says you have to start at the beginning. If you can't write the opening sentence, perhaps you can write another part of the paper. You can start in the middle, the end, or any part of your paper where you feel comfortable writing.

As with freewriting, you shouldn't worry about being perfect (unless it's the night before your paper is due). Concentrate on writing that you're comfortable with. Focus on expressing yourself in a way that feels right for you. Leave a blank if you can't think of the right word. Direct your energies to committing as many words to paper as you can so you build momentum.

The more you write, the more you will be motivated to finish. And it goes without saying that the more you write, the closer your paper will be to actually being finished. If you can get past that stumbling block of getting the first words down, the paper will begin to take shape and assume some structure. As it does so, you'll probably find that the wording of that pesky introductory sentence will become clear to you.

Now, obviously you don't want to take imperfection to extremes. Committing words to paper for the sake of committing words to paper won't help you unless your words make at least some coherent sense. But by the time you've come this far with your paper, your words presumably will make sense. Your research and any of the prewriting techniques you may have chosen—your outline, journal, mind map, results of your brainstorming, your database of preliminary components—can help you make sense.

**HINT**

Do allow yourself enough time to revise and edit after you Just Do It. Since your goal has been getting words down on paper rather than your best writing, you'll want to polish your work and improve the writing before handing your paper in. A good way to budget your time is simply to divide the available time in half. If you have two days before the paper is due, spend the available time on the first day doing your rough writing and your time on the second day revising. See Technique 24 (page 55) and chapter 6 for efficient ways to do that.

# Technique 21: Quick and dirty (but good) writing— under deadline pressure

**Let's say that,** despite all your best intentions, you've procrastinated writing your paper, and suddenly it's due the next day. (We're sure that *never* happens to you!) Or what if you simply forgot or got your dates confused? Your back is against the wall, and you don't have time for all the "gimmicks" in this chapter to jump-start your writing. You probably don't even have time for much revising. What can you do?

You can still write a decent paper, but let's hope you've done some research and employed an organizing technique—outlining, brainstorming, abstracting, mind mapping—early. Writing a paper under this kind of pressure truly requires some kind of road map. If you haven't organized up to this point, sketch out a quick outline or its equivalent now. At the very least, have a good handle on your purpose for writing—your main point or thesis.

Take comfort from knowing that sometimes too much planning results in stilted and labored writing—a paper that's actually overwritten. Be confident that your spontaneity will work for you.

Of all the writing situations you can be in, this "under-the-gun" circumstance is the one that most requires creating a conducive environment (Technique 1). Be sure you mitigate your difficult predicament by creating the optimal surroundings for writing.

A technique that can work for you and get you started is writing by speaking (Technique 15), but don't bother with the tape recorder; just write as you speak. And type as you write. It's under conditions like these that composing on the computer truly pays off.

Let your anxiety work for you instead of against you. Don't let time terrorize you; let it empower you. Say to yourself, "I do my best work under pressure." It's not as though you've never been in this situation. After all, this is exactly what it's like when you take an essay exam. As long as you know your material (or at least have your material close at hand) while remaining cool and confident, you can pull it off.

Don't get stuck over the perfect beginning. As with other techniques, it's fine to start in the middle or at the end. Writing a compelling opening paragraph when you have written more of the paper will be much easier.

As noted in Technique 3, be sure to save the computer document often. As a friend and recent doctoral student points out, "Computers seem to know when you're under pressure."

Revise as you go along or plan as much time as you can for revising. Employ such tools as spell checkers and grammar checkers. Read the paper aloud to yourself or ask a friend to read it, if time permits.

If, despite all your confidence, you end up feeling that the resulting paper is a disaster, talk to your instructor. *Show* him or her that you've completed the paper, but explain that you feel you could improve it enormously if you just had one more day to work on it. You may have to weigh the degree to which you feel you can improve the paper against any possible penalty for a late paper. Let's say you estimate the paper you've written is a D paper that you feel capable of turning into a B paper—but the instructor's policy is that every day of lateness means a drop in letter grade. If your predictions about the paper are on target, you'll end up with a C, which is better than a D, so the extension is worthwhile. Be prepared, however, for inflexibility from your professor. Many profs feel strongly that a deadline is a deadline, and it's not fair to your classmates for you to get a break. If your instructor won't agree to an extension, ask if you can later rework the paper to improve your grade.

# Technique 22: The security of following a formula

**If you're an insecure** college writer, you can benefit from following a writing formula that you can apply to many situations. That way, you always know exactly how to approach almost any writing situation. You can avoid some procrastination and fear because you have a step-by-step plan that enables you to plunge right into the writing of the piece.

This formula works best for shorter pieces, such as essays, and papers written over a relatively short period that don't require enormous amounts of research. You can apply the principles to the long research paper, but the basic building blocks of the formula are five paragraphs. In essence, the formula expands on the idea of the outline; if you take the main sentence from each paragraph, you should have a coherent outline.

As described by Carol Kanar in *The Confident Student*, the five-paragraph formula is as follows:

Paragraph one: Introduction, a three-part thesis statement

Paragraph two: Supporting argument for first point in thesis statement

Paragraph three: Supporting argument for second point in thesis statement

Paragraph four: Supporting argument for third point in thesis statement

Paragraph five: Conclusion and Implications

Donald Hall suggests in *Writing Well* five effective ways to conclude:
- a final anecdote that reinforces the central idea
- a strong final quotation
- a forecast, prediction, or warning based on facts developed in the paper
- a suggestion for remedial action
- a return from the specific to the general, relating the findings of the paper to a general trend

To expand on the formula for longer pieces, simply write as many subheadings and paragraphs as necessary for each part of the formula.

Here's an example of the introduction and topic sentences for subsequent paragraphs in a paper written according to the five-paragraph formula:

Paragraph one: If Americans intend to solve the nation's garbage crisis, they must learn the Three R's: Recycle, Reduce, Reuse.

Paragraph two: Recycling involves not only recycling products and packaging such as bottles and cans, but also buying products made from recycled materials.

Paragraph three: The typical American throws away an average of 500 pounds of garbage annually; compare this to the average European who tosses less than half that amount annually.

Paragraph four: Reusing involves saving containers, such as cardboard boxes, and reusing them for other purposes.

Paragraph five: The nation's trash and landfill crisis can only be solved by all Americans actively getting involved in the Three R's: Recycling, Reusing, and Reducing. By working together, we can solve this crisis.

**HINT**

The five-paragraph formula works like a dream for essay exams. It provides a superb way to organize your thoughts as you attempt to answer essay questions. When you're in a pressure-cooker situation such as an essay exam, nothing works better than having a specific structure that guides you in approaching each question. The formula also helps you avoid accidentally omitting an important point from your argument. Chapters 3 and 7 provide further tips on taking essay exams, as do these World Wide Web sites:

Tips on Writing the Essay-Type Examination at **http://www.csbju.edu/advising/ help/essayexm.html**

Five Tools for Writing Timed Essays at **http://splavc.spjc.cc.fl.us/hooks/ hooksessay.html**

Some General Advice on Academic Essay Writing at **http://www.erin.utoronto. ca/academic/writing/essay.htm**

Essay Writing: Tips and Pitfalls at **http://shakti.trincoll.edu/~helton/syllabi/ essayhlp.html**

# Technique 23: Overcoming the terror of writing for teachers

**Thinking of your professor** as the great, all-powerful judge of your paper and decider of your grade can be quite daunting. So, don't. Instead enlist him or her as a partner in every step of the writing process. Let your instructor buy into your paper. Let his or her investment become so great that your teacher has almost as much of a stake in your grade as you do.

Identify your attitude about writing classes and writing instructors in general. If you need to, clear your mind of any negative comments you may have received from past writing instructors. Then, make sure that you understand what is expected of you for *this* assignment from *this* instructor. If that involves asking your instructor for a definition of the audience and purpose, then ask; if it involves asking your instructor for a list of grading criteria, then ask. Try to build a partnership with your instructor.

# "Write the paper with the purpose of the assignment in mind, not the grade."

*—a professor of communications disorders at a medium-sized public university*

Ask questions about the assignment and what your teacher seeks. If you're too embarrassed to ask in class in front of your peers, visit your prof's office.

Ask about the specific purpose of the paper and its audience. The audience may seem obvious—the professor. Peter Elbow argues, however, that writing for a teacher can seem so unnatural because normal communication involves explaining something to someone who doesn't understand it; when you write for a teacher, you're explaining something to a reader who understands the subject better than you do. The prof may be able to frame the assignment in a way that avoids that unnatural communication flow. One prof we know gives take-home essay exams that require his business students to write memos to imaginary corporate players convincing them of ways to better market their products.

As a teacher himself, Elbow reports the striking frequency with which students hand in papers with the comment, "I hope this is what you wanted." If you want to write successful papers and attain good grades, make it your business always to find out what the teacher wants.

# "Follow guidelines and instructions given, and take a detailed look at examples provided."

*—a biology professor at a large public university*

**"Thoroughly understand the assignment and include all parameters requested. Don't omit…dimensions of the assignment."**

*—a professor of communications disorders at a medium-sized public university*

**"Follow directions. Ask for help if you need it rather than doing something halfway."**

*—a journalism professor at a medium-sized public university*

**"Follow the evaluation criteria for the assignment."**

*—an education professor at a large public university*

You may even want to go as far as determining how your teacher wants your paper packaged (a subject explored in greater depth in chapter 5). Does the instructor want it paper-clipped? Stapled? Folded lengthwise? Bound in a fancy report cover? Is a cover page required? Packaging probably won't make or break your grade, but if you persist in packaging your papers in ways that annoy the professor, he or she may unconsciously downgrade your paper. Do be sure to read the syllabus or any other written handout about the assignment carefully before asking questions that the professor has already answered.

"**Read** the guidelines for each paper as though you were reading directions for programming a VCR or changing the oil in your car. If you don't understand them, see [the professor]. There is no such thing as a dumb question; don't be afraid to ask."

—a psychology professor at a large public university

Get your prof's opinion of your topic. Theoretically, your teacher knows the field well enough to know how much research material is available on your topic. Solicit your instructor's ideas on the best ways to research the paper. Show him or her your outline. See if your prof is willing to read and comment on your first draft.

Don't forget the e-mail option for communicating with your instructor. If you're on a campus where students are networked with faculty, e-mail can be a marvelous way to work with your instructor. It's a terrific mode if you're shy about talking to the prof in class or in his/her office. And it gives the teacher the opportunity to respond at his or her convenience instead of being put on the spot. You may not get an answer right away, but you can ask questions and make requests at virtually any hour of the night or day.

Will some professors become annoyed if you attach yourself to them, leech-like, during every step in your paper writing process? Maybe, especially if you attend a large university in which the professors have a heavy teaching load and many students in each class. But most professors will be glad to help you write a better paper. After all, it's no fun to *read* a poorly researched, badly written paper. And the better writer you become, the less you will have to consult with your profs.

If nothing else, seeking paper writing guidance from your instructor tells him or her that you really care about doing well. Such a demonstration of concern is not a guarantee of a better grade, but those students who appear as though they care about succeeding tend to be looked upon more favorably than those who never talk to their teachers about their work.

"**Get** feedback on a draft from your teacher even if he/she doesn't invite you."

—a literature and composition professor at a large public university

If you get a curmudgeonly prof who won't give you as much help as you need, try going to another professor in the same department with whom you have rapport or your adviser, and ask if he or she will assist you with your paper. Or perhaps your prof has a graduate assistant who could guide you. If your school has a writing lab, you may be able to get the help you need there. If your school doesn't have a writing lab or writing center, you can find a number of on-line writing labs/centers on the Internet. Interactive help is sometimes available even to those students who are not enrolled at the writing center's home university. See chapter 8 for a list of these labs/centers.

"**Don't** be afraid to ask for help. Ask the professor for clarification, go to the campus writing center, use a tutor, talk to your peers. It's OK to *learn* how to write. Not everyone knows automatically."

—an English professor at a small private university

## HINT

If, despite your best efforts, your grade still comes back lower than expected, by all means talk to your professor about how you can do better. It is important to ask if you can rework the paper to improve your grade. Your disappointing grade simply may be the result of not understanding what the teacher wanted. One student, Nicole, wrote what she thought was a terrific paper for a literature class. She was devastated when it came back with a C+ on it. When she went to see the professor, Nicole learned that while she had written a fine summary and description of the piece of literature at hand, the teacher wanted a far more analytical piece. True, the professor had asked for analysis when she gave the assignment, but Nicole had difficulty discerning the difference between summary and analysis. Once Nicole learned from her teacher how to write this type of analytical paper, she aced the rest of the papers for that class.

If your prof seems reluctant to meet with you, try other measures. For soliciting more feedback than professors normally provide, Elbow suggests such techniques as attaching a sheet to your paper in which you ask him or her to respond to such questions as "What is the quickest, simplest change I could make that would create the greatest improvement?" and "What one thing do you think I should try to work on or think about in my next piece of writing?" He also suggests you might supply your prof with a cassette tape on which to make verbal comments about your paper. In either case, ask your professor first if he or she would be willing to respond to either of these devices.

# Technique 24: Quick revising

**Although this technique** seems to belong in chapter 6 on revisions, we include it here because it is the companion piece to some of the techniques we've suggested for getting words on paper. As the name implies, quick revising is what you have to do when your deadline is looming and you have no choice but to revise quickly. This technique is the one you need to employ when it's the night before your paper is due, and your writing has been either intentionally or unintentionally haphazard. You are fighting against not only the deadline but your own anxiety, so you need a surefire process to accomplish a revision that makes the grade.

If time is extremely short, you will probably have no choice but to perform this process on a computer.

First, calm your fears by believing that your paper is going to turn out just fine. Try reciting the mantra "It will all come together." Detach yourself from your paper so that you neither hate it so much that it discourages you nor love it so much that you can't change it.

In fact, detach yourself so that you put yourself in the place of the audience who will be reading the paper. Read the paper through the eyes of your professor.

Next, identify what's good about the paper. Signal all the cogent, well-written passages with a mark in the margin.

Now, determine your thesis statement and arrange all those good passages into an order that supports your thesis. You may at this point notice that you've left out important arguments that would bolster your premise. Insert these arguments.

Next, put together an almost-final draft using all your best passages and new insertions in logical order—but omit your opening paragraph. Where necessary, construct or improve transitions to get you smoothly from one passage to the next.

Write a compelling opening paragraph that entices the reader and coherently states your thesis or main point. Check to make sure you've logically arrived at your conclusion and that it's well expressed.

Now, read the paper aloud. It's a great way to flag down awkward constructions, bumpy sentences, missing transitions, and just plain murky writing.

Finally, correct spelling and grammatical errors—perhaps with some help from your computer software (see chapter 8).

**HINT**

Another "guest hint" from Mike Barker about the raw material you'll be quick-revising: "Do more than the minimum! If the paper needs three major points, write up six, then condense. If the paper needs 500 words, start by writing up a couple thousand, then trim. And so on. Knowing that you are going to revise makes those 'starting pains' a lot easier. This version isn't the final draft; this is just raw material for the sculpting. You have to start with a lot of mud to make one pot, so start mixing."

# Technique 25: The buddy system

**We've placed this last** technique at the end, close to the following chapter on research tools, because strictly speaking, this is more of a research technique than a writing technique. We include it in this chapter, however, because the snowballing effect of procrastination often means that students put off researching their papers. The longer you put off research, the less time you'll have for writing. This technique not only motivates you to do research but opens the door for you to write a better researched paper.

The idea is to share your topic with your classmates. You can do so either informally with one or more congenial classmates, or you can suggest to your instructor that the whole class describe their topics.

Once you all know each other's topic, you can help each other with research. Chances are that since you're all in the same class, topics will bear at least some relationship to each other. There's a reasonable chance that as your friend Joe is researching his topic, he'll come across material that applies to yours and turn you onto it. And naturally you'll do the same for him.

Let's say the topic for your psychology paper is instrumental conditioning, and your classmate Judy's is classical conditioning. Judy could very likely come across information that would help in your research, just as you could spot material that could assist in hers.

The buddy system lends itself to other techniques as well. Additional participants almost always enhance brainstorming (Technique 6, page 15).

You can also employ the buddy system in creating a conducive atmosphere for writing your paper (Technique 1, page 3). If you're the type who is best motivated when you're working with others around you, you can cheer each other on as you go to the computer lab together to write and type your papers. If you or a friend has a laptop computer, you could park it in the same dorm room with another's desktop computer as you and your bud work together. Finally, this system can be invaluable for proofreading, editing, and revising. Most people are better at spotting errors in the writing of others than in their own writing. If you and your friends proof each other's papers, you'll likely catch mistakes you wouldn't have caught by checking your own paper. Just be sure to allow enough time to plug in revisions after your friend has read your paper. You may also wish to form small sharing/feedback groups so your writing can be reviewed by an audience other than instructors, which can often be enlightening.

**H I N T**

A collegial writing session that turns into a gabfest or a party can obviously have disastrous effects on everyone's papers. Be sure to enlist as your buddy a friend that you know will be generally quiet. The idea is to motivate each other, push each other on, and keep each other company. Occasional questions are fine ("How do you spell 'antediluvian'?" "What's another word for 'intrepid'?" "Tell me if this sentence sounds OK."), but nonstop yakking will not get the job done for either of you.

# 2 Cutting-Edge Research Tools and Techniques

WHILE THE FOCUS OF THIS CHAPTER IS ON CUTTING-EDGE RESEARCH TECHNIQUES, WE BELIEVE THAT A REVIEW OF GENERAL RESEARCH TECHNIQUES AND TERMINOLOGY IS IMPORTANT ENOUGH TO HIGHLIGHT FIRST. REMEMBER TO DISCUSS SOURCES WITH YOUR PROFESSOR BEFORE YOU BEGIN YOUR SEARCH SINCE MANY INSTRUCTORS MAY REQUIRE BOTH PRIMARY AND SECONDARY SOURCES FOR YOUR PAPER. WHEN CONDUCTING A LITERATURE SEARCH, YOU SHOULD BE AWARE OF THE SPECIFIC CLASSIFICATION SYSTEM FOR SOURCES:

Primary sources are published original writings, reflections, and reports that can be found in books, periodicals, monographs, conference proceedings, patents, and theses and dissertations.

Secondary sources are published writings and reports that analyze, critique, or report on a primary source and can be found in periodicals and reference books.

Tertiary sources aid the researcher in using primary and secondary sources and include indexes, directories, guides, and bibliographies.

Nondocumentary sources are nonpublished forms of communication and information, which can include conversations with faculty members, other students, and experts in the field.

The focus of this chapter, of course, is on identifying and explaining those tertiary sources that will help you identify, find, and use the primary and secondary sources you need for your paper's topic. Furthermore, while this chapter is designed to give you the information you need to complete the research portion of your writing project, in no way do we want to undermine the role of reference librarians. Reference librarians are experts in locating and using research materials efficiently and effectively, and we encourage you to work with these professionals as you complete your research.

Depending on your writing project, research is a three- or four-step process:

1.  If you are researching primary or secondary sources for information published before 1980, you will want to hit the reference books first. In certain libraries, some of these reference books are still available only in print form, so that's another reason to investigate them first.

2.  If you are searching for information published later than 1980, or after you've examined the print resources, the next step is using the CD-ROM (Compact Disk–Read Only Memory) reference material. CD-ROM technology allows the storage of enormous quantities of information on a single computer disk. The reference material on CD-ROMs is growing practically daily, and once you get accustomed to using this kind of reference tool, you won't want to go back to print sources. Searching for information stored on a CD-ROM is much easier (especially since you can manipulate your search by combining terms or limiting your search) than searching through volumes of books. While each distributor of CD-ROMs has slightly different search rules, once you have completed your first successful search, you'll be able to navigate them all.

3.  If you need still more information, the next step is logging onto the Internet and the World Wide Web and examining the databases and library catalogs available on the Net. The Net is a large collection of computer networks (7,000+) linked together with a common communication protocol. Recent estimates have more than twenty million people using the Net. The easiest and most common way to search the Net is using a graphic browser (such as Netscape *Navigator*) or text-based browser (such as *Lynx*) to connect to the World Wide Web. Another way to search the Net is through a text-only resource called Gopher. Finally, you can connect to computer systems other than your own (such as the Library of Congress) through a procedure called Telnet.

4.  The final step, if the previous steps have still left you lacking adequate sources, is turning to an on-line service, such as Dialog, available at your local library. The reason on-line searches are the line of last resort is

that there is a cost for on-line services, and the more you search, the more you pay.

So, let's start your research journey with print reference material and go from there.

# Reference books

**Reference books have come** to mean a specific kind of publication in which you can find certain types of information. These books contain facts compiled from many sources and are organized for quick and easy use. They include encyclopedias; dictionaries; yearbooks, almanacs, and handbooks; biographies; atlases; and indexes. Each of these reference materials has a different purpose in your research quest, which we'll explain as we introduce each one.

## ENCYCLOPEDIAS

An encyclopedia is designed to give you an overview of a topic, including providing a definition, description, background, and bibliographic references. They are an excellent source for literature summaries and often may include a bibliography, which can then lead you to more in-depth research. Encyclopedias are also a good place to start when you need a broad understanding of a subject, which in turn will allow you to narrow down the topic of your paper. Some examples of general encyclopedias:

*Academic American Encyclopedia* (Grolier Educational Corporation)
*The Canadian Encyclopedia* (Hurtig Publishers, Ltd.)
*Chambers Encyclopedia* (Pergamon Press)
*Collier's Encyclopedia* (Macmillan Educational Corporation)
*The New Encyclopedia Britannica* (Encyclopedia Britannica)
*The Encyclopedia Americana* (Grolier Educational Corporation)
*The New Columbia Encyclopedia* (Columbia University Press)
*The Random House Encyclopedia* (Random House)
*The World Book Encyclopedia* (World Book, Inc.)

## DICTIONARIES

A dictionary contains information about words: meaning, derivation, spelling, pronunciation, syllabication, and usage. Some dictionaries also include synonyms, biographical information, historical information, and pictures or other graphics. Why are dictionaries in this chapter? Well, partly because they traditionally are part of the discussion of reference materials, but also because you might use them in the early stages of your research. For example, suppose the topic of your paper is examining the history of gaudy jewelry in the Far East. By using a dictionary, you can find synonyms (in this case, tawdry, garish, flashy, and meretricious) that may help you in your search for detailed information. Some examples of dictionaries:

*A Dictionary of American English on Historical Principles* (University of
    Chicago Press)
*American Heritage Dictionary of the English Language* (Houghton Mifflin
    Company)
*Funk & Wagnall's New International Dictionary of the English Language*
    (World Publishing)
*The Oxford English Dictionary* (Oxford University Press)
*The Random House Dictionary of the English Language* (Random House)
*Webster's New International Dictionary of the English Language*
    (Merriam Webster)
*Webster's New World Dictionary* (Prentice Hall)

## YEARBOOKS, HANDBOOKS, AND ALMANACS

Yearbooks are publications issued annually to provide current information in narrative, statistical, or directory form. The several types of yearbooks include encyclopedia annuals, almanacs, and directories. Handbooks are typically small books that treat broad subjects in brief form and serve as a record of current knowledge. Say, for example, that you were investigating the effects of Catholicism on the success of governmental efforts to decrease family size through birth control in Mexico. An almanac would be a good place for you to find government statistics on family size and birth records. A few of the major ones include:

*Americana Annual* (Grolier, Inc.)

*Britannica Book of the Year* (Encyclopedia Britannica)

*Famous First Facts* (H.W. Wilson Company)

*Information Please Almanac, Atlas & Yearbook* (Information Please
    Publishing Company)

*Washington Information Directory* (Congressional Quarterly, Inc.)

*Webster's Dictionary of Proper Names* (Merriam Webster)

*The World Almanac and Book of Facts* (Newspaper Enterprise
    Association, Inc.)

*Thomas' Register of American Manufacturers* (Thomas Publishing
    Company)

## BIOGRAPHIES

Biographical dictionaries contain brief information about the lives of individuals, often including descriptions of events that occurred during the time the person lived. Biographies can be general or subject-specific, and can include persons living or dead. While biographical information can often be found in other sources (such as encyclopedias, dictionaries, and almanacs), biographies provide the most depth. For example, if you were assigned to discover Walter Philip Reuther's influence in American history, you would find that he was a leader in the labor movement during the middle of this century. Some examples:

*Almanac of American Women in the 20th Century* (Prentice Hall)

*Chambers Biographical Dictionary* (Cambridge University Press)

*International Dictionary of 20th-Century Biography* (New American
    Library)

*McGraw-Hill Encyclopedia of World Biography* (McGraw-Hill)

*New Century Cyclopedia of Names* (Appleton-Century-Crofts, Inc.)

*Webster's New Biographical Dictionary* (Merriam Webster)

## ATLASES

An atlas is a collection of maps, usually bound together in one volume; however, many atlases today are more than collections of maps and often include descriptive data, demographic information, political history, and business conditions. Atlases can be classified into two categories, political or physical, and by themes, such as climatology, statistics, or meteorology. For example, if you were assigned to provide a snapshot of Norway's seasonal weather patterns, a climatological atlas would be an excellent source. Some examples:

*Hammond Atlas of the World* (Hammond)
*National Atlas of the United States of America* (National Geographic)
*National Geographic Atlas of the World* (National Geographic)
*The Prentice-Hall Great International Atlas* (Prentice Hall)
*The Times Atlas of the World* (Times Books)

## INDEXES

An index is designed to provide bibliographic information on articles, essays, speeches, poems, or other written works published in periodicals or as collected works. Many—if not all—of these indexes are now on CD-ROM (see next section), but the printed version often allows you to go back much farther chronologically than the CD-ROM version. A good college library generally includes:

*America: History & Life* (ABC-Clio). Abstracts articles on the history of the United States and Canada published throughout the world. From 1964 to present.

*Applied Science and Technology Index* (H.W. Wilson). Covers approximately 335 periodicals in the fields of aeronautics and space science, automation, chemistry, computer technology, electricity, mathematics, physics, telecommunications, and related subjects. From 1958 to present.

*Art Index* (H.W. Wilson). Indexes publications in the fields of archaeology, architecture, art history, city planning, design, graphic arts, landscape architecture, photography and films, and related subjects. From 1929 to present.

*Arts & Humanities Citation Index* (Institute for Scientific Information). A multidisciplinary index of more than six thousand journals covering the literature of the arts and humanities. From 1976 to present.

*Biography Index* (H.W. Wilson). A cumulative index to biographical material found in books and magazines. From 1946 to present.

*Biological Abstracts* (BioSciences Information Service). Provides indexing and abstracts of worldwide research in biology. From 1926 to present.

*Biological & Agricultural Index* (H.W. Wilson). A cumulative subject index to periodicals in the fields of biology, agriculture, and related sciences. From 1964 to present.

*Book Review Digest* (H.W. Wilson). A digest and index of selected book reviews in about seventy-five English and American general-interest periodicals. From 1905 to present.

*Book Review Index* (Gale Research Company). Indexes book reviews appearing in about 450 periodicals. From 1965 to present.

*Business Periodicals Index* (H.W. Wilson). Indexes about 350 journals in business, finance and investment, advertising and public relations, accounting, insurance, labor and management, and economics. From 1958 to present.

*Chemical Abstracts* (American Chemical Society). Abstracts in detail documents from publications in more than fifty languages. From 1907 to present.

*Computer Literature Index* (Applied Computer Research). Indexes computer-related trade publications, general business periodicals, and publications of computer and management-oriented professional societies. From 1980 to present.

*Current Index to Journals in Education* (Oryx). Published as part of the U.S. Office of Education's Educational Resources Information Center (ERIC) program, this service provides indexing for articles in more than 800 education journals. From 1969 to present.

*Economic Literature Index* (American Economic Association). Indexes articles from more than 340 journals in economics. From 1969 to present.

*Education Index* (H.W. Wilson). A cumulative author/subject index to a selected list of educational periodicals and yearbooks. From 1929 to present.

*Environmental Abstracts* (Environment Information Center, Inc.). An indexing and abstracting source covering both print and nonprint materials related to environmental issues. From 1971 to present.

*Essay and General Literature Index* (H.W. Wilson). Often referred to as Essay Index, it emphasizes articles in the humanities and social sciences. From 1934 to present.

*Facts on File: World News Digest with Index* (Facts on File). A weekly digest of news arranged under mainly geographical headings. From 1940 to present.

*General Science Index* (H.W. Wilson). Indexes more than a hundred general science periodicals not completely covered by other indexes. From 1978 to present.

*Higher Education Abstracts* (Claremont Graduate School). Abstracts some 120 scholarly journals, as well as conference papers and monographs. From 1984 to present.

*Humanities Index* (H.W. Wilson). Subject fields indexed include archaeology and classical studies, area studies, folklore, history, language and literature, performing arts, philosophy, religion, theology, and related subjects. From 1974 to present.

*INSPEC* (Institution of Electrical Engineers). Provides access to literature about physics, electrical engineering, electronics, and computing. From 1969 to present.

*International Political Science Abstracts* (International Political Science Association). Offers abstracts to articles selected from more than a thousand international journals. From 1951 to present.

*Magazine Index* (Information Access Corporation). Indexes roughly 435 popular periodicals. From 1976 to present.

*MLA International Bibliography* (Modern Language Association of America). Indexes books and articles on modern languages and literature. From 1921 to the present.

*NewsBank Index* (NewsBank, Inc.) Indexes articles focusing on socioeconomic, political, international, and scientific fields from more than a hundred U.S. newspapers. From 1982 to present.

*PAIS International in Print* (Public Affairs Information Service Inc.). An interdisciplinary, international index to periodicals relating to public issues and policy. From 1991 to present.

*Philosopher's Index* (Bowling Green University). Indexes and abstracts an international collection of books, periodicals, monographs, and dissertations related to philosophy. From 1967 to present.

*Psychological Abstracts* (American Psychological Association). Comprehensive index to the literature of psychology, indexing more than 1,200 periodicals. From 1927 to present.

*Reader's Guide to Periodical Literature* (H.W. Wilson). A cumulative index covering approximately 174 periodicals of general interest. From 1901 to present.

*Resources in Education* (U.S. Government Printing Office). Contains abstracts of items in the ERIC collection of some 400,000 research reports, papers from professional meetings, government documents, and related materials. Does not index journal articles. From 1975 to present.

*Science Abstracts* (Institution of Electrical Engineers). Coverage is international and includes periodicals, reports, books, dissertations, conference papers, and patents related to the sciences. From 1967 to present.

*Social Science Citation Index* (Institute for Scientific Information). An international interdisciplinary index to literature of the social, behavioral, and related sciences. From 1973 to present.

*Social Sciences Index* (H.W. Wilson). Author and subject index to periodicals in the fields of anthropology, area studies, community health and medical care, economics, family studies, minority studies, social work, sociology, and related subjects. From 1974 to present.

*Sociological Abstracts* (Sociological Abstracts, Inc.). Provides indexing and abstracts from international sources on sociology and related disciplines. From 1953 to present.

*Women Studies Abstracts* (Rush Publishing Company). Abstracts articles from thirty-five journals covering a wide range of subjects related to women's studies. From 1972 to present.

# Reference material on CD-ROM

**A significant number of** reference materials are on or soon to be on CD-ROM technology. Periodical indexes—those databases that search magazines, newspapers, and academic journal articles—were the first to go on CD-ROM. In more recent years, however, encyclopedias and dictionaries have gone to CD-ROM, and now even some periodicals have put their indexes and back issues on CD-ROM. The number and uses of CD-ROM are increasing rapidly. Furthermore, some of this material is also going on the Internet's World

Wide Web—at least in some form—such as the ERIC database, as well as a number of other databases and other reference material.

## PERIODICAL INDEXES

Computerized information retrieval using CD-ROM databases adds a powerful tool in helping you complete your research. The use of Boolean logic, available with most of the databases, allows you to retrieve citations based on a user-specified relationship of terms, or you can search by author, title, subject, or key terms. Make sure before you start your search that you know how the database handles "and" and "or." It also helps to list the major concepts of your topics and think of synonyms for these concepts. Some of the most widely used databases—and what you should find in a good college library—follow:

*ABI/INFORM* indexes and abstracts articles in more than 800 business and economics journals and trade publications published worldwide and is the key business database. The abstracts are lengthy and often provide key data for expanded searches.

*Academic Search* indexes and abstracts articles from more than two thousand periodicals, covering general interest magazines, some scholarly journals from the social sciences, humanities, and sciences, as well as the *New York Times* and *Wall Street Journal*. This database is an excellent source for information on current events.

*America: History and Life* contains citations, with abstracts, from more than 2,100 journals to social-science and humanities scholarly literature on all aspects of U.S. and Canadian history, culture, and current affairs from prehistory to the present.

*American Business Disc* provides basic directory information for approximately ten million businesses within the United States. This database is searchable by company name, SIC code, or "Yellow Pages" subject heading.

*Biography and Genealogy Master Index* contains biographical information on about four million current and historical persons in all fields.

*Business NewsBank* indexes selected newspaper articles pertaining to business and economics from more than 500 U.S. cities. More recently, this database has begun providing full text of the articles directly on the CD-ROM.

*CD NewsBank* provides full text of selected articles from nearly forty U.S. and Canadian newspapers, as well as from six wire services. Focus is on national and international news.

*Compact Disclosure* provides financial information on approximately twelve thousand public companies extracted from documents filed with the U.S. Securities and Exchange Commission (SEC).

*County & City Data Book* provides full-text demographic, economic, and governmental data from various census surveys.

*Dissertation Abstracts* contains bibliographic citations and abstracts of doctoral dissertations and masters theses in the humanities, social sciences, sciences, and engineering.

*EconLit* is a comprehensive indexed bibliography with selected abstracts of economic literature from around the world.

*ERIC* indexes more than 750 journals in all areas of education as well as special ERIC documents. Full Boolean search capabilities are available for this premier education-related database.

*Ethnic Newswatch* includes current events and political articles from newspapers and magazines published by ethnic presses in the United States.

*Facts on File* contains news summaries of national and international events as well as approximately 300 maps.

*FBIS (Foreign Broadcast Information Service) Index* is a collection of English translations of news reports, radio broadcasts, and government releases from around the world. Produced by the U.S. government.

*GeoRef* contains worldwide technical literature on geology and geophysics.

*Government Periodicals Index* provides information about periodicals and journals issued by agencies of the U.S. government.

*Historical Abstracts* contains citations and abstracts of articles, books, and dissertations on world history and related areas of the social sciences and humanities.

*MATHSCI* includes world literature on mathematics, as well as mathematically related research in computer science, statistics, econometrics.

*NESE (National Economic, Social, and Environmental) Data Bank* includes full-text articles and statistics about a wide variety of economic, sociological, environmental, education, and business information about the United States.

*National Trade Data Bank* (NTDB) is a full-text database that contains statistics on imports and exports, international transactions, and other trade and employment information collected by U.S. governmental agencies.

*NewsBank Plus* is an index to a microfiche collection of selected newspaper articles from more than 500 U.S. cities, focusing on current events, people in the news, and reviews of the arts.

*Newspaper Abstracts Ondisc* indexes articles in four major newspapers: *Christian Science Monitor*, *New York Times*, *Wall Street Journal*, and *Washington Post*.

*PAIS (Public Affairs Information Service)* indexes and abstracts articles, books, and government documents covering public affairs and public policy.

*Periodical Abstracts* contains abstracts from about 1,800 periodicals, including general interest magazines and the most important scholarly journals in the humanities, social sciences, and sciences.

*Philosopher's Index* indexes and abstracts literature on philosophy published in English, providing information about aesthetics, epistemology, ethics, logic, and metaphysics.

*PsycLIT* indexes and abstracts articles from about 1,300 journals worldwide. It is the premiere database for psychology.

*Religion Index* includes citations for literature on all aspects of religion and theology.

*Science Citation Index* (SCI) is a multidisciplinary database covering all areas of science and technology.

*Social Sciences Citation Index* covers 1,400 major social science journals across fifty disciplines.

*Sociofile*, focusing on sociology and related social sciences, abstracts articles from 1,600 journals, as well as dissertations from *Dissertation Abstracts*.

*World Tables* provides economic and demographic information for 216 countries and regions around the world.

## ENCYCLOPEDIAS

*Microsoft Bookshelf*. This collection of reference books contains *The Concise Columbia Encyclopedia, American Heritage Dictionary*,

*Original Roget's Thesaurus, Columbia Dictionary of Quotations, Hammond Intermediate World Atlas, People's Chronology, The World Almanac and Book of Facts,* and the *U.S. National 5-Digest ZIP Code and Post Office Directory. Bookshelf* allows the user to search all the books, or only one or two.

*Britannica CD.* What many call the gold standard of print encyclopedias is the basis for this CD-ROM version. Most reviewers site its lack of multimedia as its biggest flaw, yet the quality of its text and strong search engine make it a top choice.

*Compton's Interactive Encyclopedia. Compton's* has more than sixteen hours of multimedia and contains thirty-five thousand articles, both more than any of the other multimedia encyclopedias on the market.

*Encarta '96.* Several reviews hail *Encarta* as the best overall multimedia encyclopedia, especially for ease of use and overall technical virtuosity.

*Grolier Multimedia Encyclopedia '96.* If *Britannica* is the gold standard of print encyclopedias, *Grolier* is the gold standard of electronic encyclopedias. Most reviewers suggest that it lacks the sizzle of *Encarta* and *Compton's* but argue that its strength is in the depth of its coverage.

*Guinness Encyclopedia.* Most reviews of the newest entrant to multimedia encyclopedias suggest that the *Guinness* will not be able to function as the primary encyclopedia for any normal reference collection, but should be included as a supplement.

*Infopedia.* This is a hybrid of *Bookshelf* and *Encarta* in that it combines a complete encyclopedia with additional sources, including *Roget's 21st Century Thesaurus, The World Almanac and Book of Facts, Hammond World Atlas, Merriam-Webster's Collegiate Dictionary, Dictionary of English Usage, Dictionary of Quotations,* and *Webster's New Biographical Dictionary.*

*Webster's Interactive Encyclopedia.* Based on a British concise encyclopedia, *Webster's* tends to cover material thinly, according to most reviews.

*World Book Multimedia Encyclopedia.* Based on the widely used print version, *World Book* appears geared more for schools and libraries than for home or dorm use.

## DICTIONARIES

*Black's Law Dictionary.* Contains more than sixteen thousand legal terms and definitions.

*Choice Words.* Combines *Webster's Concise Electronic Dictionary* with *Webster's Thesaurus.*

*Concise Dictionary of 26 Languages.* Translates more than a thousand words in twenty-six different languages.

*Funk & Wagnall's Standard Desk Dictionary.* Contains definitions for 100,000 words.

*McGraw-Hill Technical Dictionaries.* Includes six different technical dictionaries covering biology, chemistry, engineering, and physics.

*The New Dictionary of the Living World.* Defines 2,600 biological terms from abaxial to zygote, with hundreds of photos, maps, and other multimedia tools.

*Random House Unabridged Electronic Dictionary.* Contains almost 315,000 entries with plenty of illustrations. Highly rated by reviewers.

*Stedman's Medical Dictionary.* Provides definitions of sixty-eight thousand medical terms.

*Webster's New World Professional Thesaurus.* Offers the full four million synonyms of the text version of the same name.

# Searching on the Internet

**Your next step in the** research process should be on the Net. You can obtain information from the Net in four ways:

Many World Wide Web pages may directly relate to the information you seek. (For example, if you were examining the social and historical consequences of the sinking of the *Titanic,* you could find more than twenty Web sites with information.)

A number of organizations on the Web now provide access (most for a fee) to large databases, as well as free access to library catalogs and other reference material.

If you don't have Web access, you can Gopher to many informational sites.

Another way to get information from the Net if you don't have Web access is to Telnet to a number of library sites on the Net.

For the most up-to-date listing of Web sites, Gopher sites, and Telnet addresses, please visit our Write Your Way to a Higher GPA Web site **(http://www.stetson. edu/~hansen/gpa.html)**.

Your keys to gaining access to this wealth of resources are a computer with a modem and an Internet account (usually with your college's computer network). To view the vast Web resources, you'll also need a Web browser (such as Netscape). If you are a novice to the information superhighway, most reference librarians can direct you to guides for surfing the Net, and as more schools "wire" their libraries, you can probably do your Web searching at the library.

## SEARCHING THE WEB

Web sites exist on practically every subject imaginable, and the number of Web sites is growing exponentially. This rapid growth means that the best way to find the information you need is to use one (or more) of the powerful Web search engines. One warning, though: each search engine has different search principles and different methods of searching. As with searches on CD-ROM databases, think carefully about your search terms and know how the search engine deals with "and" and "or." It also helps to list the major concepts of your topics and think of synonyms for these concepts. Once your search is completed, simply double-click a Web site that interests you and you are automatically connected to that site.

As this book went to press, the following were the major Web search engines—along with their Web addresses.

*ALTA VISTA,* which claims to be capable of indexing and searching twenty-one million Web pages and Usenet news groups up to 100 times faster than existing search engines. Web address: **http://www.altavista. digital.com/**

*EXCITE,* which searches more than eleven million Web sites and two weeks of Usenet News. Web address: **http://www.excite.com**

HOTBOT, a venture between *HotWired* and Inktomi, wants to be known as the search engine that has the capacity to index and search the entire Web. Web address: **http://www.hotbot.com/**

INFOSEEK GUIDE, which is the only search engine that fully integrates Internet directory browsing and Internet searching. Web address: **http://guide. infoseek.com/**

LINKSTAR, which claims that its search engine is designed to be a "next-generation search engine—one that provides an accurate, searchable directory that is freely available to any Web user." Web address: **http://www. linkstar.com/**

LYCOS, which is a comprehensive Internet database that allows Boolean "and" and "or" combinations of words in searching more than nineteen million Web sites. Web address: **http://www.lycos.com/**

MAGELLAN, which reviews and rates Web sites, with more than four million sites, out of which forty-five thousand have been fully reviewed and rated. Web address: **http://www.mckinley.com/**

OPEN TEXT, which allows searching for a complete phrase, a combination of words and phrases, or particular words. Web address: **http://www.open-text.com/omw/f-omw.html**

WEBCRAWLER, which operates by navigating the Web and either building an index for later use or by searching in real time. Web address: **http: //webcrawler.com/**

WORLD WIDE WEB WORM, which searches three million Web sites and allows Boolean "and" and "or" combinations when searching. Web address: **http://wwww.cs.colorado.edu/wwww**

YAHOO, which is a fairly comprehensive subject index, but its search engine is weak. Web address: **http:www.yahoo.com/search.html**

## INTERNET REFERENCE RESOURCES ON THE WEB

As fast as reference material is being converted to CD-ROM format, reference materials and resources are moving even faster onto the Web.

**Libraries with Web sites.** Many university libraries have Web sites, but those on the list that follows have extraordinary Web sites, with exceptional links to other research resources. Most of the addresses are to the "Reference Desk" area of the libraries, but if you so desire, you can back into the main sites of the libraries as well (usually by clicking a button labeled "Home Page").

The Library of Congress. Web address: **http://www.loc.gov/**

The U.S. Navy's Ruth H. Hooker Research Library and Technical Information Center. Web address: **http://infonext.nrl.navy.mil/catalogs_and_databases/**

Libweb, a listing of more than a thousand libraries in more than forty-five countries on six continents. Web address: **http://sunsite. berkeley.edu/ Libweb/**

The New York Public Library. Web address: **http://www.nypl.org/**

The Berkeley Public Library. Web address: **http://www.ci.berkeley.ca.us/bpl/ bkmk/index.html**

The World-Wide Web Virtual Library. Web address: **http://www.asap.unimelb. edu.au/hstm/hstm_bio.html**

The Electric Library. Web address: **http://www.elibrary.com/**

The Internet Public Library. Web address: **http://www.ipl.org/ref/RR/**

Columbia University's Bartleby Library. Web address: **http://www.cc.columbia. edu/acis/bartleby/**

University of Washington. Web address:**http://www.washington.edu/home/com-plib/databases.html**

The University of Oregon Library's ORBIS, a library catalog that combines information from eleven academic libraries into a single unified data-base. Web address: **http://orbis.uoregon.edu/**

Mansfield University Library. Web address: **http://www.mnsfld.edu/depts/ lib/index.html**

University of Minnesota's Rodney A. Briggs Library. Web address: **http: //www.mrs.umn.edu/library/net-index.html**

Nova Southeastern University Library. Web address: **http://www.nova.edu/ Inter-Links/reference.html**

Carnegie-Mellon University Library. Web address: **http://www-cgi.cs.cmu.edu/ web/references.html**

University of Toledo Library: Web address: **http://www.cl.utoledo.edu/ ref_sources/refindex.html**

Galileo: Georgia Library Learning Online. Web address: **http://galileo.gsu.edu/ Homepage.cgi**

University of California at San Diego Library. Web address: **http://gort.ucsd. edu/ek/refshelf/reshelf.html**

Library Resources on the Web. Web address: **http://www.utirc.utoronto.ca/ Lists/Libraries.html**

**Reference material on the Web.** Again, for new sites added after this book's publication, please visit our Write Your Way to a Higher GPA Web site: **http://www.stetson.edu/~hansen/gpa.html**.

SilverPlatter Databases over the Internet. SilverPlatter's Internet subscription option provides access to SilverPlatter databases on a subscription basis via the Internet. Web address: **http://www.silverplatter.com/erlrmote.html**. A listing of the databases available on SilverPlatter can be found at: **http:www.silverplatter.com/erldb.htm**.

EBSCOhost. An on-line system that allows users to search dozens of citations and full-text databases and order documents via the Internet. Web address: **http://www.ebsco.com/eisbro4.htm**

Online Computer Library Center (OCLC) Reference Services. OCLC offers both FirstSearch and OCLC Electronic Journals Online. Find information about books, articles, films, and computer software. Web address: **http://www.ref.oclc.org:2000/html/rs_homepage.htm**. A listing of the databases available on FirstSearch can be found at: **http://www.oclc.org/oclc/promo/9085fs/9085.htm**.

AskERIC. The Internet-based education information service of the Educational Resources Information Center (ERIC) System. Web address: **http://ericir.syr.edu**

Hoover's Online. The ultimate source for company information, including corporate information and web addresses. Some information is member-accessible only. Web address: **http://www.hoovers.com/**

Internet Database Service. A subscription-based service that provides access to more than sixty database products published by Cambridge Scientific Abstracts and several other publishing partners. Web address: **http://www.csa.com/ids.html**

UnCover. An on-line article delivery service, a table of contents database, and a keyword index to nearly seventeen thousand periodicals. Web address: **http://www.carl.org/uncover/unchome.html**

DIALOG. A service of Knight-Ridder Information, Inc., provides a number of services for DIALOG users and potential users. Web address: **http://www.dialog.com/dialog/index.html**

Britannica Online. With a subscription, allows full search capabilities. Web address: **http://www/eb.com**

Familiar Quotations. John Bartlett's *Familiar Quotations* (9th ed.), with full search capabilities. Web address: **http://www.cc.columbia.edu/acis/ bartleby/bartlett/**

The Elements of Style. William Strunk Jr.'s *The Elements of Style* (1918 ed.). Web address: **http://www.cc.columbia.edu/acis/bartleby/ strunk/**

Webster's Dictionary. Provides a hypertext interface that provides definitions and suggestions for misspelled words. Web address: **http://c.gp.cs.cmu. edu:5103/prog/webster**

APA Publication Manual Crib Sheet. Contains some of the more commonly used rules and reference formats, but is not meant as a substitute for the 368-page *Publication Manual of the American Psychological Association* (4th ed., 1994). Web address: **http://www.gasou.ed/pscyweb/ tipsheet/apacrib.htm**

APA Style of Citation. Offers numerous categories of bibliographic material, with good examples. Web address: **http://www.uvm.edu/~xli/reference/ apa.html**

MLA Style of Citation: Provides numerous categories of bibliographic material, with good examples. Web address: **http://www.uvm.edu/~xli/ reference/mla.html**

Guide for Citing Electronic Information. Supplies some good general rules and basic formats of referencing, with examples. Web address: **http://www.wilpaterson.edu/wpcpages/library/citing.htm**

Citing Electronic Materials with New MLA Guidelines. Provides information about citing electronic references in MLA format. Web address: **http://www-dept.usm.edu/~engdept/mla/rules.html**

Research and Writing Guides. Maintains a bibliography of style guides in print. Web address: **http://weber.u.washington.edu/~krumme/readings/ res+writ.html**

Guides for Better Science Research and Writing. Contains a fairly lengthy bibliography of style guides in print for writing in biology, chemistry, engineering, geology, and math. Web address: **http://www.indiana.edu/ ~cheminfo/14-05.html**

Research Institute for the Humanities—References: Maintains a directory of lots of good foreign language dictionaries. Web address: **http://www. arts.cuhk.hk/Ref.html#dt**

Guides for Writing About Art. Offers style guides for writing in the arts and humanities. Web address: **http://info.rutgers.edu/rulib/artshum/art/writing.htm/**

Handbook of Terms for Discussing Poetry. Contains information for analyzing poetry, including poetic types and genres. Web address: **http://www.cc.emory.edu/ENGLISH/classes/Handbook/Handbook.html**

Elementary Grammar. Everything you ever wanted to know about grammar, including discussions of word order, nouns, adjectives, and other things grammatic. Web address: **http://www.hiway.co.uk/~ei/intro.html**

Roget's Thesaurus. Allows searches of headwords or full text of *Roget's Thesaurus* (version 1.02), released to the public domain by MICRA and the Gutenberg Project. Web address: **http://humanities.uchicago.edu/forms_unrest/ROGET.html**

World Wide Web Acronym and Abbreviation Server. Allows you to search for acronyms or add your own. Web address: **http://www.ucc.ic/info/net/acronyms/acro.html**

## Navigating the Net using Gopher

Gopher allows you to tunnel your way through information resources on the Net using a series of easy-to-navigate menus that appear as numbered lists.

While the University of Minnesota Gopher is the "mother" of all Gopher sites—Gopher was so named after the University of Minnesota's mascot, the Golden Gopher—a number of other unique and information-rich sites include:

Carnegie Mellon University. Gopher address: **english-server.hss.cmu.edu**
Dictionary Server. Gopher address: **wombat.doc.ic.ac.uk**
Electronic Journals. Gopher address: **gopher.cic.net**
Internet Directory Services. Gopher address: **internic.net**
Library of Congress. Gopher address: **marvel.loc.gov**
Television News Archive at Vanderbilt University. Gopher address: **tvnews.vanderbilt.edu**
University of Michigan Library. Gopher address: **gopher.lib.umich.edu**
University of Minnesota. Gopher address: **gopher.micro.umn.edu**
University of North Carolina Archives. Gopher address: **sunsite.unc.edu**
University of Texas. Gopher address: **tcsul.texshare.utexas.edu**
U.S. Department of Education. Gopher address: **gopher.ed.gov**
Weather Maps. Gopher address: **wx.atmos.uiuc.edu**

## Getting information from the Net via Telnet

Telnetting allows you to log onto a remote computer connected to the Internet and access its database, such as logging onto the Library of Congress computer and doing a literature search. In the early days of the Internet, Telnet was one of the few tools available but has since been overtaken by the Web. Still, most colleges and universities on the Internet provide Telnet access.

With most Telnet sites, you simply need to type in the address of the site at the appropriate command line and you'll have access to the site's database. And most sites also have on-line help systems. For some sites, however, you'll need an account and password. What we've included here are some good sites that are gateways to lots more information about Telnet and about what's available through Telnet.

Hytelnet is a database of computerized library catalogs and other databases available through Telnet. Telnet address: **access.usask.ca**. At the login prompt, type **hytelnet**.

Colorado Alliance of Research Libraries (CARL) maintains databases for libraries throughout the West. Telnet address: **pac.carl.org**.

Dictionary Server provides access to an on-line Webster's dictionary. Telnet address: **cs.indiana.edu 2627**. At the login prompt, type **webster**.

Electronic News allows you to gain access to many electronic journals. Telnet address: **enews.com**. At the login prompt, type **gopher**.

Geographic Server contains geographic information, including population, elevation, and more by city or area. Telnet address: **martini.eecs.mich.edi3000**.

The Library of Congress Information Service has several databases, including the Library of Congress "card catalog," as well as current and past legislation. Telnet address: **locis.loc.gov**

LIBS provides gateway access to many Telnet services, including numerous library card catalogs. Telnet address: **nessie.cc.wwu.edu**. At the login prompt, type **LIBS**.

Rutgers University's Campus-Wide Information Service has an on-line dictionary, thesaurus, and database of familiar quotations, as well as the Bible, the Koran, the Book of Mormon, and the U.S. Constitution. Telnet address: **info.rutgers.edu**.

The University of Maryland maintains a repository of information on a wide variety of topics. Telnet address: **info.umd.edu**. At the login prompt, type **info**.

The Science and Technology Information System (STIS) is maintained by the National Science Federation and provides access to many NSF publications. Telnet address: **stis.nsf.gov**. At the login prompt, type **public**.

# On-line searching

**Your final line of research** is to do an on-line search using one of the three major commercial bibliographic databases to which your library probably subscribes: DIALOG, SDC, or BRS. DIALOG is a subsidiary of Lockheed Corp. SDC stands for the System Development Corporation, which offers a search service known as ORBIT. BRS stands for Bibliographic Retrieval Services. All three services cover more than 250 different databases, though DIALOG offers the broadest range. A computer search allows you—with the help of a librarian or other trained searcher—to scan thousands of citations to journal articles in virtually any subject area, including multidisciplinary fields such as energy or the environment. The result, in most cases, is a printed bibliography tailored to your specific requirements. Most searches conducted at academic libraries for students or other university personnel will probably cost between five to thirty-five dollars for each database searched.

Because on-line searches can get expensive, you should discuss with a librarian beforehand which databases you should search on-line. Keep in mind that many databases available from the on-line services are identical to their CD-ROM and print versions. You can also get detailed information about the coverage and depth of databases from several directories, including:

*Manual of Online Search Strategies* (G.K. Hall & Company), which provides strategies and "inside" information designed to help you be more effective with on-line searching, including an appendix that lists all the databases mentioned in the book along with the host(s) where they can be found.

*Encyclopedia of Information Systems and Services* (Gale Research), which describes about fifteen hundred databases and tells you whether the ones you want are available through the DIALOG, SDC, or BRS systems.

*Datapro Complete Guide to Dial-Up Databases* (Datapro Research Corp.), which provides full descriptions of more than fourteen hundred databases along with a subject index.

*Online Database Search Services Directory* (Gale Research), which provides a list of facilities that will do on-line searches for you if you are not currently affiliated with a university library.

# After the research

**One of the hardest** aspects of your research will not be finding the information you're seeking, but determining how—or if—you'll use all the sources you find. A related issue is determining what to do with the sources once you find them. Many of the books on college writing that we list in the bibliography in chapter 8 will tell you to take notes on index cards as you examine and read articles. Once your research is complete, these books say that you should refer to these index cards as you write your paper. Another method—and certainly a more expensive one—is to photocopy your key sources; you still need to read the sources and take notes, but this method ensures that the entire text is available to you as you write your paper. Some experts warn that photocopying is a lazy method of research, but we have used this method for years and found it extremely invaluable. A final method is to use one of the bibliography software programs we mention in chapter 8, and let one of those programs keep track of your references and notes and then automatically format your references according to the style your professor assigns you.

Another issue with which students and faculty are struggling is the availability of full-text articles that can be downloaded into a computer. Virtually every school has an honor code that prohibits plagiarism—the use of someone else's work as your own—and consequences for plagiarism are usually severe. Be careful when you download your articles that you don't simply start cutting and pasting. Proper planning and allowing enough time to write should ensure that you don't resort to plagiarism. When time is short, you may be tempted to cut corners, but resist the urge as best you can.

One final note: Once you've finished your research and are beginning to write your paper, numerous books and Web sites provide useful information and help for writers. For this information, turn to chapter 8.

# 3 Getting Acquainted with All Kinds of Academic Writing

**YOU** WILL ENCOUNTER MANY DIFFERENT TYPES OF WRITING ASSIGNMENTS IN YOUR COLLEGE CAREER, SO IT HELPS TO GO INTO YOUR CLASSES PREPARED FOR ALL THE VARIOUS NUANCES OF "THE COLLEGE PAPER." OUR AIM IN THIS CHAPTER IS TO GIVE YOU AN OVERVIEW OF THE TYPES OF ASSIGNMENTS THAT MAY COME YOUR WAY AND SOME SUGGESTIONS ON HOW YOU MIGHT APPROACH EACH TYPE. BECAUSE WE ARE NOT COMPOSITION, LITERATURE, OR ENGLISH PROFESSORS, HOWEVER, WE CAUTION THAT THIS CHAPTER IS NO SUBSTITUTE FOR ENSURING THAT YOU UNDERSTAND EXACTLY WHAT YOUR PROFESSOR EXPECTS FROM EACH TYPE OF PAPER ASSIGNED. THIS CHAPTER CAN SERVE AS A GUIDELINE THAT WILL ENABLE YOU TO CLARIFY THE ASSIGNMENT INTELLIGENTLY WITH YOUR PROFESSOR IF YOU HAVE ANY DOUBTS ABOUT WHAT HE OR SHE IS LOOKING FOR. IF YOUR PROFESSOR ASSIGNS YOU, FOR EXAMPLE, A CHARACTER ANALYSIS ESSAY AND YOU HAVE QUESTIONS ABOUT IT, YOU CAN CHECK THE DESCRIPTION IN THIS CHAPTER, AND THEN GO TO YOUR PROFESSOR AND SAY: "MY UNDERSTANDING OF THE CHARACTER ANALYSIS ESSAY IS THAT IT'S AN ANALYSIS OF THE AUTHOR'S REPRESENTATION OF A HUMAN BEING AND THAT CHARACTER'S MOST DISTINCTIVE TRAITS, INCLUDING THE CHARACTER'S OUTWARD APPEARANCE, ACTIONS, AND HOW THE CHARACTER DEVELOPS OVER THE COURSE OF THE NARRATIVE. IS THAT HOW YOU DEFINE IT?"

More details about all the resources we list in this chapter can be found in chapter 8.

# Two major categories of college writing

**Definitions of a few basic** terms are in order. Nearly all college writing is either *expository* or *creative*. Both are extremely general terms, and many variations fall within each category. Creative writing (which usually contains some expository elements) consists of fiction, short stories, plays, poetry, and related genres. Not many opportunities present themselves in college to do creative writing outside creative writing classes. Occasionally, you will have the option of crafting some sort of creative work as a way of expressing yourself about the subject matter in other classes. But the vast majority of papers you will write in college will be expository. In the most simplistic terms, an expository paper is one that explains. Edward Proffitt defines expository writing in the glossary of his *Reading and Writing about Literature* as "writing designed to explain something in a clear, concise manner. [Expository] essays, which may support a theme or argue a thesis, are aimed at communicating thoughts with clarity, and ideally, with pleasure." Most of the genres of papers in this chapter are expository. (Some excellent ideas for tackling expository writing, incidentally, can be found in Peter Elbow's *Writing with Power: Techniques for Mastering the Writing Process*.) Autobiographical writing and journal writing may be considered hybrids—part creative and part expository.

A large portion of expository writing in college consists of writing about other writing. In English composition and literature classes, you'll do expository writing about literature, while in other classes, you'll probably do expository writing about the writings in those disciplines. Writing about literature, by the way, is also sometimes called *criticism*. In classes such as business and communications, you'll likely write expositorily from sources that may include writing but may encompass other sources as well.

The many genres of college writing may be viewed as something like a Chinese menu. The chart on page 84 illustrates this point. Your professor may choose to have you take an overall approach from "Column B" and a specific way of looking at the paper from "Column D." For example, your professor's assignment might be as follows: "Write an expository essay (using only the primary piece of literature, a work of fiction, as a source) analyzing the novel's structure." Or "Write an expository research paper (using a primary source, a book

# THE CHINESE MENU OF COLLEGE WRITING GENRES

| Type | Type of Source | Use of Sources | Approach | Component Examined | Type of Writing Examined |
|---|---|---|---|---|---|
| Expository | Primary—*A Piece of Writing* | Essay | Précis/Abstract | Plot | Fiction |
| | | | Summary | Character | Poetry |
| | | | Analysis | Point of View | Film |
| | Secondary—*Outside Sources* | Research Paper | Explication | Setting | Drama |
| | | | Evaluation | Structure | Nonfiction |
| | | | Response | Theme | |
| | | | Synthesis | Symbolism | Writings |
| | | | Compare/Contrast | Tone | from |
| | | | | Style | disciplines |
| | | | Review | Specific Problem | outside |
| | | | Argumentation | | literature |
| | | | Persuasion | | |
| | | | Literature Review | | |
| | | | Report | | |
| | | | | | |
| | | | *Applied:* | | |
| | | | Journalism | | |
| | | | Public Relations | | |
| | | | Business | | |
| | | | Speechwriting | | |
| | | | Scientific | | |
| Hybrid | | | Autobiography | | |
| | | | Journal Writing | | |
| Creative | | | Novel | | |
| | | | Short Story | | |
| | | | Poetry | | |
| | | | Drama | | |
| | | | Screenplay | | |

by a famous philosopher, and secondary sources who have something to say about the primary source) to evaluate a specific problem in the work." Or "Write a review of a play." Or "Write a poem." This chapter describes many—although not all—possible combinations.

College papers are also subject to a variety of terminologies, and not all professors use the terms to mean the same things. As we define them, *paper* and *term paper* mean the same thing. An *essay* is generally a piece of writing about another piece of writing (or writings) or on a specific topic without the use of outside sources. Some professors might substitute the older term *theme*. A *research paper* is any paper that uses sources beyond a primary source. While an essay about a piece of writing would deal only with your own thoughts about the piece of writing (using passages from the writing itself to support your ideas), a research paper about a piece of writing would include your thoughts about the piece of writing supported not only by passages from the piece of writing but also by the thoughts expressed by others in secondary sources (literary criticism, for example). When applied to literature or other writing, a research paper may also be called an *original-argument paper using sources* or a *literary research essay*. Again, since definitions vary, be sure you know how your professors define these terms before tackling their assignments.

A large number of World Wide Web sites, such as Essay Writing: Tips and Pitfalls, contain information and guidance on writing college papers. These sites are listed in chapter 8.

## EXPOSITORY ESSAYS ABOUT WRITING

The first two genres of expository writing about other writing—precis/abstract and summary—employ the approaches of encapsulation and summarization.

### Type of paper: Précis (pronounced pray-SEE or PRAY-see) or Abstract

WHAT IT IS: A capsule description of a written work, which may range from 100 to 1,000 words (but usually about 350 words).

WHAT THE INSTRUCTOR IS LOOKING FOR: A concise description of the work that would enable anyone reading your abstract to grasp the main idea and usefulness of the work.

Note that a professor might assign a different type of abstract—one for a paper you are writing. The professor might assign you to submit an abstract of an assigned paper in advance of turning in the full paper or accompanying the full paper. Here, the abstract may be closely related to the opening paragraph of your paper, which contains your thesis sentence.

A GOOD WAY TO STRUCTURE THIS TYPE OF PAPER: Align the structure with the structure of the work you are abstracting.

AVOIDING POSSIBLE PITFALLS: Because you must condense a work down to its bare bones, it's possible to distort the facts. The need to be concise also means you must winnow the work down to its most important details without writing short, choppy sentences. Use your own words and avoid drawing conclusions.

RESOURCES THAT CAN HELP WITH THIS TYPE OF PAPER: Go to the library and look at any of the countless abstracts that appear in print or on CD-ROM to get a feel for how an abstract is done. Also: *Writing about Literature* by Edgar Roberts

## Type of paper: Summary

WHAT IT IS: An essay that captures the essence of the plot of a work of fiction or the details and main idea of a non-narrative work.

WHAT THE INSTRUCTOR IS LOOKING FOR: Some professors want you merely to summarize in your own words, primarily as a study aid, while others want you to develop your own interpretation of the central idea of the work.

A GOOD WAY TO STRUCTURE THIS TYPE OF PAPER:

   I.   Introduction
           Identifies the work and the type of work
           Introduces most important character(s)
           Tells the primary characteristics about the work (what stands out, what's
               distinctive about the way it's written)
           States thesis sentence that interprets central idea of the work
   II.  Actual summary of the work that supports your thesis sentence

AVOIDING POSSIBLE PITFALLS: Be careful not to include too much detail.

RESOURCES THAT CAN HELP WITH THIS TYPE OF PAPER: *Writing about Literature* by Edgar Roberts

## APPROACHES TO ESSAYS ABOUT LITERATURE

The next group of genres, representing individual components or aspects of written work, can be approached through analysis, explication, evaluation, response, synthesis, or compare/contrast. *Writing about Literature*, by Lynn Klamkin and Margo Livesey, is an excellent source on most of these approaches. We present them as analysis papers, but you can apply any of these approaches, as described below.

ANALYSIS: Examining and interpreting components or aspects (such as plot, character, setting, structure, theme, symbolism, tone, or style) of relatively large units of writing such as entire works or major parts of entire works. Breaking the work into components or aspects is key to analysis. Religion and philosophy professor Tom Bridges, on his World Wide Web page, notes that a successful analysis distinguishes among the various elements of the text and then makes a judgment about the relative importance of each element for an understanding of the work as a whole. "A good analysis of a text takes apart what is said and reconstructs it in an enlightening way," he writes. (Learn more about analysis on Bridges' Web page at **http://www.chss.monclair.edu/philrelg/tomwrit1.html**.) Another good source on analysis is *A Short Guide to Writing about Literature* by Sylvan Barnet.

EXPLICATION: A narrower analysis of a work, requiring examination and interpretation of components or aspects of comparatively small units of writing such as paragraphs, lines, sentences, and words. As Donald Hall puts it in *Writing Well*, explication entails "tracing the full meaning and implications of the writer's language."

RESPONSE: Your own personal reaction to a work and how it connects to your own experience, thoughts, and ideas. The response essay is usually the only type of essay written entirely in the first person.

EVALUATION: A step beyond a response essay, an evaluation essay is a judgment about a work, generally about whether the work is good or bad or meets certain literary standards. In *Writing about Literature*, Edgar Roberts suggests judging the work by such standards of evaluation as truth, the degree to which the work affirms life or humanity, the full effect of the work, its vitality or beauty—or simply whether it meets your own preferences.

SYNTHESIS: An essay that shows how two or more works—or two or more components or aspects of one or more works—are connected without taking the further step of comparing/contrasting the works or parts of works.

COMPARE/CONTRAST: An essay that points out the similarities and/or differences in two or more works—or two or more components or aspects of one or more works (or two or more authors, or in fact, two or more of *anything*). Because the compare/contrast essay is a favorite of professors, especially for essay exams, it's useful to know a couple of time-honored ways to structure this type of paper.

### Parallel order comparison:
1. First similarity
    a. first work (or component/aspect of work)
    b. second work
2. Second similarity
    a. first work
    b. second work
3. First difference
    a. first work
    b. second work
4. Second difference
    a. first work
    b. second work

### Point-by-point comparison:
1. First point
    a. similarities between the two works (or component/aspect of work)
    b. differences between the two works
2. Second point
    a. similarities between the two works
    b. differences between the two works
3. Third point
    a. similarities between the two works
    b. differences between the two works

**HINT**

Many resources are available on compare/contrast papers. A World Wide Web site from the Texas A&M English Writing Center called Hyper-handouts has a section on compare/contrast papers and can be found at **http://engserve. tamu.edu/files/writingcenter/handouts.html**.

**Type of paper: Character analysis essay** (**May be approached using explication, evaluation, response, synthesis, or compare/contrast instead of analysis.**)

WHAT IT IS: Analysis of what Edgar Roberts calls "the author's representation of a human being" and that character's most distinctive traits, including the character's outward appearance, actions, and how the character develops over the course of the narrative.

WHAT THE INSTRUCTOR IS LOOKING FOR: An essay that shows you understand the most important aspects of the character and how the character functions within the work, using sustained evidence culled throughout the work.

A GOOD WAY TO STRUCTURE THIS TYPE OF PAPER:

  I.   Introduction with thesis statement that provides the descriptive main thread relating to, for example, certain characteristics of the fictional person you're analyzing or the development of the character that runs through your character analysis

  II.  Body of your paper, giving evidence that supports your main idea, such as by describing events and dialogue that reveal aspects or developments of the character

  III. Conclusion tied not only to your thesis statement but to how the character functions within the work as a whole

AVOIDING POSSIBLE PITFALLS: Ensure that the events and actions you retell support whatever assertions you've made about the character.

RESOURCES THAT CAN HELP WITH THIS TYPE OF PAPER: *Writing about Literature* by Lynn Klamkin and Margo Livesey, *Reading and Writing about Literature* by Edward Proffitt, *Writing about Literature* by Edgar Roberts, *A Short Guide to Writing about Literature* by Sylvan Barnet

**Type of paper: Essay analyzing point of view** (May be approached using explication, evaluation, response, synthesis, or compare/contrast instead of analysis.)

WHAT IT IS: An essay analyzing the way a story is told. Who is telling the story? What is the narrator's role, if any, in the story? Unique literary terms describe the various points of view—*first person, third person omniscient* (when the storyteller not only narrates the action but also seems to know the inner thoughts of all the characters), *third person limited* (when the storyteller knows the inner thoughts of only one character), and *dramatic* (when the storyteller limits the story to actions and dialogue without including anyone's inner thoughts).

WHAT THE INSTRUCTOR IS LOOKING FOR: An examination of the role that point of view plays in the work, which may include such elements as language used in dialogue or to record inner thoughts and emotions, the role of point of view in developing the narrative, and how the work would be different if told from a different point of view.

A GOOD WAY TO STRUCTURE THIS TYPE OF PAPER:

    I.   Introduction identifying point of view and its role in the work

    II.  Body that traces the development of point of view and how it is used throughout the work

    III. Conclusion that measures the effectiveness of point of view in the overall work

AVOIDING POSSIBLE PITFALLS: It's easy to confuse the point of view from which the story is being told with the point of view of the author. Your professor may want you to leave the author out of your paper. It's also easy to get off on a tangent, bringing in too many details; use details from the work only to the extent that they support what you have to say about point of view, and be sure to examine the full work, not just dialogue and the recounting of inner thoughts.

RESOURCES THAT CAN HELP WITH THIS TYPE OF PAPER: *Writing about Literature* by Lynn Klamkin and Margo Livesey, *Reading and Writing about Literature* by Edward Proffitt, *Writing about Literature* by Edgar Roberts, *A Short Guide to Writing about Literature* by Sylvan Barnet

**Type of paper: essay analyzing setting** (May be approached using explication, evaluation, response, synthesis, or compare/contrast instead of analysis.)

WHAT IT IS: An analysis of the physical environment against which a work is set and the role of setting in the work.

WHAT THE INSTRUCTOR IS LOOKING FOR: When a professor assigns an analysis of setting, it's usually because setting plays a particularly important role in the work. The author may have featured setting prominently in place of describing action or as a metaphor or organizing mechanism. The instructor wants you to recognize and write convincingly about the importance of setting in the work, perhaps noting how different the work would be in an altered setting.

A GOOD WAY TO STRUCTURE THIS TYPE OF PAPER:

  I.   Introduction in which you describe the setting and set forth a thesis statement about the role of setting in the work and what setting reveals about what the author is trying to express
  II.  Body that details the use and development of setting, supporting your thesis statement
  III. Conclusion that aligns with your thesis statement and summarizes the effectiveness of using setting in the way the author has chosen

AVOIDING POSSIBLE PITFALLS: Don't forget to consider all the details of atmosphere, environment, and mood (elements such as light and dark, heat and cold, predominance of certain colors) to the extent that they contribute to your thesis.

RESOURCES THAT CAN HELP WITH THIS TYPE OF PAPER: *Writing about Literature* by Lynn Klamkin and Margo Livesey, *Reading and Writing about Literature* by Edward Proffitt, *Writing about Literature* by Edgar Roberts, *A Short Guide to Writing about Literature* by Sylvan Barnet

**Type of paper: Essay analyzing theme** (May be approached using explication, evaluation, response, synthesis, or compare/contrast instead of analysis.)

WHAT IT IS: A paper that traces the thematic thread that runs through the entire work and unites it as a whole.

WHAT THE INSTRUCTOR IS LOOKING FOR: A cohesive paper that signifies to the instructor that you understand at least one key idea that gives the work its feel and focus.

A GOOD WAY TO STRUCTURE THIS TYPE OF PAPER:

  I.   Introduction that states the theme and makes a thesis statement about how and why the author sustains the theme throughout the work
  II.  Body showing specific way the author carries out the theme
  III. Conclusion that refers to the thesis statement and assesses the effectiveness of the theme in meeting the author's aims

AVOIDING POSSIBLE PITFALLS: It's important to choose a theme that unifies the work as a whole and is evident throughout the work.

RESOURCES THAT CAN HELP WITH THIS TYPE OF PAPER: *Writing about Literature* by Lynn Klamkin and Margo Livesey, *Reading and Writing about Literature* by Edward Proffitt, *Writing Well* by Donald Hall, *A Short Guide to Writing about Literature* by Sylvan Barnet

## Type of paper: Essay analyzing structure (May be approached using explication, evaluation, response, synthesis, or compare/contrast instead of analysis.)

WHAT IT IS: An analysis of the way a work is organized. Some typical literary structures include logical structure, chronological structure, or a structure organized around conflict or emotions.

WHAT THE INSTRUCTOR IS LOOKING FOR: An essay that demonstrates your understanding of the importance of the structure the author has chosen.

A GOOD WAY TO STRUCTURE THIS TYPE OF PAPER:

  I.   Introduction describing structure and making a thesis statement about the role of structure in the work
  II.  Body that aligns with the structure of the work and supports your thesis statement
  III. Conclusion that recalls your thesis statement and evaluates the effectiveness of the structure in accomplishing what you've asserted that the author tries to accomplish

AVOIDING POSSIBLE PITFALLS: Be sure you truly understand the structure the author employs. Outlining the work is a great help in analyzing structure. To develop a thesis statement, it always helps to ask: How would the story have been different with a different structure? Could the author have organized it differently? Could any parts have been left out without damaging the narrative effectiveness?

RESOURCES THAT CAN HELP WITH THIS TYPE OF PAPER: *Writing about Literature* by Edgar Roberts

## Type of paper: Essay analyzing style (May be approached using explication, evaluation, response, synthesis, or compare/contrast instead of analysis.)

WHAT IT IS: An examination of the writing style an author employs to achieve a given effect in a work. Writing style, according to Edgar Roberts, can be analyzed in terms of:

> Diction—the meanings of words and the relationships among words in context
>
> Grammar—the way the author structures phrases, sentences, and paragraphs
>
> Rhythm and Sound—how groups of words work together to create a rhythm in the writing
>
> Rhetoric—the effectiveness of the writing style in conveying ideas

WHAT THE INSTRUCTOR IS LOOKING FOR: An analysis that shows you can recognize an author's writing style and show its effect in the work as a whole. You can probably analyze the style of only a portion of the work, yet you'll need to relate your analysis to the full work.

A GOOD WAY TO STRUCTURE THIS TYPE OF PAPER:

I. Introduction that identifies the portion of the work whose style you are analyzing and places it in context with the full work. The introduction should also make a thesis statement about the style and how you intend to analyze it.

II. Body that traces and discusses the effectiveness of the style

III. Conclusion that gauges how successfully the author employs the style

AVOIDING POSSIBLE PITFALLS: Be careful not to confuse the author's style with the style of the characters' speech within the dialogue.

RESOURCES THAT CAN HELP WITH THIS TYPE OF PAPER: *Reading and Writing about Literature* by Edward Proffitt, *Writing about Literature* by Edgar Roberts

**HINT**

Reading a work aloud can help you to analyze style. An oral reading gives you a better feel for the sound of the words, sentences, and phrases, and the rhythm of the writing.

**Type of paper: Essay analyzing tone** (May be approached using explication, evaluation, response, synthesis, or compare/contrast instead of analysis.)

WHAT IT IS: You can think of tone as a subset of style. Tone, says Edgar Roberts, is the quality of the writer's style that reveals his or her attitude. Of all the components you can analyze in an essay, tone is the one that most requires you to get inside an author's head and guess what he or she is feeling about the subject matter and trying to convey. Think of tone in writing as analogous to the tone of voice the author would use if he or she were telling you the story instead of writing it. Comedy and irony can be elements of tone.

WHAT THE INSTRUCTOR IS LOOKING FOR: This type of paper requires you to be particularly analytical—to truly "read between the lines." Just as with the essay about setting, your instructor probably wants you to notice that the work's tone stands out.

A GOOD WAY TO STRUCTURE THIS TYPE OF PAPER:

I.  Introduction in which you describe the tone that the author uses throughout the work or is contained within just part of it and relate it to an attitude the author is trying to convey

II.  Body in which you analyze the tone and show how the author uses it to express attitude

III.  Conclusion in which you judge the effectiveness of the author's tone in conveying the attitude you've described in the introduction

AVOIDING POSSIBLE PITFALLS: Since your professor may expect you to detect something particularly distinctive about the tone of the assigned work, you especially may want to check with the instructor as your paper progresses to ensure that you're on the right track.

RESOURCES THAT CAN HELP WITH THIS TYPE OF PAPER: *Writing about Literature* by Edgar Roberts (Edward Proffitt deals with tone in poetry in *Reading and Writing about Literature;* as we will see in the section on writing about poetry [page 96], many of the same components that can be explored in fiction can also be explored in poetry.)

### Type of paper: Essay analyzing symbolism (May be approached using explication, evaluation, response, synthesis, or compare/contrast instead of analysis.)

WHAT IT IS: An essay analyzing an element of a work that has significance beyond itself. Simply stated, a symbol is something that stands for something else, as an American flag stands for the United States itself. The symbol is generally a unifying element in the full work.

WHAT THE INSTRUCTOR IS LOOKING FOR: The instructor wants you to recognize the symbolism and understand how it is used in the work.

A GOOD WAY TO STRUCTURE THIS TYPE OF PAPER:

    I.   Introduction identifying the symbol central to the work and making a thesis statement about how the author uses it
    II.   Body that traces the use of the symbol and supports your thesis statement
    III.   Conclusion describing the effectiveness of the symbol as a unifying theme and reflecting your thesis statement about how the author uses it as such

AVOIDING POSSIBLE PITFALLS: In this type of paper, you must be sure to justify that whatever you have identified as a symbol truly is a symbol. A certain element's repeated appearances throughout the work do not necessarily mean that element is a symbol. When in doubt, check with your instructor to see if you're on the right path.

RESOURCES THAT CAN HELP WITH THIS TYPE OF PAPER: *Writing about Literature* by Lynn Klamkin and Margo Livesey, *Reading and Writing about Literature* by Edward Proffitt, *Writing Well* by Donald Hall, *A Short Guide to Writing about Literature* by Sylvan Barnet, *Writing about Literature* by Edgar Roberts

### Type of paper: Essay analyzing a specific problem (May be approached using explication, evaluation, response, synthesis, or compare/contrast instead of analysis.)

WHAT IT IS: Analysis of a specific issue or question involving a piece of writing. The specific problem generally is beyond the scope of the elements of literary works we've already discussed (character, style, tone, structure, setting, etc.) but may include or combine some of these elements.

**WHAT THE INSTRUCTOR IS LOOKING FOR:** The specific-problem paper may tend to be one for which you develop the topic rather than one the instructor assigns. The instructor is looking for your creativity in developing a specific problem to explore, and more importantly, the solution you come up with for the problem. The instructor will regard your paper most favorably if you answer whatever question you've raised satisfactorily and support your argument effectively.

**A GOOD WAY TO STRUCTURE THIS TYPE OF PAPER:**

I.   Introduction that states the problem or question as a thesis statement
II.  Body that supports the thesis with concrete examples from the work
III. Conclusion that affirms your solution or argument

**AVOIDING POSSIBLE PITFALLS:** Be sure you adequately support your thesis! As you'll see in chapter 4, students' failure to support their theses is one of professors' biggest complaints.

**RESOURCES THAT CAN HELP WITH THIS TYPE OF PAPER:** *Writing about Literature* by Edgar Roberts

**HINT**

Reading literary criticism about the work or author in question can provide excellent food for thought for topic development of this kind of paper. Never borrow or steal a literary critic's idea, but do allow the ideas of literary critics to inspire your own ideas.

## Type of paper: Essay on poetry

**WHAT IT IS:** You can approach poetry in many of the same ways as you can prose, using analysis, explication, evaluation, response, synthesis, or compare/contrast. You can also write about many of the same elements in poetry that you can about prose: character, setting, structure, theme, symbolism, tone, and style. Poetry presents some unique additional elements about which your instructor may want you to write: prosody (the rhythm of poetry), voice, diction, figurative language, irony, and patterns of sound.

**WHAT THE INSTRUCTOR IS LOOKING FOR:** Your instructor probably seeks a demonstration of your understanding of the mechanics that go into poetry.

A GOOD WAY TO STRUCTURE THIS TYPE OF PAPER:

    I.   Introduction that makes a thesis statement relating to your approach to the poet's technique
    II.  Body that supports your thesis statement and cites examples of the technique
    III. Conclusion affirming your thesis statement and discussing the effectiveness of the poet's technique

AVOIDING POSSIBLE PITFALLS: If your instructor asks you to write about an aspect of poetry with which you are not familiar, be sure you have a clear understanding of how your professor defines the terms.

RESOURCES THAT CAN HELP WITH THIS TYPE OF PAPER: *Writing about Literature* by Lynn Klamkin and Margo Livesey, *Reading and Writing about Literature* by Edward Proffitt (who, in fact, writes exhaustively on writing about poetry in this volume), *Writing about Literature* by Edgar Roberts. Handbook of Terms for Discussing Poetry, a World Wide Web site, contains information for analyzing poetry, including poetic types and genres. Web address: **http://www.cc.emory.edu/ENGLISH/classes/Handbook/Handbook.html**

The Texas A&M Department of English Writing Center site on the World Wide Web has a section called Hyper-handouts that includes a handout on writing about poetry, which lists some excellent questions the student writer can use to determine how to attack an essay about poetry. The site can be found at **http://engserve.tamu.edu/files/writingcenter/handouts.html**.

With the next group of genres, we leave the territory of essay genres that are primarily assigned in English, composition, and literature classes and enter the realm of essays that may be assigned in a wide variety of disciplines.

## Type of paper: Essay on a film/play

WHAT IT IS: As with poetry, you can approach film and drama using analysis, explication, evaluation, response, synthesis, or compare/contrast and discuss the same elements as you would the printed version of the film or drama: plot, character, setting, structure, theme, symbolism, tone, and style. Visual and aural elements enter the mix when you write about film; beyond the elements found in print, you also encounter camera techniques, editing techniques, lighting, use of color, and sound. Visual elements such as set design, costume design, and lighting may also be part of an essay about a play. You may have more occasion to write about a play in its written version than its performed form, while the opportunity to view and write about the written versions of films is infrequent.

WHAT THE INSTRUCTOR IS LOOKING FOR: Instructors have various reasons—linked to the subject matter being taught in the class—for assigning their students to write about films and plays. Some are concerned with content, others with literary elements, and others with filmmaking and playcrafting techniques. It's best to ensure that you understand your instructor's objectives in asking you to write about a film or play.

A GOOD WAY TO STRUCTURE THIS TYPE OF PAPER:

  I.  Introduction that makes a thesis statement relating to your approach to the film/play and/or the filmmaker's/dramatist's technique
  II.  Body that supports your thesis statement citing examples of the technique
  III.  Conclusion affirming your thesis statement and discussing the effectiveness of the filmmaker's/dramatist's technique

AVOIDING POSSIBLE PITFALLS: Don't confuse an essay about film with a review unless a review is what your instructor has assigned (see the following entry).

RESOURCES THAT CAN HELP WITH THIS TYPE OF PAPER: *The Elements of Writing about Literature and Film* by Elizabeth McMahan, *A Short Guide to Writing about Film* by Timothy Corrigan, *Writing about Literature* by Edgar Roberts (film), *Writing about Literature* by Lynn Klamkin and Margo Livesey, *Reading and Writing about Literature* by Edward Proffitt (drama)

**HINT**

If you're writing about a film, see the film more than once, if possible. Obtain the video of the film if it's available so you can study the film closely. Since many films are derived from plays, an interesting approach to these genres is to compare the film version with the play version.

## Type of paper: Review

WHAT IT IS: A review is an essay combining summary and evaluation approaches. Your instructor may ask you to review a book, story, play, film, article, or any other work. Reviews tend to be brief: 500 to 1,500 words.

WHAT THE INSTRUCTOR IS LOOKING FOR: Frequently instructors assign reviews as a way of ensuring that students read or view certain works, so you should write your review in a way that demonstrates you are thoroughly familiar with the work. Instructors may also seek to acquaint students with writing about works other than those that the students typically write about. Finally, your instructor may wish to help you develop your summation and evaluation skills. As always, ask the instructor to clarify the objectives of the assignment if you are unsure.

A GOOD WAY TO STRUCTURE THIS TYPE OF PAPER:

    I.   Introduction describing the nature and scope of the work
    II.   1–2 paragraphs summarizing the work
    III.   Paragraph that discusses the thrust or overriding theme of the work
    IV.   1–2 paragraphs evaluating the work's strengths
    V.   1–2 paragraphs evaluating the work's weaknesses
    VI.   Concluding paragraph evaluating the work as a whole

(Adapted from *A Short Guide to Writing about Literature* by Sylvan Barnet)

AVOIDING POSSIBLE PITFALLS: Because you have a wide latitude of freedom within a review to evaluate the work as you see fit, it's sometimes difficult to whittle down what you wish to say. Be careful not to go off on tangents as you write the review.

RESOURCES THAT CAN HELP WITH THIS TYPE OF PAPER: *Writing about Literature* by Lynn Klamkin and Margo Livesey, *Writing about Literature* by Edgar Roberts, *A Short Guide to Writing about Literature* by Sylvan Barnet

HINT

Reading reviews of the medium you're reviewing can give you a good feel for the summary and evaluation approaches.

The genres we've seen up to this point are generally those used to write about one or more primary sources without the use of outside secondary sources. With the next group of genres, we begin to enter the area of papers that may be written partially or entirely using secondary uses. With *argumentation* and *persuasion*, you may write using only a primary source, but you may also use secondary sources, depending on what your instructor assigns. *Literature reviews* by definition require secondary sources.

## Type of paper: Argumentation

WHAT IT IS: The argumentative paper answers the question "how did you reach that conclusion?" The paper sets forth a premise and then takes the reader—in sequence—through the writer's thought process to show how the writer arrived at his or her conclusion. Types of argumentative papers include:

induction—drawing general conclusions from individual observations

pro and con—giving both sides of the argument

cause and effect—explaining the factors that have brought about a given situation

analysis of alternatives—showing various solutions to a problem, eliminating the less desirable choices until the best alternative emerges

The argumentative paper has its roots in the world of logic; thus, the more you know about such logic terms as syllogisms, premises, and valid deductions, the better you will be at argumentation.

WHAT THE INSTRUCTOR IS LOOKING FOR: The instructor seeks clear, concise, convincing evidence that you have thought through the matter at hand.

A GOOD WAY TO STRUCTURE THIS TYPE OF PAPER: The structure of your paper will depend on which approach to argumentation you take:

Induction:
I.   Premise
II.  Individual paragraphs, each containing a set of facts/observations related to the premise
III. Conclusion that considers all the preceding facts

Pro and con:
I.   First premise
II.  Detailed examples of first premise
III. Opposing premise
IV.  Detailed examples of opposing premise
V.   A balanced conclusion

Cause and effect:
I.   Premise/problem
II.  First cause

   III.  Second cause

   IV.  Third cause

   V.  Conclusion/solution

Analysis of alternatives:

   I.  Premise/problem

   II.  First alternative

   III.  Second alternative

   IV.  Third alternative

   V.  Conclusion/solution

AVOIDING POSSIBLE PITFALLS: In *Words and Ideas,* Hans Guth cautions against these problems with argumentative papers:

> Using examples that have strong impact but are not typical and therefore don't hit home with the reader
>
> Using examples that are too narrow to be representative
>
> Making superficial or premature generalizations
>
> Making sweeping generalizations
>
> Making arguments that are too abstract

RESOURCES THAT CAN HELP WITH THIS TYPE OF PAPER: *Writing about Literature* by Lynn Klamkin and Margo Livesey, *Writing Well* by Donald Hall, *Words and Ideas* by Hans Guth. A World Wide Web site from Texas A&M's Writing Center called Hyper-handouts has a section on argumentative papers and can be found at **http://engserve.tamu.edu/files/writingcenter/handouts.html.**

Philosophy and religion professor Tom Bridges' Web page at **http://www.chss. montclair.edu/philrelg/tomwrit1.html** also has a section on argumentative writing.

"**Back** up whatever you assert to be so with examples, observations, details, and such to show your audience that what you say is valid."

—a composition professor at a large public university

## Type of paper: Persuasion

WHAT IT IS: The persuasive paper takes argumentation a step further, not only showing the reader how the writer arrived at a given conclusion, but persuading the reader to buy into the conclusion, as well. We have a chance on any given day to study the techniques of persuasive writing simply by picking up a newspaper and turning to the editorial page.

WHAT THE INSTRUCTOR IS LOOKING FOR: The instructor wants a paper that demonstrates that your primary intent focuses on the effect you hope the paper will have on the reader. A well-organized effort that can clearly and effectively influence the reader will score points with your instructor.

A GOOD WAY TO STRUCTURE THIS TYPE OF PAPER: Hans Guth recommends persuading your audience by degrees, moving from the simple to the more difficult elements of your argument, from the familiar to the new, from the safe to the controversial.

I. Introduction that explains why the issue you are writing about is of direct concern to the reading audience

II. Section that explains the point of view you want to get across

III. Section providing evidence for this point of view

IV. Section that suggests a resolution and explains its benefits to your reading audience

V. Conclusion that suggests an action step the audience can take. The action step could be simply changing one's mind about the issue.

AVOIDING POSSIBLE PITFALLS: The following, according to Guth, can sink your persuasive efforts:

Exaggeration

Arguments so slanted that the writing is discredited with fair-minded readers

Abuse of emotional appeals

Evasion of the issue by dealing in personalities

RESOURCES THAT CAN HELP WITH THIS TYPE OF PAPER: *Words and Ideas* by Hans Guth

**HINT**

Hans Guth describes these techniques that will give your persuasive paper extra impact:

Strategic comparison—Comparing a situation with which the reader may not be familiar with one to which the reader can easily relate.

Insiders' testimony—Including inside information from people in the know to make your case.

Bandwagon effect—Showing that many people are moving toward your position to sway your reader.

Confused opposition—Showing the contradictions inherent in the view opposing yours.

Refuting objections—Attacking the objections you believe are the most influential with your reader.

The common cause—Demonstrating that you and your reader share common interests.

The cause célèbre—Using a major test case to bring your issue into focus.

"**Make** sure that you lay the argument out logically so that the reader understands and is persuaded by the evidence that you offer for your position."

—a political science professor at a large public university

### Type of paper: Review of the literature

WHAT IT IS: A lit review is generally part of any research paper, but professors sometimes assign literature reviews as a separate exercise or as a prelude to the full research paper. The idea of the lit review is that whatever argument or thesis statement you've set forth in your paper, you have demonstrated that, to the greatest degree possible, you have researched and discovered what all relevant sources have to say about your subject matter. A lit review shows the extent to which others have already researched the subject and sets the stage for you to add to the body of research with your own findings and assertions.

WHAT THE INSTRUCTOR IS LOOKING FOR: The instructor seeks a paper that avoids two of the top writing flaws listed by our surveyed professors—little evidence of adequate research and little evidence of understanding the topic. A thorough lit review can overcome both these flaws, showing the professor you've done comprehensive research and you understand your topic completely.

A GOOD WAY TO STRUCTURE THIS TYPE OF PAPER:

I. Introduction with thesis statement
II. Paragraph for each point related to your thesis statement on which sources you've researched have something to say
III. Conclusion that assesses the state of the research. What's the next step in the research? What questions are still open for further inquiry? In a full research paper, you would probably take that next step or answer some of those questions, but in a lit review, you stop at this point

AVOIDING POSSIBLE PITFALLS: Strike a balance between conducting a thorough lit review and one that covers too much ground or goes far afield of your topic. You will certainly want to include all research that closely relates to your topic. You may, however, want to limit your coverage to the most recent works, say those written in the last ten years. On the other hand, you should be sure to include any landmark works that are important to the topic area, no matter how old they are.

RESOURCES THAT CAN HELP WITH THIS TYPE OF PAPER: Writing Academic Essays and Mini-Dissertations is a World Wide Web site that provides useful information about lit reviews and can be found at **http://www.aber.ac.uk/~ednwww/ writess.html**.

### H I N T

Students too often limit their literature reviews based on the span of years covered by the CD-ROM database on which they're searching. To discover landmark works published before the mid 1980s, you'll need to search the print indexes. See chapter 2 for more details.

## Type of paper: Report
WHAT IT IS: While the report is primarily the province of elementary, middle, and high school, professors will occasionally assign reports in college. A report is an organized collection of information about a single topic. You may gather the information from one or more primary sources, but your professor will probably direct you to secondary sources, depending on his or her objectives.

The report is closely akin to a summary essay about a single piece of writing (page 86), but its focus is the content or information that the writing or writings divulge rather than the writings for their own sake. The report is also related to the literature review (page 103) except that you are not taking a position or making an argument about your topic; you are merely summarizing information in your own words. The book report is a variation on the report. Most documents written for science classes are also called reports and are covered under "scientific writing," page 115.

WHAT THE INSTRUCTOR IS LOOKING FOR: The instructor's objective in assigning a report is usually content-driven. He or she wants you to answer a specific question, find out about a given topic, or show that you've read a certain book. It's the instructor's way of helping you learn or study about a particular subject. Writing skills are as important with the report as with any other type of paper, but content is likely your instructor's most important grading criterion.

A GOOD WAY TO STRUCTURE THIS TYPE OF PAPER:

    I.   Introduction identifying the question you're answering, topic you're summarizing, book you've read
   II.   Summary of the most relevant information about the topic, organized logically
  III.   Brief conclusion providing highlights of summary

AVOIDING POSSIBLE PITFALLS: Because you don't have the creative latitude afforded by asserting and defending your own argument, summarizing information for a report in your own words may be difficult. (Remember in grade school when you looked up passages in the encyclopedia and struggled to write the information in your own words?) The ability to paraphrase is paramount with report writing.

RESOURCES THAT CAN HELP WITH THIS TYPE OF PAPER: *10,000 Ideas for Term Papers, Projects, and Reports* by Kathryn Lamm

## THE RESEARCH PAPER

Having looked at papers that generally use a primary source and then papers that may use both primary and secondary sources, we arrive at the monster category of the research paper. While it is a monstrous category, we won't spend a great deal of time discussing the research paper here because the focus of this entire book is on the research paper. In a very real sense, all the genres of papers we've discussed up to this point are in the minority among types of college writing you will likely do. Most of the papers you're assigned in college are research papers, so most of this book assumes you are writing research papers primarily and attempts to provide you with the tools and techniques to do so.

The research you collect for a research paper illuminates what scholars have to say concerning the argument that you've set forth, and it serves as a springboard to your conclusion. To see the relationship between the structure of papers we've discussed to this point and the structure of the research paper, let's look at one of the outlines from chapter 1:

### Godlike Authority in *Elsie Dinsmore* and its Uses in Gendered Social and Religious Discourse

I. Introduction/Thesis Statement: The major characters in *Elsie Dinsmore* possess a Godlike authority that results in power shifts between them.

  A. Horace Dinsmore serves as Godlike authority

    1. The evolving Horace as metaphor for "feminization" of Godlike authority

    2. Horace as promulgator post-Calvinist theology of Bushnellian Christian Nurture, and hence, "secular authority nonpareil," between which and heavenly authority, Elsie must mediate

      a. Health and fitness

      b. Personal finances

**Introduction** containing *Thesis Statement*

**Body of paper**—essentially a literature review (page 103) in which secondary sources are employed to support these arguments, all of which bolster the central argument or thesis statement

B. Use of Godlike authority in both Horace and Elsie for chastening/incest/patrimatrimony

C. Elsie Dinsmore as Godlike authority

    1. Elsie as Evangelist—promulgator of Sunday School didacticism

        a. Moral superiority

        b. Access to power as a result

    2. Promulgator of Calvinist faith vs. works theology

    3. Christlike figure who converts through resurrection

II. Conclusion: Who has more power? — **Conclusion** that refers to the *thesis statement*

In some classes, professors will ask that you go beyond making a simple argument and discussing it based on what other scholars have contributed to the discourse. In social science, business, and natural science classes, for example, your instructor may ask that you conduct original research, such as a study or experiment. In those situations, you likely will structure your paper like this:

I. Introduction/thesis statement/hypothesis

II. Literature review

III. Explanation/methodology of study/experiment/original research

IV. Results of study/experiment/original research

V. Discussion/suggestions for further research/limitations of original research

VI. Conclusion

What do professors want most from students who write research papers? Chapter 4 expands on what they want, but essentially, instructors reward student research-paper writers who understand their paper topic, support their theses with solid research, organize their papers well, write clearly, and avoid the major student writing flaws that are constant irritants to most professors. See also the many excellent resources listed in chapter 2 to help you research your paper and in chapter 8 to assist you in writing a research paper.

## THE ESSAY EXAM

The essay exam may involve one or more primary sources, but more likely, it will require the use of both primary and secondary sources, among which a major one may be lecture notes given by your professor. The essay exam carries many of the same requirements of other student papers—good organization, clarity, understanding of the topic, support for your argument—but the exam also demands that these requirements be met under duress and under less-than-ideal conditions. In most cases, for example, you'll have to write your exam by hand under extremely tight time pressure without the benefit of spell checkers and any of the other useful technological tools we present in Chapter 8. Those difficult circumstances usually behoove a professor to be a bit more lenient in grading the writing quality of the exam than he or she would be in grading, say, a paper that you wrote on a computer after having had the entire semester to work on it. Still, the way you write responses to an essay exam is important to your grade, so give it your best shot.

"**Assume** your professors expect you to make connections between the readings and the lectures in [your] writing."

—a social-sciences professor at Michigan Technological University

Among the obstacles you may encounter with an essay exam are:

    lack of preparation
    lack of sufficient time
    disorganized thoughts
    stress, fear, panic, drawing a blank

Here are some techniques for conquering each demon.

Lack of preparation—Studying is the obvious remedy for lack of preparation. If you've studied sufficiently, you'll feel prepared. But what college student ever really feels he or she has enough time to study sufficiently, and how do you know you've studied enough? First, be sure you're clear on the breadth and scope of the material to be covered on the exam. Ask your instructor which material is fair game to be included in the exam if you have any doubts. You want to study neither too much nor too little material. Next, be sure you've borrowed lecture notes from a good note-taker for any classes you may have missed. Develop a study plan that includes a breakdown of the time you feel you should spend studying each topic. Use study techniques that work for you. For example, if it helps you to have a friend quiz you, include a quizzing session in your plan and allow time for it. One shortcut, described in detail in chapter 7, is to anticipate test questions. If you know what to expect, you'll have a pretty good idea if you've studied enough. And having anticipated, you may even want to write out some practice answers to questions you think will be on the test. That way, you'll be much more likely to retrieve what you want to write when you're under the gun.

Exam questions typically use verbs such as these. Being poised to answer questions with these verbs will help prepare you for the test:

Compare/contrast
Differentiate/distinguish
Apply a principle
Criticize/evaluate
Comment
Define
Identify
Demonstrate
Describe
Discuss/explain
Give cause and effect
Enumerate/list
Illustrate/give an example
Interpret
Justify/prove/support
Outline/detail/diagram
Relate
Summarize/review
Trace the development of

Lack of sufficient time—Wear a watch to the exam. Once the professor has handed out the tests, quickly develop a plan of attack for the essay questions. Allot a certain amount of time for each question and another chunk of time to go back over all your answers. If the exam has four questions—all weighted equally in point value—and you have fifty minutes to complete the exam, allot ten minutes to each question and ten minutes to review and edit all your answers. If the questions have different point values, allot time segments that correspond with those values. It's usually best to start with the question for which you know you'll be able to give the best response. Answering that question will boost your confidence, and you'll know that on that answer, at least, you can probably expect full credit. If you're in the middle of a question, and time is about to run out, try to outline what the rest of your response would have been; your professor may give partial credit for the outline.

Disorganized thoughts—Be sure you read the questions and understand what each is asking. If you don't understand what a question is asking, don't hesitate to ask the instructor for clarification. You may want to include some of the key words from the question in your opening paragraph, as well as in your conclusion so your professor knows you've kept your answer aligned with the topic. The English Department at the University of Victoria, Canada, suggests analyzing each question from these angles:

Why is it being asked?
Is it a multilayered question, one that can be answered on more than one level?
Does it invite a largely factual response?
Is it looking for a specific critical stance?

Pay attention, too, to the instructor's written instructions on the test. Sometimes professors give, say, seven questions, but you need only answer three. Sketch out a quickie outline for each answer, using the five-paragraph formula described in chapter 1:

Paragraph One: Introduction, with thesis statement
Paragraph Two: Supporting argument for first point in thesis statement
Paragraph Three: Supporting argument for second point in thesis statement
Paragraph Four: Supporting argument for third point in thesis statement
Paragraph Five: Conclusion and implications

Use the most important information in the earliest paragraphs; if you run out of time, your answer will contain the most critical information. If your answer requires more than five paragraphs, of course, add additional paragraphs in the body as needed. Outlining your answers will help you deal with the time crunch. It will also help you attain a better grade. The professor doesn't just want to see that you can memorize a collection of unrelated facts; he or she wants to see that you can construct a cohesive statement that answers the question.

Stress, fear, panic, drawing a blank—If you've employed all the techniques described, you can probably avoid these feelings. But let's say you've done it all, and you come across a question that you either simply don't know the answer to or that you know but you draw a blank on. Before panic really sets it, take a deep breath. Put the troublesome question(s) aside for now, and concentrate on the ones you know you can answer well. But be sure to allot time to come back to the problem question(s). If you don't know or can't remember the answer, you probably can't outline, but you can jot down on the back of your test paper all the words you can think of that relate to the question. That process of word association may trigger something in your mind that will enable you to answer the question sufficiently. If you can't answer it, it's probably best to write down some sort of answer related to the topic, even if your response doesn't exactly answer the question. If you demonstrate some knowledge of the subject matter, the instructor may award you partial points, which are better than the zero points you would get for leaving the question blank. If there's an answer you don't know, but an extra-credit question to which you do know the answer, by all means, try to make up for the lost points on the unanswered question by responding to the extra-credit question.

Despite the difficult conditions, try your best to avoid the writing flaws described in chapter 4. Also write as legibly as you can. Studies have shown that, even when instructors have been told to grade solely on content, they tend to downgrade sloppy exam papers. Go back to check for spelling, punctuation, grammar, sentence structure, and word usage. Above all, ensure that you answer the question, organize your answer, and support your answer with evidence.

RESOURCES THAT CAN HELP WITH PREPARING FOR AND TAKING ESSAY EXAMS: *How to Study in College* by Walter Paulk, *The Confident Student* by Carol C. Kanar.

A World Wide Web site called Tips on Writing the Essay-Type Examination can be found at **http://www.csbju.edu/advising/help/essayexm.html**. Perfecting the mechanics of the essay-exam response is the subject of a Web site created by Professor Jeff Hooks called Five Tools for Writing Timed Essays; you can access it at **http://splavc.spjc.cc.fl.us/hooks/hooksessay.html**.

**HINT**

You can sometimes score extra points with your professor if you bring a relevant point into your essay answer that comes from a source other than one assigned for class. Literary criticism, as described in chapter 7, is excellent for this purpose. Your professor can scarcely avoid being impressed if you've investigated the topic beyond what is required for the class.

## APPLIED FORMS OF STUDENT WRITING

Still in the realm of the expository, the next group of student writing genres may be thought of as applied forms of writing because you can apply them directly to their corresponding career fields. A rich variety of resources is available to assist you with these genres because a great deal is written not just for students, but for professional practitioners in these disciplines. We've listed just a few of those resources here, but many more are available in any library or bookstore and on the Internet.

**Journalistic writing**—You may encounter assignments of journalistic writing in communications, journalism, or public relations classes. Its extraordinary conciseness, its objectivity, and its formulaic approach to the reporting of events distinguish journalistic writing from other forms of expository writing. Many special rules of journalism are required because newspaper stories must fit within tight spaces. Newswriting uses what's called the *inverted pyramid style,* in which the most important information is at the top of the story, and all subsequent details are of decreasing importance. Newspaper reporters write that way so that when editors need to cut stories for space, they won't cut the most important details of the story. Newspaper writers endeavor to include the *five Ws*—who, what, why, when, and where—in or near the opening paragraph, called the lead, of each story. The best news stories rarely report on events chronologically but according to what is most newsworthy. If your journalism professor, for example, assigns you to cover a meeting of local government, you should ask yourself, "What's the real news here?" You would then write the story, not in the order in which the meeting unfolded, but with the most newsworthy development of the meeting as your lead. Although newswriting style has loosened up in recent years, it is still a rather terse, concise, bare-bones style of writing that lacks flowery descriptions and colorful language. Reporters must attribute any opinion given in a news story to a source; the writer never injects his or her own opinion. Facts are extremely important in journalistic writing, and they must be accurate. When we went to journalism school, fact errors meant automatic failure for the assignment. Journalistic writing employs its own set of stylistic rules, usually those of the *Associated Press Stylebook.*

Among variations on journalistic writing is *feature writing,* distinguished from newswriting because it is not tied to breaking news. Feature writing, usually looser and more colorful than newswriting, is often used for profiles of interesting people and portraits of programs of community interest. *Writing for broadcast media*—television and radio news—is another variation. Here, writing must be even more concise to fit into brief moments of broadcast time, and news must be written for the ear, not the eye.

RESOURCES THAT CAN HELP WITH JOURNALISTIC WRITING: *Associated Press Stylebook, News Reporting* by Melvin Mencher, *Language Skills for Journalists* by R. Thomas Berner, *On Writing Well* by William Zinsser, *The Writing Craft* by Edward D. Yates, *Working with Words* by Brian Brooks and James Pinson. The Columbia Journalism Review's Web page can be accessed at **http://www.cjr.org**.

**Public relations writing**—The goal of public relations practitioners, who work in companies, nonprofit organizations, and the public sector, is to publicize and promote the products and services of their employers. Yet because the print and broadcast media are the major conduits for such publicity, public relations writing is a subset of journalistic writing. Public relations writers must follow all the basic rules of journalism if they hope to see and hear stories about their employers' products and services in the media. The challenge for public relations writers is to write about products and services in a way that's newsworthy and not merely shallow puffery. The press release (also called news release, media release) is a major tool of public relations, and it is written very similarly to journalistic writing.

RESOURCES THAT CAN HELP WITH PUBLIC RELATIONS WRITING: *Associated Press Stylebook, Handbook for Public Relations Writing* by Thomas Bivins, *The Publicity Handbook* by David R. Yale, *Public Relations Writing* by Doug Newsom.

**Speechwriting**—People usually give speeches to affect the behavior of the audience, whether to motivate, amuse, educate, or persuade; thus, speechwriting is closely related to the persuasive and argumentative genres of writing. In fact, speechwriting combines elements of several disciplines. Speechwriters sometimes come from the ranks of business, but also frequently from the public relations field. Speechwriting is a distant cousin to journalistic writing, and while it is most closely related to editorial writing, speechwriting also includes some elements of broadcast writing because of the necessity to write for the ear instead of the eye. At some point in your college career, you will likely take a public speaking class. You'll be graded in large part on how well you deliver speeches, but you can gain an advantage by writing good speeches that are easy to deliver. The most important element in speechwriting is the audience. A good speechwriter knows as much about the audience as possible—how many members, what their interests are, what ideas they are most likely to respond to, what their attention span is, and so on. Most speeches should be as brief as possible because most audiences have poor attention spans. The speechwriter should also cater to the audience's short attention span by peppering speeches with anecdotes, startling statistics, humor when appropriate, quotations, and inspiring language. The speechwriter should also include signposts—phrases such as "in conclusion"—so the audience knows how much more they have to listen to.

RESOURCES THAT CAN HELP WITH SPEECHWRITING: *Writing Effective Speeches* by Henry Erlich, *The Elements of Speechwriting and Public Speaking* by Jeff Cook. The Web Pages of David Slack is a site on the World Wide Web that provides tons of useful information about speechwriting and contains links to other helpful sites. The site can be found at **http://speeches.com/index.shtml.**

**Business writing**—This extremely broad category covers many types of writing primarily directed at employees, suppliers, and customers. Included under the business writing heading are business letters, memos, reports, proposals, and presentations. Also included are the kinds of documents individuals use to write to businesses when they seek employment—resumes and cover letters. The business courses you take, even those outside business communications classes, will probably present you with the opportunity to craft some applied writing that simulates what employers may require of you in the business world. In one marketing class we know of, for example, the professor often requires exam responses to be in memo form.

In the real world, much business writing is garbled, unclear, self-important, and pompous. Thus, clarity, simplicity, and straightforwardness count for a great deal, not only in the business classroom, but in the business world. Clear, concise business writing can give you an edge in both venues.

RESOURCES THAT CAN HELP WITH BUSINESS WRITING: *Write to the Top: Writing for Corporate Success* by Deborah Dumaine, *How to Write First-Class Business Correspondence* by L. Sue Baugh, Maridell Fryar, and David A. Thomas, *WritePro for Business* software by Sol Stein. The World Wide Web site called Internet Technical Writing Course Guide, while primarily about technical writing, has some information relevant to business writing; it can be accessed at **http://uu-gna.mit.edu:8001/uu-gna/text/wamt/acchtml/acctoc.html**. Another site, Business Writing, can be found at **http://www.interlog.com/~ohi/www/ biz.html**.

**Scientific writing**—From the lab reports you write in college to reports on research you may create if you pursue a career in the sciences, scientific writing is quite specialized. Ebel, Bliefert, and Russey note in *The Art of Scientific Writing* that the definitive source for the style of scientific writing is *The Chemist's English* by Robert Schoenfeld. The authors also state that quality scientific reports, both at the student and professional levels, have several common elements:

▲ They are written with the reader in mind so that the researcher includes the right amount of information. Overexplaining will bore and irritate your reader, whether it's your professor or your boss, while underexplaining will suggest you didn't perform enough of the work that the report is intended to detail.

▲ They serve as an independent record of your scientific endeavors.

▲ They include a literature review (see page 103) that puts your work into the context of the greater body of research in a given area.

▲ They suggest what the next step in the research should be.

▲ They are properly identified. Check with your professor about what kind of title page or heading is required.

A GOOD WAY TO STRUCTURE A COLLEGE-LEVEL SCIENTIFIC REPORT:

    I.   Heading

    II.   Introduction, including lit review

    III.   Methodology

        a. steps performed

        b. observations

    IV.   Results

    V.   Discussion: Interpretation and significance of results

    VI.   Conclusion

RESOURCES THAT CAN HELP WITH SCIENTIFIC WRITING: *The Art of Scientific Writing* by Ebel, Bliefert, and Russey, *The Chemist's English* by Robert Schoenfeld. Writing a Research Report is an Australian site on the World Wide Web that provides useful information about writing scientific reports and can be found at **http://www.macarthur.uws.edu.au/ssd/ldc/Research_report.html**, while a Canadian site, Writing the Formal Report, can be found at **http://library-www. scar.utoronto.ca/Subject/Physical_Sciences/AA05.html**. Guides for Better Science Research and Writing is a Web site that contains a fairly lengthy bibliography of style guides in print for writing in biology, chemistry, engineering, geology, and math. Web address: **http://www.indiana. edu/~cheminfo/14-05.html**.

## Hybrid forms of student writing

While still expository in many respects, autobiographical writing and journal writing also have characteristics of creative writing. Both types of writing can have strongly imaginative elements and take flights of fancy. Autobiographical writing and journal writing are similar in that both center on the writer's memories, thoughts, feelings, ideas, and impressions. But autobiographical writing is likely to be just a one-time assignment, while journal writing may be an ongoing activity in a class. Autobiography tends toward chronicling one event or era that may have occurred in the distant past, while journal writing tends to be concerned with the present and very recent past.

**Autobiographical writing**—Ever since the day you wrote your first paper on "What I Did on My Summer Vacation," you've been writing autobiographical papers for school. One reason teachers like to assign them is that they know that the easiest thing to write about is one's own experience. Fiction writers are constantly being cautioned to "write about what you know." For many students, writing about their own experience is easy. But others are uncomfortable about writing about themselves, revealing their innermost experiences, and exposing themselves to their instructor. You may be more comfortable if you think of this kind of writing as an extension of something you've been doing all your life—relating events about your life to others. In the not-too-distant past, students used to write a lot of letters to friends and family, and maybe you still do. Today, the chronicling of your life is more likely to take other forms, perhaps e-mail or simply talking on the phone or face-to-face.

Sometimes students have difficulty writing about themselves because they think nothing interesting has ever happened in their lives. But there's no denying that a life—even one that has reached only eighteen or so years so far—is full of experiences. Even experiences that you don't think a teacher will find exciting can make for rich writing. Remember that nothing in human experience is trivial because human life is something we all share. Going back to your childhood can be especially rewarding. Think of people and places that have played important roles in your life.

The best autobiographical writing not only relates events in our lives but also gives meaning to those events. Not every teacher would admit it, but another reason they assign autobiographical papers is that the papers are a great way of getting to know students better and opening a little window on their personalities. If you can write autobiographical papers in a way that gives meaning to your experiences and helps your instructor get to know you better, you'll be well on your way to successful college writing.

RESOURCES THAT CAN HELP WITH AUTOBIOGRAPHICAL WRITING: *Writing Incredibly Short Plays, Poems, Stories* by James H. Norton and Francis Gretton, *Writing Well* by Donald Hall. A World Wide Web site called Eye to I: Writing the Personal Essay has good information related to autobiographical writing; it can be accessed at **http://www.nando.net/prof/poynter.wrtper.html**.

**Journal writing**—Instructors assign students to keep journals for all kinds of reasons, and they have many ways of grading them. Some teachers want you to keep a journal purely for jotting down thoughts and ideas that you will use for future writing assignments. Others want to you record your responses to content presented in class or readings done outside class. A professor we know who teaches a course on how business is portrayed in the movies, for example, requires his students to write their responses to the movies they view in class and to tie all journal entries to a central theme. Another assigns students to write journal entries about cultural events and exhibitions they attended throughout the semester.

The teacher who assigns journal writing as a self-help tool may never collect and grade those journals, while other teachers may collect journals only at the end of the term. Still others may collect and grade them at regular intervals, and some may not announce when journals will be collected. They ask you to hand your journal in at an unannounced time just to make sure you're making regular entries in your journal.

Since instructors assign journal writing with so many different learning objectives in mind, no single piece of advice on what instructors seek will quite fit. Overall, however, instructors want journals that are thoughtful and that show you have put some effort into the entries. The writing probably doesn't need to be as formal as with other papers, but neither should it be riddled with writing flaws. Since most journals are handwritten, your writing should be reasonably legible.

RESOURCES THAT CAN HELP WITH JOURNAL WRITING: *Journaling Handbook* by Carol Barton, *Telling Your Own Stories: For Family and Classroom Storytelling, Public Speaking, and Personal Journaling* by Donald Davis. The Write Place is a site on the World Wide Web that contains a section on journal suggestions and samples and can be found at **http://www.rio.com/~wplace/**. Writer's Resource Center is another World Wide Web site with a section on journal and essay writing; it can be found at **http://www.azstarnet.com/~poewar/writer/pg/essay.html**.

## CREATIVE WRITING: FICTION, POETRY, DRAMA, SCREENPLAYS

Since more creative writing is done outside academia than inside, vast resources are available to the would-be novelist, poet, dramatist, or screenwriter—as well as to the student creative writer. But what is the instructor looking for in a piece of student creative writing?

As we mentioned under autobiographical writing, teachers are constantly exhorting creative writers to write about what they know—their own experience. As Donald Hall puts it, "Fiction writing is writing out of your life with imagination added." As a beginning creative writer, you can write about something that happened to you, add a few imaginative details, change the names, and voilà—you have a piece of fiction. And no one can quibble with how true-to-life it is because it comes from your own experience. Not that fiction has to be true-to-life; after all, look at fantasy and science fiction. Still, the feelings and evocation of your own human experience are bound to come through so the reader can identify with them.

Keeping a journal is an excellent way to develop ideas for creative writing. If you carry your journal with you at all times, you can record little vignettes from your daydreams, fantasies, observations, and experiences that you can weave into, say, a story, poem, or play someday. How many times have you seen or thought about something that made you say, "That would make a good movie." Those movies in your head are perfect fodder for creative writing.

Poetry-writing is difficult for some students. While you probably won't take a poetry-writing course unless you feel you have poetry within you, you may be assigned to write a poem in another class. Peter Elbow has an excellent chapter on poetry-writing in his book *Writing with Power: Techniques for Mastering the Writing Process.* Among many inspiring poetry-starting exercises, he suggests treating poetry-writing as if it were no big deal. Instead of fretting about what to write a poem about, Elbow says, assign yourself to write a poem about a certain thing, and don't hesitate as you write it. Just write it all down, and don't worry about making it a good poem until afterwards. If you feel that poetry is completely foreign to you and you'll never be able to relate to it or create it, just think about popular music. The lyrics are a form of poetry that you can relate to, and you probably won't find it that difficult to replicate their style in a poem of your own.

Similarly, some students fear they couldn't possibly latch onto anything worth dramatizing in a script or screenplay. James Norton and Francis Gretton have written a nifty little volume called *Writing Incredibly Short Plays, Poems, Stories* in which they state that all that is necessary for good drama is conflict plus consequences. The authors suggest a number of typical situations in a student's life in which conflict and consequences may play a part.

Some creative writing instructors conduct very free-form classes; they don't want to hamper your creativity by imposing a lot of rules and structure on your writing. Others insist that you learn basic techniques such as description, narrative, and dialogue in fiction; rhythm patterns and figurative language in poetry; stage directions in drama; and cinematographic instructions in screenwriting. If yours is one who values the basics, learn them well, and apply them in your writing if you want to succeed in the class. Whichever style your teacher adopts, he or she will be your best possible resource for success as a creative writer in that class. Many creative writing teachers are writers themselves who truly cherish the nurturing and development of a talented student writer. If you find your instructor is giving you low grades on your creative writing, go to see him or her to learn how you can make it better.

RESOURCES THAT CAN HELP WITH CREATIVE WRITING: *Writing with Power: Techniques for Mastering the Writing Process* by Peter Elbow, *Writing Incredibly Short Plays, Poems, Stories* by James H. Norton and Francis Gretton, *The Poet's Handbook* by Judson Jerome, *Writing Well* by Donald Hall, *Fade In: The Screenwriting Process* by Robert A. Berman, *The Elements of Screenwriting: A Guide for Film and Television Writers* by Irwin R. Blacker, *The Way to Write: A Stimulating Guide to the Craft of Creative Writing* by John Fairfax, *Write-Pro* software by The WritePro Corporation, *Dramatica* software by Screenplay Systems, *FictionMaster* software by The WritePro Corporation, *StoryCraft* software by StoryCraft Corporation. World Wide Web sites that can aid the creative-writing process include:

Electronic Poetry Center. Web address: **http://wings.buffalo.edu/epc/**
Essays on the Craft of Dramatic Writing. Web address: **http://www.teleport. co.uk/~ei/intro.html**
Journal and Essay Writing. Web address: **http://www.azstarnet.com/~poewar/ writer/pg/essay.html**
The Playwrights Project. Web address: **http://www.vnet.net/users/phisto/**
Poetry Portals for the World Wide Web. Web address: **http://www.infi.net/tcc/ tcresourc/faculty/dreiss/pomweb.html**
Poetry Writing Tips. Web address: **http://www.azstarnet.com/~poewar/writer/ Poet's_Notes.html**
Poets & Writers. Web address: **http://www.pw.org/**
Screenwriters and Playwrights Home Page. Web address: **http://elaine. teleport.com/~cdeemer/scrwriter.html**

Screenwriters Online. Web address: **http://screenwriter.com/insider/**

Script Tutor. Web address: **http://scripttutor.com/**

Ultimate Poetry Links. Web address: **http://www.kiosk.net/poetry/links.html**

Zuzu's Petals Literary Resource. Web address: **http://www.lehigh.net/uzu/
index.htm**.

# The Top Ten Writing
# 4 Flaws That Lead
# to a Lower Grade

LET'S ASSUME YOU WANT TO GET BETTER GRADES ON THE PAPERS YOU WRITE. THAT'S A SAFE ASSUMPTION SINCE YOU'RE READING THESE WORDS. MAYBE YOU DON'T HAVE THE TIME OR INCLINATION TO MASTER EVERY DETAIL ABOUT HOW TO WRITE A PERFECT COLLEGE PAPER. YET IF YOU KNEW THE MISTAKES IN STUDENT PAPERS THAT MOST TICK PROFESSORS OFF, YOU COULD AVOID THEM AND GET A BETTER GRADE, RIGHT? WELL, YOU'VE COME TO THE RIGHT PLACE.

We surveyed 146 college professors nationwide who place significant weight on writing as a part of the coursework they assign, and we identified the top ten writing flaws that make for a lower grade. These are the ten flaws that professors see most often, most irritate them, and make them most likely to lower your grade. In this chapter, we provide the tools and guidance to enable you to overcome the Top Ten. If you can master these ten, you will be well on your way to better grades.

Keep in mind, however, that at least nineteen additional writing flaws annoy your professors and influence the way they grade you, although not as dramatically as do these ten. We'll list those also-rans later in the chapter with some broad suggestions for how to overcome them.

The top ten writing flaws that make for a lower grade:

1. Poor organization
2. Failure to support your thesis
3. Misspellings
4. Inadequate citation of sources
5. Confusing sentence structure

6.   Typos/Sloppiness
7.   Sentence fragments
8.   Run-on sentences
9.   Incorrect word usage

and tied for tenth:

10.   Little evidence of research
10.   Little evidence of understanding the topic

Yes, we realize we've actually listed eleven flaws. However, since number three (misspellings) and number six (typos/sloppiness) are closely related and have similar root causes, we'll examine them together.

# "Following technical instructions is an easy way to improve your grade and a silly thing to resist."

—a women's studies professor at a large university

**"Master the basics: spelling, grammar, punctuation, capitalization. No matter how strong the content of information, it is always overshadowed by the errors in writing."**

—a business professor at a medium-sized public university

Now let's take an in-depth look at each flaw and what you can do to avoid it.

# 1. Poor organization

**The poorly structured paper**—the number one complaint of college professors—frequently results from procrastinating and failing to plan adequately. The major points of your paper should flow logically from each other and build upon each other. In short, your paper should make sense.

The first, and perhaps most significant, way to avoid a poorly organized paper is to start early. Faulty organization often results from waiting until the last minute and then slapping together all the points of your paper haphazardly. If you start as soon as the paper is assigned, you'll have plenty of time to construct a paper that makes sense and builds to a logical conclusion.

Starting early will also give you enough time to employ one of the planning and organizing techniques outlined in chapter 1. The following techniques can be especially helpful in producing a well-organized paper: Technique 9 (page 20), Technique 10 (page 25), Technique 11 (page 26), and Technique 12 (page 28).

Each of these techniques essentially is a form of outlining, the most reliable method of ensuring a well-organized paper. Again, if a point seems out of place in your outline, it will seem even more askew in your paper, and your professor will notice.

In the same way that you use headings to organize your outline, you may wish to use subheads in your paper, if your professor allows them, to help organize your paper and direct the professor's attention to the way it's organized.

Think of your paper as a building, with your thesis sentence or paragraph as a foundation. Each additional paragraph must be a building block that not only logically bolsters but also follows coherently on the preceding paragraphs. Your conclusion tops off the building in a way that aligns symmetrically with its foundation. You can also think of your paper as a rhetorical argument that supports a thesis you've developed.

Remember back in elementary or middle school when you learned about topic sentences in paragraphs? Apply that knowledge to the organization of your paper, and note how one element builds on the next:

> Your introduction sets forth your thesis.
> Coherent paragraphs contain a topic sentence that relates your main point to your thesis, as well as a concluding sentence.
> Each paragraph should flow rationally from the preceding paragraph.
> Your conclusion should summarize your argument and should relate directly to the thesis statement you made in your opening paragraph.

Some writing instructors are not quite so stodgy in their insistence on topic and concluding sentences in every paragraph. They recommend, instead, that each paragraph convey an "organic coherence," meaning that "each sentence must relate to the one before it like a branch to a tree or a twig to a branch. Paragraphs can grow in any number of directions as long as the sentences link to one another in a way that makes sense," writes James Raymond. You will likely feel less uptight and inhibited about writing if you use the organic coherence strategy, but make sure your professor is comfortable with that approach.

One of our colleagues at Stetson University, American studies professor Paul Jerome Croce, includes the following outline for a well-organized paper in a writing handout he provides to his students:

**Organization/Structure**

1. Examples to illustrate theme
2. One point for every paragraph
3. Smooth flow of ideas, transitions
   a. sentence to sentence
   b. paragraph to paragraph
4. Clear relation of parts
5. Thorough pursuit of ideas
   a. explanations until whole idea is written
   b. interpretations or demonstrations to back up opinions
6. Introduction
   a. inform reader of theme
   b. draw reader into your viewpoint
   c. raise a question or questions
7. Conclusion
   a. summarize briefly
   b. show significance of your point
   c. offer an answer

The final checkpoint for determining whether your paper is well organized, of course, is to read it and ask yourself after each paragraph if that paragraph seems to be in place and contributes to your argument. Be sure to allow yourself enough time, in case you need to overhaul the structure of your paper completely. Your task may be as simple as rearranging a couple of paragraphs. However, be prepared, too, to scrap any paragraphs that simply refuse to "go with the flow." One of the professors we surveyed described what he calls his "Rude Little Question" test that students should apply to each paragraph as they proofread. The Rude Little Question is "So what?" and if you can't come up with an answer to that rude little question for each paragraph, the paragraph probably ought to be tossed out.

Knowing that the disorganized paper is the number one writing flaw that pushes professors' buttons, you should stop at nothing to ensure that your paper will delight your professor with the coherent way you develop and prove your argument. Remember, it never hurts to ask someone else to read it, asking them to pay particular attention to how it's organized and how well it flows.

"**One** of the most important aspects of good writing is good organization of your ideas. The more you think about what you want to say in your argument, the better the argument will be.**"**

—a political science professor at the University of Utah

"**Take your time and understand that clear, organized writing cannot be accomplished in one sitting; it takes some effort and care.**"

—a political science professor at a medium-sized public university

"**Organize, organize, organize, dammit.**"

—a professor of constitutional law at a small public university

"**I would advise students to know how to ORGANIZE their compositions. Effective organization can contribute to a composition that appears knowledgeable and substantive.**"

—a professor who teaches English at a university in Mexico

"**Start by outlining your thesis, the shape of your argument, supporting evidence, and conclusions.**"

—an adjunct professor at a private university in Virginia

"**Start with a strong thesis and use it to create tight organization of [your] argument.**"

—a women's studies professor at a large university

SOFTWARE TIP: Most of the top-selling word-processing software programs, such as Corel *WordPerfect* and Microsoft *Word*, have built-in outlining functions. You can also purchase outlining software, such as *In Control* (for Macintosh and Windows) and *InfoDepot* (for Macintosh). Other programs, such as *Three by Five* (Macintosh) and *Mind Mapper* and *Thoughtline* (Windows), help you better develop your thoughts. See chapter 8 for full details.

HINT

A number of books and Internet sites can help with organizing; see chapter 8.

# 2. Failure to support your thesis

**In high school, you** could sometimes get away with papers that were more like reports—essentially a collection of facts strung together. However, you can rarely write that kind of paper in college. Your college papers must explore a question, problem, or issue. You must state a thesis at the outset, also known as a hypothesis, and the rest of your paper, as we've just noted, must build a case that supports your thesis, argument, or main point. You are not merely summarizing information, as you might do with a high school paper, but taking a position with the best evidence you can find in the literature. (Note that, in this sense, "literature" refers to all the academic material written about your topic.)

Here's how our Stetson colleague, history professor Jeff Horn (who never gives A's unless papers are clearly superlative), expresses this concept in the writing guidelines he distributes to his students: "All papers must have a thesis. Providing information is not enough. There must be a point to your work. The thesis of your paper should be a declarative sentence that makes an argument of some kind and shows why a topic or idea is significant."

An important aspect of adequately supporting your thesis is developing a viable thesis in the first place. The techniques from chapter 1 related to topic development (Techniques 4 and 8) can be valuable in this pursuit. It's important not only to choose a topic about which you feel comfortable making an argument but about which you are likely to find enough literature to help you support that argument. Those topic development techniques are: Technique 4 (page 9), Technique 5 (page 13), Technique 6 (page 15), and Technique 7 (page 17).

Beyond topic development, outlining and similar techniques can help you develop points that will support your main point. Thorough research will help even more. Accumulating research literature and citing authors that bolster each aspect of your argument should enable you to convince your instructor that you've supported your thesis. You can test out the success of your paper by reading it and asking yourself: "Have I proven my point? Are my thesis and supporting arguments convincing?"

"**Be** specific. Support what you say with concrete examples and details."

—an English professor at the University of Maryland

"**What is the point you are trying to make? Concentrate on explaining it in a clear and concise manner.**"

—a communications professor at a medium-sized public university

"**Take some time to really think about what your opinion is on this topic. Then construct a thoughtful argument that uses evidence and logic to persuade the reader why this is a valid analysis to make.**"

—a sociology and anthropology professor at a Canadian university

SOFTWARE TIP: A number of good brainstorming and idea-generating software products are available, including, for the Macintosh, *Three by Five, Genius Handbook, IdeaFisher, Inspiration,* and *MindLink Problem Solver;* and for Windows, *Axon Idea Processor, Brainstormer, Creative Whack Pack, Creativity Machine, Genius Handbook, IdeaFisher, Idea Generator Plus, Inspiration, MindLink Problem Solver,* and *Thoughtline.* See chapter 8 for full details.

HINT

A number of books and Internet sites also help you creatively develop your topic; see chapter 8.

# 3. Misspellings and 6. Typos/Sloppiness

**Ah, that old bugaboo**—spelling. Spelling need not be as much of a problem for today's college students as it was for those a few years ago. Sure, you can learn to be a better speller. But today's college student has an invaluable shortcut. Most decent word-processing programs have spell checker features. Unfortunately, you'd be amazed at how often college students write their papers in such a rush that they neglect to employ the spell checker. That's why it's so important to develop a workable timetable for writing your paper (Technique 2, page 5) so you won't be caught short with no time to spell check.

Just what is the difference between a typo and a misspelling anyway? A misspelling is a word that you deliberately write or type incorrectly because you don't know the correct spelling, while a typo is a word that you may know perfectly well how to spell, but you mistype it so that it appears as a misspelled word—or the wrong word. With that in mind, it's important to remember that spell checkers will not catch a word that is spelled correctly but is not the correct word for the context. For example, we frequently mistype "from" as "form." "Form" is spelled correctly, but its meaning is very different from the meaning of "from."

Sloppiness has the same root cause as misspellings and typos—finishing your paper in such a rush that no time remains for spell checking, proofreading, and fixing errors. Sloppiness can comprise anything from ink marks all over a typed paper where you've attempted to indicate corrections to a poorly typed paper that lacks margins to leaving words out (we're famous for such omissions).

That's where careful proofreading comes in. While spell checking is key to catching most misspellings, thorough proofing is essential for catching the misspellings that appear as out-of-context words, as well as for spotting typos and sloppiness. Most of us are notoriously bad proofreaders of our own work. Thus, the more distance we can put between ourselves and our writing, the better proofreaders we'll be. One of the best ways to achieve this distance is to allow enough time to proofread your paper once, put it down overnight (longer if your schedule allows), and then take a fresh look at it the next day— or better yet, ask a friend to view it with fresh eyes. See also the revising tips in chapter 6.

SOFTWARE TIP: Most of the top-selling word-processing software programs have spell checkers, but you can also buy both general and subject-specific spell checkers for Macintosh *(Spelling Coach, SpellsWell)* and Windows *(Spell Check 3.3)*. For more information, see chapter 8.

# 4. Inadequate citation of sources

**Integrating sufficient research** into your paper won't matter if you don't know how to cite your sources properly. English, the humanities, and literature tend to use the citation style set forth by the Modern Language Association (MLA), while business and the social sciences use the style dictated by the American Psychological Association (APA). Your professor can tell you which of these styles to use—or whether to refer to an altogether different style manual (such as *The Chicago Manual of Style* or one that is subject-specific) for citing sources. Both MLA and APA publish hard-copy handbooks outlining their styles, and versions of the handbooks are also available in virtual form on the World Wide Web. See chapter 8 for addresses.

Even more important than using the correct style to cite your sources is the understanding that when you use ideas, facts, and opinions that are not your own—even when you don't use the author's exact words—you must give appropriate credit to the author as you incorporate his or her ideas into your paper. If you don't do so, you're committing plagiarism, one of the most serious offenses in academe. You can also footnote sources that won't fit into your paper because of space or flow. As Jeff Horn the history professor notes, it's better, when in doubt, to over-cite than under-cite.

SOFTWARE TIP: Software programs also are available that allow you to choose one of numerous academic styles and have the software create your citations in the correct style. Some programs even help you build your bibliography as you use the sources in your paper. Examples include, for the Macintosh, *Bibliography Builder, Bookends Pro, End Note Plus,* and *ProCite;* and for DOS/Windows, *Citation 7, EndNote Plus, Library Master, Perfect Scholar, Square Note,* and *ProCite.* See chapter 8 for more information.

# 5. Confusing sentence structure

**The best way to avoid** sentences that trip up your professor and hamper readability is to read your paper aloud. Chances are, a sentence that doesn't read well orally is too complex or confusing in print as well.

You can usually simplify by breaking a sentence into two or more sentences and by ensuring that all modifiers (adjectives and adverbs) and clauses (groups of related words that contain both a subject and a predicate and that function as part of a sentence) are structurally close to the elements to which they refer. You can also cut out unnecessary clauses and phrases (groups of related words without a subject and a predicate that function as a single part of speech). Of course, you should also avoid going to the opposite extreme of having too many short, choppy sentences in your paper since professors in our survey identified short, choppy sentences and paragraphs as number twenty on their list of student writing pet peeves. When you can join two sentences gracefully and without adding confusion, by all means join them. But if compound subjects, compound verbs, and numerous clauses have obscured the meaning of your sentences, it may be time to simplify.

In his book *Edit Yourself*, Bruce Ross-Larson offers some excellent suggestions for improving the flow and readability of your sentences. He advises listing the elements of a sentence—pairs, series, compound subjects and predicates in order from short word to long word, from simple to compound. In listing series of words, those with the most syllables should come after shorter words. In listing series of phrases, those with the most words should come last. Compound elements, whether compound noun phrases or compound predicates (the portions of the sentence containing the verb), should also come last.

Similarly, Strunk and White note in *Elements of Style* that the words on which you wish to place the most emphasis or make most prominent should come at the end of the sentence.

"I think that students should concentrate on being clear and lucid first of all, and then use style manuals or writing resource centers to correct the fine points. I find that clear thinkers make good writers."

—a professor at a small Canadian university

**SOFTWARE TIP:** Most of the top-selling software word-processing programs have grammar checkers. As we discuss in chapter 6, you need solid knowledge of grammar rules to make use of grammar checkers effectively, but the programs still may be useful in helping you identify crippled sentences.

# 7. Sentence fragments

**Sentences need to have** a subject and a verb. If a sentence does not have both, it's a fragment, which you can often successfully attach to another sentence. Take the sentence you just read. A clumsy student might write: "If a sentence does not have both, it's a fragment. Which you can often successfully attach to another sentence." The student can perform a quick fix by turning the sentence fragment into a clause, setting it off with a comma, and attaching it to the sentence to which it belongs. Make sure all your sentences have both a subject and a verb, and when appropriate, perform reattachment surgery on those that don't.

SOFTWARE TIP: Most of the top-selling software word-processing programs have grammar checkers. As we discuss in chapter 6, you need solid knowledge of grammar rules to make use of grammar checkers effectively, but the programs are excellent for identifying incomplete sentences.

# 8. Run-on sentences

**We can think of the** run-on sentence as the evil twin of the sentence fragment. Where the sentence fragment lacks a subject or verb, the run-on sentence has too many of both. There's nothing wrong with joining two sentences into one compound sentence as long as you use an appropriate connector between the two sentences. An appropriate connector is either a conjunction, such as *and, but, yet, so, however,* or punctuation—such as a semicolon or colon. (*Not* a comma.) Joining two complete sentences with a comma results in the most common type of run-on sentence.

A good check for run-ons can be performed by reading your paper aloud. Every time you naturally feel the need to pause in the spoken version of your paper, ensure that appropriate punctuation marks the pause and ensure that if two sentences are on either side of the punctuation, a conjunction, semicolon, or colon has joined them.

**SOFTWARE TIP:** Most of the top-selling software word-processing programs have grammar checkers. As we discuss in chapter 6, you need solid knowledge of grammar rules to make use of grammar checkers effectively, but the programs are effective at alerting you to sentences that are inappropriately joined.

# 9. Incorrect word usage

**You remember all those** confusing pairs: *affect* and *effect, less* and *fewer, among* and *between, farther* and *further, lay* and *lie, who* and *whom, that* and *which*...the list goes on and on. And did you know that *presently* doesn't mean the same as *currently* and *utilize* is just a stilted way to say *use?* Our advice on this troublesome writing flaw is simple: Obtain a copy of Strunk and White's *The Elements of Style,* available in an inexpensive paperback, and read and refer to the chapter called "Words and Expressions Commonly Misused." The entire book is worth its weight in gold to the student writer who wants to earn better grades, but the chapter on word usage is particularly valuable.

Be aware, too, that the word usage flaws that especially drive professors off the deep end are the most simple ones that everyone should know to avoid: *to, too,* and *two; there, their,* and *they're;* and *it's* and *its.* If you learn no other correct word usage, at least learn these easy ones.

**SOFTWARE TIP:** Most of the top-selling software word-processing programs have grammar checkers. As we discuss in chapter 6, you need solid knowledge of grammar rules to make use of grammar checkers effectively, but the programs are excellent for troubleshooting incorrect word usage.

# 10. Little evidence of research

**Inserting quotations,** citing authors that bolster your thesis, and presenting a lengthy-but-pertinent bibliography will all help show your professor that you've researched your topic well, assuming that you have, in fact, gathered sufficient research material. But evidence of copious research will succeed only if you use the research you've uncovered in a way that logically supports your thesis. Thus, the lack-of-evidence writing flaw is intricately tied to the failure-to-support-thesis flaw, as well as the poor-organization flaw.

Remember that your professor can give you the best guidance on how much research you need to do. Check in with your instructor as you're researching and writing your paper, and share your research with him or her. Your teacher can probably tell you whether the research seems adequate.

Integrating that research into the paper is trickier. Our friend the history professor offers this stringent guideline: "Every paragraph except the introduction and conclusion ought to have a reference to the primary or secondary material used for your paper. If there is not a reference to a source in the paragraph, you probably have not provided the necessary evidence to demonstrate your point." While some professors might consider such a dictum extreme, you certainly can't go wrong if you follow the "a-source-in-every-paragraph" guideline.

"**Give** yourself sufficient time to define your topic and research for information."

—political science professor at a small private university

HINT

Chapter 2 shows you the vast resources available to you to ensure that you perform adequate research.

# 10. Little evidence of understanding the topic

**This writing flaw most** frequently results when the professor assigns the topic. Since it's not a topic you developed on your own, there's a greater margin of error for understanding how the professor wants you to explore the assigned topic. The best way to make sure you understand what the professor wants before your start? Ask. (Also, see Technique 23 on page 51.) A surprising number of the professors we surveyed said that the one piece of advice they would most like to give student writers is students should make sure they understand the assignment. If you don't want to seem stupid or take up the instructor's time in class, schedule a meeting outside class and go over the topic to ensure you not only understand the topic but you grasp how the professor wants you to attack it in your paper. If you go away from that meeting still harboring some doubts, ask your professor if you can show him or her an outline or rough draft to confirm your understanding of the topic. Some professors have a certain agenda when they assign a topic; they want you to come up with the "correct" conclusion in your paper. Thus, it's crucial that you do everything possible to understand the agenda and discover what the correct conclusion is. The agenda may especially pertain when the topic assignment comes directly from class lecture or reading material or when the assignment is, for example, a take-home essay exam.

Sometimes you can also display poor understanding of a topic you have chosen yourself—or you can fail to demonstrate how the topic relates to the course content. Here's where it's important to feel comfortable with the topic you've developed, perhaps using the topic development techniques described in chapter 1. It's also important to ensure that you can find enough outside research material to help you understand your topic better—and to prove to your professor that you understand the topic. Again, discussing your topic and research with your professor will go a long way toward assuring him or her that you understand the topic—or will prompt him or her to suggest that you develop better understanding of the topic before proceeding or even that you pick a different topic.

# "Don't try to cover too much. Choose one narrow topic, and focus your efforts on that."

—a political-science professor at a small Midwestern private university

**"Plan to allow enough time to research the topic well."**

—a business professor at a medium-sized public university

Now let's take a quick look at the flaws that didn't make the Top Ten but that are still plenty aggravating to your professor and influential in lowering your grade. Our format here is a brief explanation of what the flaw is and how to find guidance for fixing it if it's a problem that plagues your academic writing.

## 12. Poor punctuation

**What the problem is:** Improper or nonuse of punctuation marks, especially commas.

**Where to turn for help:** Few substitutes exist for simply knowing the rules. If you don't know them, you can refer to a good grammar book or use a grammar checker on your computer (see chapter 8). Another helpful technique is to read your paper aloud. Think of punctuation marks as traffic signs that tell you to stop or pause. If your paper lacks the appropriate stops and pauses, it probably won't read well and will benefit from periods, commas, and other punctuation.

## 13. Comma splices

**What the problem is:** Essentially, another way to look at a run-on sentence. A comma splice refers to using only a comma to join two complete sentences that you should join with a conjunction, semicolon, or colon.

**Where to turn for help:** See number 8, page 132.

## 14. Poor or nonexistent transitions

**What the problem is:** You've made little or no effort to connect your paragraphs; your paper lacks flow.

**Where to turn for help:** Since this problem relates to poor organization (see page 123), improving your paper's organization will set the scene for improved transitions. Test your transitions by reading aloud to determine whether each paragraph flows coherently from the preceding paragraph. Note also these transitions words commonly used to improve writing flow:

▲ Sequence—again, also, and, and then, besides, finally, first...second...third, furthermore, last, moreover, next, next in importance, still, too, in addition to

▲ Time—after a bit, after a few days (hours, weeks, months, years), after a while, afterward, as long as, as soon as, at last, at length, at that time, before, earlier, formerly, from now on, from then on, immediately, in the meantime, in the past, lately, later, meanwhile, now, presently, shortly, simultaneously, since, so far, soon, then, thereafter, until, when, subsequently, also, at the same time, while, following

▲ Comparison—again, also, in the same way, likewise, once more, similarly, in comparison, equally important, or, in addition

▲ Contrast—although, but, despite, even though, however, in contrast, in spite of, instead, nevertheless, nonetheless, notwithstanding, on the contrary, on the one hand…on the other hand, regardless, still, though, yet, whereas, conversely, in another sense, despite

▲ Examples—after all, even, for example, for instance, indeed, in fact, of course, specifically, such as, the following example, to illustrate

▲ Cause and Effect—accordingly, as a result, because, consequently, for this purpose/reason, hence, so, then, therefore, thereupon, thus, to this end, if…then

▲ Place—above, adjacent to, below, beyond, closer to, elsewhere, far, farther on, here, near, nearby, opposite to, there, to the left, to the right

▲ Concession—although it is true that, granted that, I admit that, it may appear that, naturally, of course, in any event, accepting the data

▲ Subordination—although, as, as if, as though, because, if since, so that, that, though, unless, until, when, whenever, where, wherever, whether, while

▲ Summary, Repetition, Intensification, or Conclusion—above all, add to this, as a result, as has been noted, as I have said, as we have seen, as mentioned earlier, finally, in any event, in conclusion, in other words, in short, more important, on the whole, therefore, to summarize, accordingly, consequently, for these reasons, hence, that is, thus, briefly, in brief, indeed, in particular, in summary, of course, to sum up, ultimately

## 15. WORDINESS

**WHAT THE PROBLEM IS:** You've used more words than are necessary to express your ideas, probably rendering your sentences too complex and your paper too long.

**WHERE TO TURN FOR HELP:** See "Write tight" on page 145.

## 16. NONAGREEMENT OF SUBJECT AND VERB

WHAT THE PROBLEM IS: Singular subjects must take singular verbs, and plural subjects take plural verbs. It's a fairly easy problem to avoid with simple sentences but can be harder to detect in more complex sentences.

> Wrong: Every student, especially seniors, know the cafeteria's hours.
> Right: Every student, especially seniors, knows the cafeteria's hours.

WHERE TO TURN FOR HELP: Grammar books and grammar checkers (chapter 8) can provide shortcuts if you don't have a firm grasp of this grammatical concept.

## 17. MEANINGLESS MODIFIERS

WHAT THE PROBLEM IS: Overuse of adverbs and adjectives that add no meaning to your writing. Notoriously meaningless modifiers include *very, extremely, rather, little,* and *basically.*

WHERE TO TURN FOR HELP: As you proof your paper, test every modifier for whether it truly adds meaning to your words. If you can eliminate the modifier without changing the sentence's meaning, chances are your sentence is better off without it.

The following two flaws are tied for eighteenth:

## 18. VAGUE PRONOUN REFERENCE

WHAT THE PROBLEM IS: Using pronouns, such as *this, it,* or *these,* in place of nouns in an unclear fashion. When you use such pronouns, a referent must accompany them generally. Check every personal, impersonal, relative, and possessive pronoun to be sure no question exists as to what noun the pronoun refers to.

> Wrong: Saigon fell to the Communists in 1975. This disheartened many Americans.
> What is *this?* You need to make clear what *this* refers to.
> Right: This event disheartened many Americans.

You can argue that the meaning of *this* is clear in the above example, but determining the meaning can still slow some readers down. The referent for *this* is far less clear in the next example.

> Wrong: A new political climate developed when Saigon fell to the Communists in 1975, and many refugees escaped Vietnam in boats. This disheartened many Americans.
>
> What is *this?* This new political climate? The event of Saigon's fall to the Communists? Or the escape of the Vietnamese refugees in boats?
>
> Right: This series of events disheartened many Americans.

WHERE TO TURN FOR HELP: Ensure that no pronouns stand naked without referents in your paper.

## 18. OVERUSE OF PASSIVE VOICE

WHAT THE PROBLEM IS: A passive verb is always a verb phrase consisting of a form of the verb *to be* followed by a past participle. The subject of an active verb acts, while the subject of a passive verb is acted upon. The passive form of the sentence we used as the preceding example would be:

> Wrong: Many Americans were disheartened by this event.
> Right: This event disheartened many Americans.

Some professors, including our friend the history professor, allow no passive verbs in their papers and automatically deduct points for use of the passive voice.

WHERE TO TURN FOR HELP: The tip-off to whether a verb is passive is if you can tack a prepositional phrase beginning with "by" to the end of the sentence: Many Americans were disheartened *by* this event. Check for actual or potential "by" phrases as you read over your paper. One of the most effective features of your word-processing software's grammar checker (chapter 8) is its ability to spot passive constructions.

## 20. SHORT, CHOPPY SENTENCES AND/OR PARAGRAPHS

WHAT THE PROBLEM IS: Professors dislike short, choppy sentences and paragraphs only slightly less than they abhor long, complex ones. Let's look at the same sentences we used in the last two examples:

> Choppy: Saigon fell to the Communists in 1975. This disheartened many Americans.

These sentences would sound less choppy and would flow better if we joined them into one.

> Smoother: Saigon fell to the Communists in 1975, disheartening many Americans.

WHERE TO TURN FOR HELP: As you read over your paper, look for opportunities to join choppy sentences together—without creating sentences that are too long and complex. Our colleague Paul Jerome Croce advises students to "end choppy phrasing by combining, deleting, or elaborating."

The following two flaws are tied for twenty-first:

## 21. FAILURE TO FOLLOW A PARTICULAR ACADEMIC WRITING STYLE

WHAT THE PROBLEM IS: We noted under writing flaw #4 that the various academic disciplines use different style manuals for citation of sources. The same is true for general writing style conventions (for example, the way certain rules of punctuation, capitalization, and so forth, are treated in the various style manuals).

WHERE TO TURN FOR HELP: Be sure you clearly understand the academic style your professor requires you to use, obtain a copy (print or on-line) of the manual for that style, and use it as you write your paper. See chapter 8 for more information about print and on-line style guides.

"**Buy** a style manual and read it. Then read it again."
—a marketing professor emeritus at UCLA

## 22. POOR VOCABULARY

WHAT THE PROBLEM IS: Your writing lacks the sophistication and level of vocabulary that your professor expects of a college student.

**WHERE TO TURN FOR HELP:** The thesaurus feature that comes with or can be added to many word-processing programs is a godsend for students with underdeveloped vocabularies. An Internet thesaurus site is listed in chapter 2. A thesaurus in print form can't hurt either. See chapter 8 for more information.

## 23. OVERUSE OF JARGON

**WHAT THE PROBLEM IS:** Your paper contains too much technical language or terminology. Courses in the sciences and applied subjects (such as business) often require you to master technical terminology. You can overuse these terms, however, and turn your paper into a collection of jargon rather than of thoughts and words.

**WHERE TO TURN FOR HELP:** If you know that jargon is a problem for you, ask the professor or another professor to look over a rough draft and advise you about whether the writing depends too much on technical terms. You could also give it to someone with little knowledge of the discipline to read it, and see if he or she is tripped up by unexplained technical jargon. Another clue is when your spell checker keeps stopping on words you've spelled correctly, but because they are technical terms, the spell checker doesn't have them in its default dictionary.

## 24. DANGLING CLAUSES

**WHAT THE PROBLEM IS:** A clause or phrase at the beginning of a sentence must refer to the grammatical subject.

> Wrong: Knowing that you are an expert on career development, you probably hear frequent questions about resumes.

If you ask yourself who is doing the knowing, you realize that it's an understood *I*.

> Right: Knowing that you are an expert on career development, I'm sure you hear frequent questions about resumes.

**WHERE TO TURN FOR HELP:** Grammar books and grammar checkers (chapter 8).

## 25. LACK OF PARALLELISM

WHAT THE PROBLEM IS: When you list a series of items, the items must be in a parallel format.

> Wrong: Diane Arbus and Alice Neel had in common feeling depressed, thoughts of suicide, and trying to capture human psychology in their artwork.
>
> Right: Diane Arbus and Alice Neel had in common bouts of depression, thoughts of suicide, and the tendency to try to capture human psychology in their artwork.

WHERE TO TURN FOR HELP: Grammar and writing style books (chapter 8).

## 26. VERB TENSE CHANGES

WHAT THE PROBLEM IS: You bounce back and forth between present and past tense in your writing.

> Wrong: Alcott writes with a decidedly feminist point of view in *Diana and Persis*. She seemed to disapprove of women giving up their careers to marry.
>
> Right: Alcott writes with a decidedly feminist point of view in *Diana and Persis*. She seems to disapprove of women giving up their careers to marry.

WHERE TO TURN FOR HELP: Grammar books and grammar checkers (chapter 8).

## 27. PAPER IS TOO LONG AND 29. PAPER IS TOO SHORT

WHAT THE PROBLEM IS: We were a bit surprised that too-long papers irritated professors slightly more than too-short ones—but the chore of having to grade too-long papers puts this flaw in focus. Several professors we know will simply stop reading at exactly their page limit and grade only the paper that fits into the assigned limit.

WHERE TO TURN FOR HELP: Make sure you know the professor's exact expectations for the length of your paper, and if you realize you will have difficulty meeting those expectations, ask your professor about his or her policy for too-long or too-short papers. It is, of course, easier to edit a lengthy paper than to stretch one of deficient length. If it appears your paper will be too short, you may want to see if you can arrange a time extension with your professor to do more research and writing.

## 28. OVERUSE OF CLICHÉS

**WHAT THE PROBLEM IS:** If your professors have told you once, they've told you a thousand times not to use trite, hackneyed expressions such as this one. Using tired, worn-out expressions is the straw that broke the camel's back for many professors, who won't beat around the bush as they lower your grade for using clichés. When all is said and done, you should avoid clichés at all costs.

**WHERE TO TURN FOR HELP:** Clichés are fairly easy to spot if you read over your paper with an eye toward eliminating them. If you have trouble spotting them, ask someone else to ferret the clichés out of your paper. A quality grammar checker can also identify them. You can practice with this book; we've used a few clichés because we have a soft spot in our hearts for them—and in the final analysis, we're aren't writing an academic paper after all.

# 5 Five Extra Tips for Writing an A Paper

**YOU** WON'T NECESSARILY FIND THE TIPS IN THIS CHAPTER IN OUR SURVEY OF TOP WRITING FLAWS. IF YOU MAKE A MISTAKE IN ONE OF THESE AREAS, YOU PROBABLY WON'T LOSE SIGNIFICANT POINTS FROM YOUR GRADE UNLESS YOUR PROFESSOR IS A REAL STICKLER OR YOU'RE TAKING AN ADVANCED-LEVEL WRITING COURSE. THESE ARE, HOWEVER, SUBTLE MEANS THAT CAN MAKE THE DIFFERENCE BETWEEN A VERY GOOD PAPER AND ONE THAT IS TRULY EXCEPTIONAL. IF YOU LEARN THESE SKILLS, YOUR PROFESSOR MAY NOT BE ABLE TO PINPOINT *WHY* YOUR PAPER READS SO MUCH BETTER THAN OTHERS, BUT HE OR SHE WILL KNOW THAT IT DOES.

## 1. Eliminate weak sentence and clause openers:

**The words *It* and *There*** are weak sentence openers that frequently entail unnecessary wordiness. When you give these low-content words the starring role in your sentence, you are spotlighting pronouns that substitute for nouns not yet defined. For example:

> Weak and wordy: It appears that Edme Morisot regretted giving up painting for marriage and family.
> Stronger and tighter: Edme Morisot apparently regretted giving up painting for marriage and family.

> Weak and wordy: It is worth noting that women who support capital punishment are more likely to be elected.
> Stronger and tighter: Women who support capital punishment are more likely to be elected.

> Weak and wordy: There are certain poets who changed twentieth century poetry.
>
> Stronger and tighter: Certain poets changed twentieth century poetry.

> Weak and wordy: There are many factors that account for the computer boom of the last twenty years.
>
> Stronger and tighter: Many factors account for the computer boom of the last twenty years.

> Weak and wordy: There was nothing more satisfying to Jim than a cold beer.
>
> Stronger and tighter: Nothing was more satisfying to Jim than a cold beer.

WHERE TO TURN FOR HELP: Bruce Ross-Larson's book *Edit Yourself.* Grammar checkers will identify at least some weak sentence-openers. See chapter 8 for more details.

# 2. Write tight:

**One complaint that** professors expressed in our survey focuses on the problem of writing that is too wordy. As you edit and revise your paper, you should scrutinize the necessity of every word. Have you used more words than are necessary to express your ideas? What words can you eliminate without changing the meaning of your sentences? Every word should contribute to your point. If "it goes without saying," why say it? "Murder your darlings," a speechwriting instructor advised us about extraneous words. As a longtime professor of freshman composition writes: "Think of each sentence in your paper as a snapshot on a roll of film; normally only a few will be worth keeping." The credo of journalists, who must tell their stories in minimal space, is "Write tight." Let that credo be yours and don't use the wordy phrases that frequently ensnare student writers, just a few examples of which appear here:

| WORDY | TIGHT |
|---|---|
| located in | in |
| as to whether | whether |
| of a scientific nature | scientific |
| in a timely manner | on time |

| | |
|---|---|
| due to, due to the fact | because |
| in light of the fact | because, considering, since |
| with regard to | about |
| She is the kind of writer who paints word pictures. | She paints word pictures. |
| in order to | to |
| in an effort to | to |
| attempt to | try |
| for the purpose of | for |
| call to your attention | point out |
| end result | result |
| on a weekly basis | weekly |
| during that period of time | when |
| by the author himself | by the author |
| event that took place on November 20, 1864 | event on November 20, 1864 |
| at this point in time, at the present time | now |
| the process of editing | editing |
| had the effect of reducing | reduced |

WHERE TO TURN FOR HELP: Ross-Larson's *Edit Yourself* has a wonderful chapter simply titled "Fat" (with the idea that you should cut all fat out of your writing). The entire second half of his book is a compendium of words and phrases that writers should edit, whether for conciseness, clarity, or correctness. Strunk and White's *Elements of Style* is a classic in describing the art of spare writing. Grammar checkers also work well to weed out wordiness. See chapter 8 for more details about these excellent guides to writing tight.

# 3. Differentiate between restrictive and nonrestrictive clauses:

**A restrictive clause defines** a noun and is introduced by *that* (or *who*). Employing *which* to introduce restrictive clauses has come into such widespread use that many people, including some in academe, consider *which* acceptable. Still, *that* is the preferred introduction, and your writing will sound less stilted if you use *that* to introduce restrictive clauses. A nonrestrictive clause supplies information about a noun but is not essential to define the noun or essential to the meaning of the sentence. A nonrestrictive clause is introduced by *which* (or *who*). The tip-off to a nonrestrictive clause is that it is almost always set off by a comma. Thus, the two keys to usage for these types of clauses are (1) use *which* and *that* correctly to introduce these clauses and (2) use a comma to set off nonrestrictive clauses.

> Wrong: Many of the stories which Louisa May Alcott wrote in later life were quite different from *Little Women*.
>
> Right: Many of the stories that Louisa May Alcott wrote in later life were quite different from *Little Women*.

> Right, but lacking punctuation: Alcott's posthumous publications include *Diana and Persis* which was not published until the 1970s.
>
> Right: Alcott's posthumous publications include *Diana and Persis*, which was not published until the 1970s.

WHERE TO TURN FOR HELP: Strunk and White's *Elements of Style*. See chapter 8.

# 4. Take advice from professors:

**Here we offer advice** from our surveyed professors in three areas that we do not cover elsewhere in the book:

1. Know your audience and write convincingly for that audience.
2. Be true to your own style and ideas.
3. Read.

We were interested in the number of professors who advised students to keep their audience—whether a real or imagined audience—in mind while writing papers. A writing professor suggests you ask, "What do I want my audience to feel, know? Think *audience*." A business professor recommends, "Write as though you were talking on paper." A social sciences professor proposes that students "think of an intelligent person who is not an expert on the subject. Then, write for that person." A history professor concurs: "Write for the intelligent layperson, not your professor." Alternatively, you could imagine you are writing for an employer, and as one marketing professor suggests, "Write persuasively as though your job depended on [it]."

"Write to communicate with (persuade, teach, clarify an issue for) your audience," notes a composition professor. "Writing is not simply a matter of recording content," he says. Beyond mere communication, proving your point to your audience is important, according to an English professor, who writes, "Back up whatever you assert to be so with examples, observations, details, and such, to show your audience that what you say is valid." Similarly, "make sure that you lay out the argument logically so that the reader understands and is persuaded by the evidence you offer for your position," advises a political science professor. It's not enough that you comprehend your own argument, cautions a composition professor. "Develop ideas so that your *reader* can understand them, not merely so that you can," the professor writes.

Being true to yourself by employing your own style and ideas was an important theme for several professors. "Say what you think, clearly and directly," counsels a literature professor. Another literature professor advises, "Develop your own ideas." Remembering that your writing is a window into what makes you tick is the advice of a business professor, who writes, "Your writing is like a [business] card; it shows your personality." A history professor suggests that students "write in their own style rather than reproducing a stiff textbook style—so that they actually pass content through their minds and make it their own." Concurs a communications professor, "Be original and creative; don't be too disheartened by all the red marks."

Intensive reading, whether of sources you use for your paper or outside material, will make you a better writer, assert some of our surveyed professors. "Read, and take adequate care to reflect on the text," cautions an English professor. "Read before you write" is the advice of a marketing professor. Finally, a management professor recommends that students "find an excellent author and read his/her work profusely; we learn from the best work of others."

# 5. Make packaging work for you:

**Should you bind your** paper or staple it? Dressing your paper up in a fancy report cover will not turn it from mediocre to outstanding. Most professors are more irritated than impressed with elaborate packaging. Some would rather have you paper-clip your paper or fold it lengthwise than staple it. Many professors don't even require or desire a title page. Some professors are not concerned in the least about format or packaging. Others are fanatics about a precise format, and they will deduct points if you don't follow their guidelines to the letter. The key is to ask how your professor wants papers packaged because instructors rarely spell out this type of minutia on a syllabus. Now, if the professor is not a format fanatic but disdains the title page that you provide, he or she is surely not likely to lower your grade anymore than if you stapled when he or she wanted you to paper-clip. But papers not packaged according to a professor's preference are an irritant. If you go to the trouble to ask how your professor wants the paper packaged, you'll score a few warm fuzzies. We've seen some fancy packaging of academic work that had a pleasing effect on the professor and enhanced what was already excellent work (see the story of Ellen's art history project on page 169). Generally, however, such over-the-top packaging works for projects for which more than simply a paper is involved. The simple, unadorned paper may be your best bet, but the only way you'll know for sure is to ask your professor.

And whatever its format and packaging, do be sure your paper is neat—no smudges, no coffee rings, no grease stains from your pizza, few (if any) marks. Make sure your computer printer doesn't leave stray marks on the paper and that the print is heavy enough to be readable. If you should use a typewriter rather than a computer, be sure no messy erasures or blots of correction fluid mar your paper, and don't use that awful, shiny erasable paper.

Remember that your paper's first impression on your professor may be significant. One professor who tells students about the importance of format and packaging notes that "the first appearance of a paper is often an indicator of its quality." Echoes Carolyn J. Mullins in *The Complete Writing Guide*, "Neatness, consistency, and faithful use of a prescribed style make a favorable, although often subconscious, impression on readers."

# 6 How Revision Can Turn an Average Paper into an A Paper

IF YOU WERE TO ASK OUR SURVEYED PROFESSORS TO PICK A FAVORITE CHAPTER IN THIS BOOK, WE BELIEVE IT MIGHT BE THIS ONE. WE ASKED THE PROFESSORS WE SURVEYED, "IF YOU COULD GIVE STUDENT WRITERS JUST ONE PIECE OF ADVICE, WHAT WOULD IT BE?" THE ANSWERS OF ALMOST A FULL THIRD OF THEM RELATE TO REVISION. A SOLID CONTINGENT STRONGLY STRESSES THAT DILIGENT REVISION IS THE KEY TO ACADEMIC WRITING SUCCESS.

Based in part on their suggestions, we compiled a comprehensive, step-by-step guide to revising your paper. If you were to follow every step, you could scarcely go wrong. Experience suggests, however, that it is unrealistic to expect students to go through this entire process—not for every paper, at least. You can see immediately that the process we describe requires a large chunk of time, perhaps as much as half the time you allot to prepare your paper. One professor we surveyed recommends that revision take 70 percent of the time you schedule for your paper; that's the amount of time required, he says, "to go from a D to an A." Rarely will you have that much time available. You'll need to weigh the time required for a comprehensive revision against the importance of the paper to your grade. For greatest success, we recommend you use at least some of the steps in the process; your time constraints will dictate how extensive the process will be. Notice that we've linked each step in the revision process to the twenty-nine writing flaws we discussed in chapter 4. The more time you allow yourself for revising, and the more of these steps you follow, the greater the number of writing flaws you can attack, especially those that most provoke professors to give you a lower grade.

Sources on revision that we particularly like include *Edit Yourself* by Bruce Ross-Larson and *The Complete Writing Guide* by Carolyn J. Mullins. While neither book is written specifically about revising academic papers—Ross-Larson aims at writers preparing manuscripts for publication and Mullins targets writers in the business world—both are useful for student writing. See chapter 8 for more information about these and other sources on revising.

This chapter concludes with a makeover of a college paper to illustrate that a paper that originally received a poor grade can be massaged into an A paper.

Steps in revising:

1.  Preparing the first draft
    This step should target the following areas:
    ▲  Organization (writing flaw #1)
    ▲  Support of your thesis (writing flaw #2)
    ▲  Content/understanding of topic (writing flaw #10—tied)
    ▲  Adequacy of research (writing flaw #10—tied)
    ▲  Length of paper (writing flaws #27 and #29)
1.a  Read the paper on the computer screen. Make spot corrections.
1.b  Spell check and grammar check.
1.c  Print the paper out.
1.d  Evaluate the areas listed above, giving the greatest attention to organization.
1.e  If necessary, repeat steps 1.a through 1.c, creating a new draft.
1.f  Ask an instructor to critique an early draft.
2.  Revising subsequent draft(s)
    This step should target the following areas:
    ▲  Sentence structure (writing flaw #5)
    ▲  Sentence fragments (writing flaw #7)
    ▲  Run-on sentences (writing flaw #8)
    ▲  Word usage (writing flaw #9)
    ▲  Transitions (writing flaw #14)
    ▲  Wordiness (writing flaw #15)
    ▲  Meaningless modifiers (writing flaw #17)
    ▲  Vague pronoun reference (writing flaw #18—tied)
    ▲  Use of passive voice (writing flaw #18—tied)
    ▲  Short, choppy sentences/paragraphs (writing flaw #20)
    ▲  Vocabulary (writing flaw #21—tied)
    ▲  Use of jargon (writing flaw #23)

&#9650;  Dangling clauses (writing flaw #24)

&#9650;  Parallelism (writing flaw #25)

&#9650;  Clichés (writing flaw #28)

2.a   Incorporate your instructor's suggestions (from step 1.f).

Repeat steps 1.a through 1.c, as needed, creating a new draft.

2.b   Set your paper aside for one to ten days, depending on your schedule.

2.c   Give your paper a fresh reading.

Repeat steps 1.a through 1.c, as needed, creating a new draft.

2.d   Read your paper aloud.

Repeat steps 1.a through 1.c, as needed, creating a new draft.

2.e   Ask someone else to read the paper.

Repeat steps 1.a through 1.c, as needed, creating a new draft.

3.   Proofreading and final polishing

This step should be a final check of grammar, punctuation, writing style, capitalization, bibliographic style, format/packaging, and neatness, targeting all remaining writing flaw areas listed in chapter 4.

3.a   Proofread.

Repeat steps 1.a through step 1.c, as needed, to create a final draft. You may not need to print out all pages.

3.b   Ensure that the paper is in the professor's preferred format (see tip #5, page 149) and hand it in on time.

Now let's look at the steps in detail.

1.   Preparing the first draft

1.a   Read the paper on the computer screen.

Once you feel your paper is just about finished, you'll probably want to give it another read-through on the computer screen before printing it out. While it's impossible to grasp the "big picture" of your paper on-screen, reading it on the computer enables you correct obvious flaws before printing the paper out, and especially before asking someone else to critique it.

1.b   Spell check and grammar check.

We've discussed the usefulness of spell checkers and grammar checkers in chapter 4, and you can learn even more in chapter 8. While these technological tools can be enormously helpful, they are still not sophisticated enough to be relied upon as a crutch. The software simulates, but cannot duplicate, human thinking. For the reasons we discussed in chapter 4, spell checking must not be considered a substitute for proofreading, but a supplement. Consider this poem by Jerry Zar, associate provost for graduate studies and research and dean of the graduate school at Northern Illinois University, which illustrates the limitations of spell checkers:

**An Owed to a Spelling Checker**

I have a spelling checker
It came with my PC
It plane lee marks four my revue
Miss steaks aye can knot sea.

Eye ran this poem threw it,
Your sure reel glad two no.
Its vary polished in it's weigh
My checker tolled me sew.

A checker is a bless sing,
It freeze yew lodes of thyme.
It helps me right awl stiles two reed,
And aides me when aye rime.

Each frays comes posed up on my screen
Eye trussed too bee a joule
The checker pours o'er every word
To cheque sum spelling rule.

Bee fore a veiling checker's
Hour spelling mite decline,
And if we're lacks oar have a laps,
We wood be maid too wine.

Butt now bee cause my spelling
Is checked with such grate flare,
Their are know fault's with in my cite,
Of nun eye am a wear.

Now spelling does knot phase me,
It does knot bring a tier.
My pay purrs awl due glad den
With wrapped word's fare as hear.

153

> To rite with care is quite a feet,
> Of witch won should bee proud.
> And wee mussed dew the best wee can,
> Sew flaw's are knot aloud.
>
> Sow ewe can sea why aye dew prays
> Such soft wear four pea seas.
> And why eye brake in two averse
> Buy righting want too pleas.

Reprinted by permission of the author and the *Journal of Irreproducible Results.*

Grammar checkers assume you know enough about grammar to make the right choices; they are most definitely not for the grammatically illiterate. In fact, if you don't know what you are doing, grammar checkers can assist you in making plenty of wrong choices. You have to know enough about grammatical rules to know whether the tool is pointing out a legitimate flaw in your writing, or if the program has simply "misread" your sentences.

Bottom line: Use spell checkers, but don't depend on them. Use grammar checkers if you know grammatical rules well enough to make the correct choices among those the program offers you.

"**I** advise students not to rely on spell check instead of proofreading papers."

—a political-science professor at a medium-sized, public university

1.c    Print the paper out.

Most people prefer editing on paper, so even if your earliest draft is not ready for the scrutiny of another, you'll want hard copy so you can go through it to mark potential changes. It's also not a bad idea to print out an early draft of your paper in case a technical problem zaps the version in the computer or on disk.

1.d    Checklist: Evaluate these areas, giving the greatest attention to organization:

Organization: Is the order of your paper as logical as it can be? Does it make sense? Is anything out of place? Didn't outline your paper before writing it? Some experts advise you to outline *after* you've written your first draft as a way of checking whether your organization is logical and effective.

Content/understanding of topic: Does the content of the paper demonstrate that you understand the topic thoroughly?

Support of your thesis: Have you proven your point? Do all your arguments support your main thesis?

Adequacy of research: Is your bibliography rich and full without being padded?

Length of paper: Is it too short? Too long? Or the right length to meet the assignment?

1.e    If necessary, repeat steps 1.a through 1.c, creating a new draft.

Even if your paper passes the 1.d checklist, it may not be ready for its public debut. If not, repeat the earlier steps. Don't move on to Step 2 until your paper's organization satisfies you. Since you'll pay more attention to the mechanics of the paper in Step 2, you won't want to waste time doing so on paragraphs that you end up eliminating because they don't fit your paper's organization.

1.f    Ask an instructor to critique an early draft.

Ideally, the instructor you ask should be the one who assigned the paper. That professor will know best how well you've met the assignment and whether the paper meets all his or her requirements. Your next best bet would be the graduate teaching assistant who works with that professor. Next in line would be any other approachable instructor. Finally, the personnel at the writing lab or writing center at your college or university would work in a pinch. If you can find no one matching these descriptions to critique your paper, you should probably skip this step. While a later step suggests you ask someone detached from this assignment to read the paper, the idea of this step is to ask someone who *thinks like an instructor* to critique the paper, particularly concerning the 1.d checklist. Ask whomever you have chosen to review your paper to pay special attention to the items in that checklist. Remember, you don't want a detailed nit-pick that zeroes in on grammar, punctuation, and other mechanics (although you will certainly not reject such scrutiny). You are more interested in a big-picture critique, an overview of the paper that assesses how well organized the paper is and how well it makes its point. If you approach someone other than the professor who assigned the paper, be sure to tell your reviewer your deadline, leaving enough time for the subsequent steps you choose to pursue. The concept of approaching your professor is further detailed in Technique 23 on page 51.

2.     Revising subsequent draft(s)

2.a     Incorporate your instructor's suggestions (from step 1.f).

Repeat steps 1.a through 1.c, as needed, creating a new draft.

Once you've received feedback from the professor, work his or her ideas into your next draft. Since you may well be adding new material at this point, you'll likely want to repeat the on-screen editing, spell checking, grammar checking, and printing steps.

2.b     Set your paper aside for one to ten days, depending on your schedule.

While many surveyed professors agreed on the value of putting your paper aside for a period so you could take a fresh look at it later, the set-aside durations they suggested ranged from ten days to just one day. You may find yourself with even less time available—overnight, perhaps, or even just an hour or two. Even when your time is incredibly tight, however, do try to put the paper aside for as long as you can.

# "Revise, revise, revise. Leave yourself time to write and reread what you've written so you can improve it."

—a political-science professor at a small college

**"Complete the assignment several days before it is due. Let it 'rest' for a day, and then review and revise as necessary."**

—a political science professor at a medium-sized public university

**"Write it; set it aside for one to two days; rewrite it; set it aside for one to two days; rewrite it; set it aside, etc., etc."**

—a professor of health and physical education at a medium-sized private university

**"Practice by writing rough drafts and letting them 'sit' for awhile before editing and revising; but revise, revise, revise."**

—a political science professor at a medium-sized public university

2.c    Give your paper a fresh reading.

Repeat steps 1.a through 1.c, as needed, creating a new draft.

Longtime writing professor James Raymond reminds us that the word "revision" means seeing something in a new way. When you read the same paper repeatedly, you grow so accustomed to the writing style that you can no longer objectively evaluate it. You also tend to overlook errors that will jump right out at you when you read your paper after not looking at it for a period. You'll see your paper in a new way—or "re-vision" it—once you've removed yourself from it a bit; it may seem much better than you thought, or it might suddenly seem in need of major surgery. Another way to re-vision your paper is to read it from the end to the beginning. Read the last paragraph, then the next-to-last paragraph, and so on. When you read it in the correct order, your brain is lulled into thinking everything's in good shape. But when you read it backwards, your brain is jarred by the re-visioning, and you're more apt to catch errors. As you give the paper its fresh reading, concentrate on these areas, using this checklist:

> Sentence structure: Are sentences as simple as they can be? Can they be untangled easily and understood?
>
> Sentence fragments: Do all sentences have a subject and a verb?
>
> Run-on sentences: Are all compound sentences joined with a conjunction or the proper punctuation (not a comma)?
>
> Word usage: Have you used all questionable words correctly?
>
> Transitions: Do sentences and paragraphs flow smoothly from each other? Have you used effective transitional words and phrases to aid the flow?
>
> Wordiness: Have you cut out all extraneous words that add nothing to your meaning?
>
> Meaningless modifiers: Have you eliminated empty words as modifiers?
>
> Vague pronoun reference: Do pronouns, such as "this," have obvious referents?
>
> Use of passive voice: Have you favored the active voice as much as possible and eliminated the passive in most cases?
>
> Short, choppy sentences/paragraphs: Have you sought to connect short sentences in cases where doing so improves their flow?
>
> Vocabulary: Have you endeavored to use a rich variety of words?
>
> Use of jargon: Have you eliminated all technical language that a layperson would not understand?

Dangling clauses: Have you ensured that all clauses or phrases that begin sentences refer to the grammatical subject?

Parallelism: Do all items in a list possess the same grammatical format?

Clichés: Have you eliminated meaningless clichés that add nothing to your paper?

"**Read** your work after having a chance to 'step away' from it."

—an accounting professor at a small private university

"**Complete the writing in enough time that you can distance yourself from it. Then, critique it harshly.**"

—a sociology professor at a large public university

2.d    Read your paper aloud.

Repeat steps 1.a through 1.c, as needed, creating a new draft.

Once you try this step, you may be amazed at how your ear picks up writing flaws that your eye cannot. You'll hear how well your paper flows, how confusing and complex its sentences are, and whether it is punctuated with the proper pauses. Other writing flaws that are easy to target with an oral rendition of your paper include run-on sentences, transitions, nonagreement of subject and verb, choppiness, and use of jargon and clichés.

"**Read** your piece into a tape recorder and play it back to yourself before completing your final draft. If it makes sense when you listen to it being played back, then it should be OK to hand in.**"

—a political science professor at a medium-sized public university

"**Edit, edit, edit, mostly by reading sentences out loud and fixing them if they don't sound right.**"

—a political science professor at a large public university

"**Read it through as if you were an [outsider]. Is it understandable? Does it sound right? Is it believable?**"

—a marketing professor at a very small public university

"**Read it back to yourself. Does it make sense?**"

—a marketing professor at a medium-sized Australian university

"**Read your work aloud, as if you were giving a speech. You will hear the mistakes you can't see.**"

—a business professor at a large Canadian university

2.e    Ask someone else to read the paper.

Repeat steps 1.a through step 1.c, as needed, creating a new draft.

Having incorporated any changes you decided to make after your fresh and/or oral readings of the paper, you are at the point at which you should ask someone who is detached from the assignment to read the paper. Here, you want to know if it makes sense and is clear to someone who does not know the assignment and may not be familiar with the subject matter. You should ask the person to evaluate the paper for its own sake; how well does it read as an isolated piece of writing? The person you ask could be almost anyone—a friend, your roommate, the person you're dating, a parent. Ask the person to target the 2.c checklist only if he or she is particularly adept at checking for those writing flaws. (Obviously, it would be advantageous to approach someone qualified to evaluate those areas of your paper.)

"**Complete** your first draft at least ten days before the assignment is due and have someone else look at it. Ask for their opinions as to how clearly the paper is written and [how well] its main ideas are expressed. Then reread it yourself and use the comments you receive and your own impressions to write an improved final draft."

—a political science professor at a large public university

"**Start early, do several drafts, have someone else critique your paper, and *proofread!***"

—a marketing professor at a medium-sized public university

"**Do several drafts and ask someone else to read each one for content, clarity.**"

—a biology professor at a very large public university

"**Have someone not intimately involved with the subject read the paper for clarity, errors, and support of the main thesis.**"

—a business professor at a medium-sized private university

3.    Proofreading and final polishing

3.a    Proofread.

Repeat steps 1.a through 1.c, as needed. You may not need to print out all pages.

You're in the homestretch. Your last step should be to proofread, which is different from the editing and revising you've done in the previous steps.

Proofreading is your last check to ensure that every flaw is fixed and the paper contains as little as possible to tempt your professor's red pen into action. Proofreading checklist:

> Grammar is correct.
> Spelling is correct.
> Correct academic writing style has been successfully employed.
> Punctuation is correct.
> Capitalization is correct.
> Bibliography is complete and in the correct style.
> Sources within the text have been accurately cited.
> Requirements of assignment have been met.
> Paper is neat and attractively presented.

"**Proof**reading counts. We're often judged more by format than by content. So make sure it looks nice, reads easily, and is grammatically correct."

—a marketing and management professor at a small public university

3.b    Ensure that the paper is in the professor's preferred format (see #5, page 149) and hand it in on time.

Just put the final polish on your paper, and proudly hand it to your professor.

# Makeover

**To show how revising** can turn a poor paper into a successful one, we present a makeover that is a short response to a question on a marketing take-home essay exam. The student received a failing grade on his deficient response. The essay question he responded to was as follows:

> *You have been just been hired as a marketing assistant at American Television Manufacturing Corporation. Top management at American Television see an opportunity to develop high-quality, low-priced television sets for the U.S. market. You've been assigned to write a short report analyzing the market, identifying a target market and niche, and then developing a market-entry strategy that focuses on retail selection.*

Here, with flaws noted by the professor, is the student's poorly written, unedited response, which he also clearly did not spell check or proofread:

---

**Target market**   (F)

*spelling*

American Television's target market would be the low-income class. American would (devlop)
*spelling*
its product for the people who can't afford the prices of the (televios) already on the market.

**Market strategy**   *wordy; sentence fragment*   *Spelling + don't capitalize*   *wordy*

First, American Television would do a (Needs Accessment) to see if there was a need for its
*wordy*
(particular) product. (In this process.) (Amerian) Television would get a better (understading) of what the
*spelling*                    *spelling*                              *spelling*
*s*                      *wordy*
market need and how to fulfill that need in a big way. Then American would (to) continue the

*don't capitalize*                          *spelling*                                    *is*
process by Prospecting to find what retailers (whould) support its product and what price range are

*ed*                                                   *n*
to be consider in manufacturer cost. Prospecting also gives American a idea of what to (espect)
*wordy + passive*                                                                    *spelling*
when it is time to put its product on the market. Next American Television would start advertising
*wordy*                                              *sentence fragment*
its product by using many different marketing strategies. One by using the low-price high quality
                                                          *makes no sense*
for its advertising (screem.)  *spelling*
                                            *, possessive*
For an example its (commerial) should have a low income person go to a retailers department
                                                                        *redundant*
store (like Wal-Mart) and purchase an American Television based on the better price for your
                                        *awkward*   *ing*
money reason. Then manufacture a sample of 25 to see just how much is manufacture cost (in
                                                                                  *s*
numbers). Before American Television is ready to start manufacturing its research team need to (do)
*wordy*                        *wordy*
research on all competitors direct and indirect to see what that they did right and what they did

wrong. Also to see what was successful and what was not successful. Last American Television
*sentence fragment + redundant*
must get a clear understanding of the laws and criteria needed to meet (to) government standards.
            *don't capitalize*

Overall critique: Note that the steps described are not in a logical order, making the paper's organization poor.

In addition to citing the obvious problems with spelling, typos, lack of punctuation, and overall poor writing, this hapless student's professor gave the essay a failing grade because of its content—or lack thereof —specifying the student's clear lack of research. While the paper needs much better research and content to achieve a *good* grade, let's see how it might earn a passing grade if all the writing flaws were fixed and the writing style improved:

---

**Target market**

American Television should target lower-income customers who can't afford the televisions already on the market.

**Market strategy**

A needs assessment would enable American Television to determine the degree of demand for its product and plan how to fulfill that need. Prospecting to discover which retailers would support its product and at what price range would crystallize American Television expectations about putting the low-cost televisions on the market.

The company's research and development team should research the strengths and weaknesses of all competitors and determine American Television's market niche.

To determine manufacturing costs, American Television could produce twenty-five prototypes.

Having studied the criteria needed to meet government standards, American Television then would use various marketing strategies to advertise its product, such as emphasizing the product's low price and high quality. American Television could establish a cooperative relationship with a discount retailer, such as Wal-Mart, and commercials could depict a low-income Wal-Mart shopper purchasing an American Television because the brand offers excellent quality at a low price.

---

Now, let's see how much the paper improves when some well-researched content is added:

**Background**

Not since the South Korean firm LG Electronics purchased Zenith Electronics has a television purchased in the United States been manufactured in the United States (Kielman 1995) — not until American Television was founded. Although nearly two-thirds of the 25 million color television sets purchased in the United States last year were assembled domestically, none were from U.S.-based manufacturers (Kielman 1995). American Television will use this information as one if its key marketing strategies by taking advantage of the nationalistic "Buy American" trend, coupled with the recent furor over the production of supposedly American products by sweatshop workers in foreign countries.

**The market**

Television-set sales have increased dramatically over the past two years, partly fueled by demand for larger sets and partly because of increased channel access options (Roach 1994). In fact, for the first time in history, sales of larger television sets (twenty-five inches or bigger) have outpaced sales of smaller sets (Coy 1994). According to Kevin Proctor, national marketing manager for Samsung, "There is definitely an upswing in the cycle.... People are investing in second and third television sets" (Roach 1994). Furthermore, Mark Stephenson, vice president of marketing for Magnavox, states, "The number one feature, the feature that ultimately sells the set, is the size of the screen" (Roach 1994).

Beyond the larger-screen television, one other feature is pushing television sales: TV/VCR combination units. The Electronic Industries Association projects that TV/VCR combination unit sales will reach one billion dollars by the end of 1995 (Roach 1994).

**Target market**

American Television should target first-time buyers as well as families in the market for a replacement or additional television set. The company's efforts should focus on three key factors: completely American-made; high quality for a low price; and superior features (such as larger screens and TV/VCR combination units).

**Product**

American Television must produce a small, but attractive line of television products, including mostly large-screen sets and at least two different TV/VCR combination units. The company must design and manufacture the sets in the United States, and must do so following stringent total quality management (TQM) standards while achieving the greatest efficiency and lowest costs.

## Market strategy

Television sets are increasingly being sold at large retail outlets, following a trend that aligns with that of many other products (Smith 1994). Smaller retailers are being replaced by "Category Killers," such as Best Buy, Office Depot, Circuit City, and others, as well as by "Power Retailers," such as Wal-Mart, KMart, and Target (Smith 1994). The local television retailer has been replaced with Best Buy, and the local department store with an electronics department has been replaced by a Wal-Mart with an electronics department.

This trend of sales toward category killers and power retailers has immediate implications for a small television manufacturer, such as American Television. The large retail outlets sell based on low price, not on service as local retailers do. Thus, for American Television to compete (and survive) in this market, the company must reduce costs as much as possible, enabling it to sell its televisions at a low price suitable to these large retailers.

Because American Television is a relatively new company and has limited production capacity, it is recommended that the company form an alliance with Wal-Mart. By forming this alliance, American Television gains access to an extremely large percentage of the United States market through just one retailer. Furthermore, with Wal-Mart's "Buy American" slogan, American Television is a perfect strategic fit with the retailer. Finally, by dealing with only one retailer, American Television simplifies its distribution methods, thereby reducing costs.

Some hazards, however, may emerge with this strategy. First, Wal-Mart has a history of ending relationships with manufacturers that cannot meet its low-cost demands. Second, while Wal-Mart publicly touts "Buy American," it also has a history of replacing American-made products with cheaper models produced outside the United States (Wallace 1994). Third, by being so closely associated with Wal-Mart in the consumer's mind, American Television may find it hard to expand to other retailers—especially more upscale retailers—once the company increases production capacity.

## Conclusion

For American Television to survive and grow in an increasing but ever-competitive market, it must limit production to a small number of larger-screen color televisions and TV/VCR combination units. The company should target first-time buyers and families looking to replace or buy an additional set. Finally, the company should strategically align itself with Wal-Mart and enter into an exclusive dealership relationship.

# 7 Beyond Writing: Ten More Tips to Raise Your GPA

**WHILE** WE BELIEVE THAT JUST USING THE WRITING IDEAS IN THIS BOOK WILL HELP RAISE YOUR GRADES, WE ALSO RECOGNIZE THAT THE STUDENT WHO CARES ENOUGH TO BE READING THIS BOOK IS PROBABLY INTERESTED IN SOME ADDITIONAL "TRICKS OF THE TRADE." THESE TIPS ARE ADDITIONAL WAYS TO BOOST YOUR GPA.

## 1. Go to class (and be on time).

**Duh. A real no-brainer.** But we've found that, because college students have for the first time in their academic lives the real freedom to choose whether or not to go to class, they tend to use that freedom to the fullest. Quite simply, if you want good grades, you should go to class. Attending class not only ensures that you won't miss important material and assignments but that you will make a good impression on your teacher. Every class you miss lowers your credibility in your professor's eyes. You could miss lots of classes and still turn in a decent paper at the end of the semester, yet your poor attendance could very well prejudice your instructor in grading your paper. Worse, you could achieve good grades on individual tests and assignments despite your many absences, but if the professor assigns points for attendance, you could seriously damage your good average. Be sure, too, that you know your instructor's attendance policy. Still not convinced you should go to class? Try prorating your tuition costs per class and figure out how much each missed class costs you or your parents.

# 2. Go to the head of the class.

**Sit in the front of** the class. If you're going to attend class, you might as well make sure your professor sees you. That notion may sound like pure brown-nosing, but studies have shown that those who sit in the front row—and on the right side of the classroom—tend to achieve better grades. Even if you're not as nearsighted as we are, sitting in front will enhance your view of the chalk-board, overheads, computer projections, or any other audiovisual devices.

# 3. Participate in class.

**Another way to achieve** visibility and impress the instructor is to ask questions, answer questions, and join in the discussion. Nothing is more disheart-ening to a professor than what we call "Glazed-Over Undergraduate Syndrome," in which the instructor tries to get a discussion going, and the entire class just sits there looking bored or hung over from last night's party-ing. Yes, we realize it takes a lot of guts to rise above the fear of asking a stu-pid question or appearing to be a geek or a brownnoser. But your professor will thank you for it and likely reward you with a better grade than the rest of your somnambulant classmates. Some professors even award points or give grade consideration for class participation.

# 4. Anticipate test questions.

**When study time is short,** it's wise to anticipate what questions (especially essay questions) will be on the test. How to anticipate? For starters, there's every professor's favorite question, "Could you tell us what's going to be on the test?" One of our favorite professors was extremely accommodating in responding to that question. When colleagues asked him why he told students what material would be on the tests, he responded, "Because that's what I want students to learn." You'll find, however, that professors give you a wide range of responses to that question. If the instructor provides a vague answer, you still have ways to anticipate. What are the professor's interests? In what areas has the professor done research? On what topic did he or she write his or her doctoral dissertation? What did he or she seem to emphasize the most in lectures? On what subjects is the professor most passionate? What was the emphasis of the material you read for class? If you ask yourself these questions and listen for verbal clues during lectures of the material's relative importance and likelihood to pop up again on a test, you'll have an advantage. Some professors, as well as some fraternities and sororities, keep old exams on file and available for your perusal. Looking at old exams will not guarantee that you can predict what material will be on your upcoming exam, but this practice can provide another window into your professor's thought process and what topics he or she considers important. Ideally, of course, you'd study all material that could conceivably be on the test. But it's not always possible to study everything. If time is short, you may be better off hedging your bets by knowing selected areas extremely well. That way, you can probably answer the questions about those areas so well that you can partially make up for deficiencies in other areas. If time permits, you might want to practice organizing and writing answers to anticipated test questions, as we describe on page 108.

# 5. Type your notes.

**"Are these authors insane?"** you ask. Yes, this suggestion probably seems like extreme overkill to many students. But when we found it increasingly difficult to study from our scrawled notes, we started typing them. The very act of typing them reinforced the concepts from class lectures. Typing our notes also enabled us to organize them coherently and correlate them with reading material. When we were finished, we possessed a high-quality study guide that was easy to use for reviewing for exams. The assumption is, of course, that you are a facile typist. If you are a hunt-and-peck person, this method will be too time-consuming to be worthwhile. Peter Elbow further suggests using writing as a step beyond taking notes about material you read for class. (Many academicians eschew the common practice of highlighting text in favor of taking notes on what you've read.) "If you want to digest and remember what you are reading," Elbow writes, "try writing about it instead of taking notes." Elbow suggests that writing your reactions about your reading will stimulate your mind, so you'll be more likely to remember what you've read. He even goes as far as to advise students not to take any notes during a lecture but to go immediately and write about the lecture afterwards.

# 6. Meet deadlines.

**Professors find it tiresome** to deal with the constant parade of students who turn in late papers or continually ask for extensions on papers and other assignments. If you're one who never misses a deadline, you'll make a favorable impression on the instructor. If you can even beat a deadline, you'll really stand out from the crowd. Turning in an assignment early is often to your advantage, but only if the assignment is complete and not a rush job just to beat the deadline. On the flip side, we have suggested in the earlier portions of this book some occasions when you may find it advantageous to ask—in advance—for an extension. Generally, however, you should avoid doing so except in extremely extenuating circumstances. Be *honest* if you can't meet a deadline; professors are tired of hearing about dying grandparents. Remember, though, that most professors deduct points for late papers, even when they have granted extensions.

# 7. Check out the smart student's Cliff's Notes: literary criticism.

**Some students rely on Cliff's** or Monarch Notes either to help them interpret works of literature, or in more extreme cases, as a substitute for actually reading the literature. We're not here to pass judgment, but we know a more creative way to achieve the same results. Any author who is remotely well known has literary criticism written about his or her work. The entire Library of Congress classification designated PS in your library is devoted to "lit crit." If you're writing a paper on a specific author or his or her work, you can certainly get some topic ideas from literary criticism, and you may very well end up using the criticism among your sources. Examining the interpretations that other writers provide about literature can also be extremely useful for exams about those works of literature. Of course, if you use an idea from another writer on your exam, you must credit that writer. Chances are, your professor will admire the fact that you've taken the extra step of looking at literary criticism. Just don't rely too heavily on lit crit. Professors want you to develop and express your own ideas. Literary criticism can jump-start your thought processes and help you develop those ideas.

# 8. Go the extra mile.

**We could also label this** tip the "wretched excess" suggestion. The idea is to go so far above and beyond the requirements of a given assignment that the instructor has little choice but to give you an A. One student we know, Ellen, was assigned to compile a journal of ten contemporary artists. The journal was to consist of photocopies of a minimum of three articles about each artist, a bibliography listing additional articles, and an essay analyzing and synthesizing the work written about the artist. Most students turned in their journals bound in one of those report covers that costs less than a dollar. Not Ellen. Ellen collected so many articles about each artist that her journal mushroomed into three volumes. To package each volume, she used a three-inch wide, three-ring binder with an elaborate indexing system. Her bibliography for each artist was about ten times longer than that of anyone else in the class, and she included color photocopies of some of each artist's best-known works. Ellen received an A+ on her journal. Clearly, there are some drawbacks to going the extra mile; such excess can be both time-consuming and expensive. But as long as *you've also met all the requirements of the assignment,* you almost have to get an A because you've put so much more work into it than your classmates have. Following the assignment is key, however; you don't want simply to do extra work but to complete the assigned requirements in greater depth. When is it appropriate to go the extra mile? You may want to outdo yourself if your performance in the class is not otherwise stellar, and you want to be sure of at least one high grade. If you are following a research stream (as discussed under Technique 5, page 13), this approach serves the dual purpose of enabling you to complete an assignment, as well as building your personal reference library of research and writing related to your interests. You may also want to employ this overkill method to make the "halo effect" technique (below) work for you.

# 9. Make the "halo effect" work for you.

**The idea here is to** do so well at the beginning of a semester and to so impress your teacher with your studiousness and work ethic that, even if your work slips a notch later in the term, the "halo effect" from your earlier performance inspires the teacher to give you the benefit of the doubt and go a little easier in the grading than he or she might for a slacker who turns in an assignment of similar mediocre quality. The trick, however, is to perform fabulously well early in the semester by showing enormous interest in the class, participating, and visiting your professor outside class—in short, use practically every suggestion in this book. This technique also works particularly well if you have a professor that you've had for an earlier class. If you performed well in a previous class, you may have the luxury of being able to rest on your laurels a bit in the next class you take with that professor.

# 10. Tell your instructor your expectations.

**This concept may seem** like the ultimate in brownnosing, and if you were ever to ask a professor if this technique works, chances are he or she would deny it. But we've never known it to fail. It's very simple: Early in the semester, find an opportunity outside class to tell the professor that you expect to do well in the class. Explain that you are a serious student, and your grades are important to you. The technique works optimally when you are already a good student. If that's the case, you can mention your GPA. Tell him or her that you expect to maintain your good average. You must tread a very careful line between telling the professor your expectations and demanding of him or her that he or she not damage your GPA. Ask the professor for suggestions about how best to succeed in the class. It never hurts to tell the instructor how much you enjoy the class, that you admire his or her teaching, and that you're getting a lot out of the class. While it may sound totally improbable that telling the professor these things could result in a good grade, we've seen it work time and again. One student we know had received decent grades on most of the speeches she gave in a public speaking class, but she had bombed badly on a particular speech. She went to the professor and told him that, despite the one deficient speech, she felt she deserved an A because she had put so much work into the class. She got it. Another student did poorly on both the midterm and final exam of his religion class. Still, he had the audacity to ask the professor for a passing grade in the course because he had gotten so much out of it. He got a C. Yes, there are professors on whom this approach will not work, but we haven't found one yet. As long as your performance is decent, and you don't ask for a grade that is totally unwarranted, you have little to lose by at least trying to approach your professor with your expectations. We've suggested in other places in this book that you should make your professor your ally. Don't wait until your grade is in trouble to make him or her your ally, but certainly go talk to your professor if you are having trouble.

# 8 Where to Turn for Guidance on Style, Word Usage, Punctuation, Grammar, and Syntax

THIS IS A CHAPTER YOU'RE NOT LIKELY TO READ IN ITS ENTIRETY, YET THIS WILL PROBABLY BE ONE OF THE KEY CHAPTERS YOU USE AS A RESOURCE AS YOU SEARCH FOR GUIDANCE IN IMPROVING YOUR WRITING. THIS CHAPTER IS DIVIDED INTO THREE SECTIONS:

▲ A bibliography of general style guides and subject-specific guides.
▲ A detailed listing of technological aids to improve your writing that includes software packages for both the Macintosh and DOS/Windows environments.
▲ World Wide Web and Gopher sites on the Internet that provide general and specific writing assistance.

## Books

**Many books are published** about writing and writing skills, and the list that follows is not meant to be all-inclusive. Rather, what we have done is talk with college professors and professional writers and editors and developed what they think is a list of the best resources for you. The "general style guides" segment provides you with information about general rules of English writing and grammar. The "subject-specific and other guides" segment includes style guides for specific types of writing, such as journalistic and scientific writing.

### GENERAL STYLE GUIDES

All the books in this section come highly recommended, but if we had to choose a few "must use" items from the collection below, we would include Bernstein's *The Careful Writer*, Strunk and White's *The Elements of Style*,

172

Cook's *Line by Line*, Ross-Larson's *Edit Yourself,* Zinsser's *On Writing Well,* and Elbow's *Writing with Power.*

*The Art of Writing* (1981) by Vincent R. Ruggiero. Sherman Oaks, CA: Alfred Publishing Company.

*The Chicago Manual of Style* (1993, 14th edition). Chicago: University of Chicago Press.

*The College Writer's Handbook* (1976, 2nd edition) by Suzanne E. Jacobs. New York: Wiley.

*College Writing: A Personal Approach to Academic Writing* (1991) by Toby Fulwiler. Portsmouth, NH: Boynton/Cook Publishers.

*College Writing Basics: A Progressive Approach* (1995, 4th edition) by Thomas E. Tyner. Belmont, CA: Wadsworth Publishing Company.

*The Complete Guide to Citing Government Information Resources: A Manual for Writers & Librarians* (1993) by Diane L. Garner and Diane H. Smith. Bethesda, MD: Congressional Information Service.

*A Dictionary of Modern English Usage* (1991, 2nd edition) by Henry W. Fowler. New York: Oxford University Press.

*Dos, Don'ts & Maybes of English Usage* (1977) by Theodore M. Bernstein. New York: Times Books.

*Edit Yourself: A Manual for Everyone Who Works with Words* (1982) by Bruce Ross-Larson. New York: W.W. Norton & Company.

*Electronic Style* (1993) by Xia Li and N.B. Crane. Westport, CT: Meckler.

*The Elements of Style* (1979, 3rd edition) by William Strunk Jr. and E.B. White. New York: Macmillan.

*Essentials of English Grammar: A Practical Guide to the Mastery of English* (1993, 2nd edition). Lincolnwood, IL: Passport Books.

*A Guide to Academic Writing* (1993) by Jeffrey A. Cantor. Westport, CT: Praeger.

*Handbook for Writers* (1983) by Celia Millward. Troy, MO: Holt, Rinehart & Winston.

*The Handbook of Good English* (1991) by Edward D. Johnson. New York: Pocket Books.

*The Handbook of Nonsexist Writing* (1988, 2nd edition) by Casey Miller and Kate Swift. New York: Lippincott & Crowell.

*How to Write a Research Paper* (1986, 2nd edition) by Ralph Berry. New York: Pergamon Press.

*Line by Line: How to Edit Your Own Writing* (1985) by Claire Kehrwald Cook. Boston: Houghton-Mifflin.

*The Little, Brown Guide to Writing Research Papers* (1994, 3rd edition) by Michael Meyer. New York: HarperCollins.

*A Manual for Writers of Term Papers, Theses, and Dissertations* (1996, 6th edition) by Kate L. Turabian. Chicago: University of Chicago Press.

*Miss Thistlebottom's Hobgoblins: The Careful Writer's Guide to the Taboos, Bugbears, and Outmoded Rules of English Usage* (1984) by Theodore M. Bernstein. New York: Simon & Schuster.

*The MLA Handbook for Writers of Research Papers, Theses, and Dissertations* (1995, 4th edition) by Joseph Gibaldi. New York: Modern Language Association.

*Modern American Usage: A Guide* (1966) by Wilson Follett. New York: Hill and Wang.

*On Writing Well* (1994, 5th edition) by William Zinsser. New York: Harper & Row.

*The Oxford Dictionary of English Grammar* (1994) by Sylvia Chalker. New York: Oxford University Press.

*Practical English Handbook* (1996, 10th edition) by Floyd C. Watkins and William B. Dillington. Boston: Houghton Mifflin.

*Prentice Hall Encyclopedic Dictionary of English Usage* (1993) by Nathan H. Mager. Englewood Cliffs, NJ: Prentice Hall.

*Publication Manual of the American Psychological Association* (1994, 4th edition). Washington, DC: American Psychological Association.

*Research: How to Plan, Speak and Write about It* (1985) by Clifford Hawkins and Marco Sorgi. Berlin: Springer-Verlag.

*Simple and Direct: A Rhetoric for Writers* (1994) by Jacques Barzun. Chicago: University of Chicago Press.

*Strategies for Academic Writing: A Guide for College Students* (1982) by Irvin Y. Hashimoto. Ann Arbor, MI: University of Michigan Press.

*The Student Writer: Editor and Critic* (1996, 4th edition) by Barbara Fine Clouse. New York: McGraw-Hill.

*The Student Writer's Guide* (1976) by Elliot D. Allen and Ethel B. Colbrunn. DeLand, FL: Everett/Edwards.

*Style: Ten Lessons in Clarity & Grace* (1994) by Joseph M. Williams. New York: HarperCollins.

*Style: Toward Clarity and Grace* (1990) by Joseph M. Williams. Chicago: The University of Chicago Press.

*A Style Manual for Citing Microform and Nonprint Media* (1978) by Eugene B. Fleischer. Chicago: American Library Association.

*10,000 Ideas for Term Papers, Projects, and Reports* (1995, 4th edition) by Kathryn Lamm. New York: Arco Publishing.

*Words and Ideas: A Handbook for College Writing* (1980, 5th edition) by Hans Guth. Belmont, CA: Wadsworth.

*The Writer's Essential Desk Reference* (1991). Cincinnati, OH: Writer's Digest Books.

*Writing for College: A Practical Approach* (1996, 3rd edition) by Robert E. Yarber. New York: HarperCollins.

*Writing for College and Career* (1990, 4th edition) by Andrew W. Hart and James A. Reinking. New York: St. Martin's Press.

*Writing Research Papers: A Guide to the Process* (1994, 4th edition) by Stephen Weidenborner and Domenick Caruso. New York: St. Martin's Press.

*Writing Research Papers: A Complete Guide* (1996, 8th edition) by James D. Lester. New York: HarperCollins.

*Writing Research Papers: A Norton Guide* (1984) by Mellisa Walker. New York: W.W. Norton & Company.

*Writing Strategies: Reaching Diverse Audiences* (1990) by Laurel Richardson. Newbury Park, CA: Sage.

*Writing Term Papers* (1988, 3rd edition) by Alan Heineman. San Diego: Harcourt Brace Jovanovich, Inc.

*Writing Well* (1991, 7th edition) by Donald Hall. New York: HarperCollins.

*Writing with Power: Techniques for Mastering the Writing Process* (1981) by Peter Elbow. New York: Oxford University Press.


## SUBJECT-SPECIFIC AND OTHER GUIDES

### Writing about literature

*The College Writer's Guide to the Study of Literature* (1970) by C.R. Reaske. New York: Random House.

*The Elements of Writing about Literature and Film* (1988) by Elizabeth McMahan. New York: Macmillan.

*A Handbook to Literature* (1992, 6th edition) by Hugh C. Holman and William Harmon. New York: Macmillan.

*Reading and Writing about Literature: Fiction, Poetry, Drama, and the Essay* (1990) by Edward Proffitt. San Diego: Harcourt Brace Jovanovich.

*A Reference Guide for English Studies* (1990) by Michael J. Marcuse. Berkeley, CA: University of California Press.

*A Research Guide for Undergraduate Students: English and American Literature* (1995, 4th edition) by Nancy L. Baker. New York: Modern Language Association.

*A Short Guide to Writing about Art* (1981) by Sylvan Barnet. Boston: Little Brown.

*A Short Guide to Writing about Film* (1994, 2nd edition) by Timothy Corrigan. New York: HarperCollins.

*A Short Guide to Writing about Literature* (1992, 4th edition) by Sylvan Barnet. New York: HarperCollins

*Writing about Literature* (1995, 8th edition) by Edgar V. Roberts. Englewood Cliffs, NJ: Prentice Hall.

*Writing Incredibly Short Plays, Poems, and Stories* (1972) by James H. Norton and Francis Gretton. New York: Harcourt Brace Jovanovich.

## Business writing

*The Complete Writing Guide to Preparing Reports, Proposals, Memos, Etc.* (1980) by Carolyn J. Mullins. Englewood Cliffs, NJ: Prentice-Hall.

*Dynamic Cover Letters* (1995, 2nd edition) by Katharine Hansen and Randall S. Hansen. Berkeley, CA: Ten Speed Press.

*How to Write First-Class Business Correspondence* (1995) by L.S. Baugh, M. Fryar, and D.A. Thomas. Lincolnwood, IL: NTC Publishing Group.

*Manipulative Memos: Control Your Career through the Medium of the Memo* (1994) by Arthur D. Rosenberg and Ellen Fuchs Thorn. Berkeley, CA: Ten Speed Press.

*Style Manual: A Complete Guide With Model Formats for Every Business Writing Occasion* (1992) by Mary A. DeVries. Englewood Cliffs, NJ: Prentice Hall.

*Writing that Works: How to Improve Your Memos, Letters, Reports, Speeches, Resumes, Plans, and Other Business Papers* (1992, 2nd edition) by Kenneth Roman. New York: HarperPerennial.

*Write to the Point* (1988) by R.T. Fruehling and N.B. Oldham. New York: McGraw-Hill.

*Write to the Top: Writing for Corporate Success* (1989) by Deborah Dumaine. New York: Random House.

## Creative writing

*Fade In: The Screenwriting Process* (1988) by Robert A. Berman. Westport, CT: Michael Wiese Films.

*The Elements of Screenwriting: A Guide for Film and Television Writers* (1986) by Irwin R. Blacker. New York: Macmillan.

*The Poet's Handbook* (1980) by Judson Jerome. Cincinnati, OH: Writer's Digest Books.

*The Way to Write: A Stimulating Guide to the Craft of Creative Writing* (1981) by John Fairfax. New York: St. Martin's.

## Science/technical writing

*The Art of Scientific Writing* (1987) by Hans F. Ebel, Claus Bliefert, and William E. Russey. Weinheim, Germany: VCH Verlagsgesellschaft.

*The Chemist's English* (1986, 2nd edition) by Robert Schoenfeld. Weinheim, Germany: VCH Verlagsgesellschaft.

*The Craft of Scientific Writing* (1987) by Michael Alley. Englewood Cliffs, NJ: Prentice Hall.

*Integrating Research: A Guide for Literature Reviews* (1989) by Harris M. Cooper. Newbury Park, CA: Sage Publications, Inc.

*Effective Writing for Engineers, Managers, Scientists* (1988, 2nd edition) by H.J. Tichy and Sylvia Fourdrinier. New York: Wiley.

*The Fine Art of Technical Writing* (1991) by Carol R. Perry. Hillsboro, OR: Blue Heron Publishing.

*How to Write and Present Technical Information* (1991, 2nd edition) by Charles H. Sides. Phoenix: Oryx.

*Science and Technical Writing: A Manual of Style* (1992). New York: Holt, Rinehart and Winston.

## Journalism and public relations writing

*The Associated Press Stylebook and Libel Manual* (1994). Reading, MA: Addison-Wesley.

*Basic Media Writing* (1996, 5th edition) by Melvin Mencher. Madison, WI: WCB Brown & Benchmark Publishers.

*Handbook for Public Relations Writing* (1995, 3rd edition) by Thomas Bivins. Lincolnwood, IL: NTC Business Books.

*Language Skills for Journalists* (1984, 2nd edition) by R. Thomas Berner. Boston: Houghton Mifflin.

*News Reporting and Writing* (1994, 6th edition) by Melvin Mencher. Madison, WI: WCB Brown & Benchmark Publishers.

*Newswriting: From Lead to "30"* (1991, 3rd edition) by William Metz. Englewood Cliffs, NJ: Prentice Hall.

*Public Relations Writing: Form and Style* (1991, 3rd edition) by Doug Newson. Belmont, CA: Wadsworth.

*The Publicity Handbook* (1991) by David R. Yale. Lincolnwood, IL: NTC Business Books.

*Working with Words: A Concise Handbook for Media Writers and Editors* (1993, 2nd edition) by Brian S. Brooks and James L. Pinson. New York: St. Martin's Press.

*Words into Type* (1974, 3rd edition). Englewood Cliffs, NJ: Prentice Hall.

*The Writing Craft* (1985, 2nd edition) by Edward D. Yates. Raleigh, NC: Contemporary Publishing Company.

*Writing for the Broadcast Media* (1985) by Peter E. Mayeux. Boston: Allyn & Bacon.

## Other writing

*The Art of Writing Nonfiction* (1987, 2nd edition) by Andre Fontaine and William A. Glavin Jr. Syracuse, NY: Syracuse University Press.

*The Elements of Speechwriting and Public Speaking* (1991) by Jeff Scott Cook. New York: Collier Books.

*The Journaling Handbook* (1994) by Carol Barton. Philadelphia: Running Press.

*Telling Your Own Stories: For Family and Classroom Storytelling, Public Speaking, and Personal Journaling* (1993) by Donald D. Davis. Little Rock, AK: August House.

*Writing Effective Speeches* (1992) by Henry Ehrlich. New York: Paragon.

## Other resource books

*The Art of Creative Thinking* (1982) by Gerard I. Nierenberg. New York: Simon & Schuster.

*The Confident Student* (1991) by Carol C. Kanar. Boston: Houghton Mifflin.

*The Mind Map Book: How to Use Radiant Thinking to Maximize Your Brain's Untapped Potential* (1994) by Tony Buzan. New York: Dutton.

*Mind Mapping: Your Personal Guide to Exploring Creativity and Problem-Solving* (1991) by Joyce Wycoff. New York: Berkley Books.

*The Philosopher's Guide to Sources, Research Tools, Professional Life, and Related Fields* (1980). Lawrence, KS: The Regents Press of Kansas.

*Research Guide for Psychology* (1982) by Raymond G. McInnis. Westport, CT: Greenwood Press.

*A Short Guide to Writing about Social Science* (1988) by Lee J. Cuba. Glenview, IL: Scott Foresman.

*Sociology: A Guide to Reference and Information Sources* (1987) by Stephen H. Aby. Littleton, CO: Libraries Unlimited.

*Sources of Information in the Social Sciences: A Guide to the Literature* (1986, 3rd edition). Chicago: American Library Association.

*Writing the Natural Way: Using Right-Brain Techniques to Release Your Expressive Powers* (1983) by Gabrielle L. Rico. Los Angeles: J.P. Tarcher.

# Computer software

**Many software options are** available for the student writer. You can brainstorm by using one of the creativity and idea-generation software programs we list. You can develop an outline for your paper by purchasing one of the outlining software we list—or, use the outline function that your word processor may have. You can write your paper using one of the general or specialized word-processing software programs we list. Finally, you can check your spelling and grammar by using one of those programs that we list—or use the spell checker and grammar checker that may be included with your word-processing software.

We have separated this section into the two dominant personal computing platforms: the Apple Macintosh and DOS/Microsoft Windows (begins on page 193). We have further subdivided each of the two categories into sub-categories:

▲ creativity and idea generation
▲ word processing—general
▲ word processing—outliners
▲ word processing—spell checkers and dictionaries
▲ word processing—writing aids.

Finally, where possible, we have included the software manufacturer's name, address, phone numbers, e-mail address, and World Wide Web address.

## APPLE MACINTOSH

### Creativity and idea generation

As we mentioned earlier in the book, sometimes the hardest part of writing is thinking up ideas and then organizing those ideas. The products included in this section are designed to question you, challenge you, excite you, and fire up your creativity.

Here are the best creativity generators, along with their main features:

*CORKBOARD/THREE BY FIVE*
MacToolKit
1234 6th Street, Suite 204
Santa Monica, CA 90401
310-395-4242
Fax: 310-393-7747

A brainstorming tool with a powerful graphical outliner, *Three by Five* allows you to organize your thoughts using the metaphor of index cards on a bulletin board, from which an outline can be produced. You actually record each idea on a separate electronic index card that you stick up on a corkboard-covered screen. You can drag the cards around and stack them, create categories and assign them to cards, and even clump cards together. Includes a powerful word processor and outliner, complete with spell checker.

### GENIUS HANDBOOK
Sierota Systems
114 Parsippany Road
Whippany, NJ 07981-1126
201-560-9072
E-mail: **waxman@ix.netcom.com**

Using the *Genius Handbook* can make your days more productive and enjoyable by helping you expand and apply your creative abilities in both big and small ways. This shareware product will help you save time and make breakthroughs—all for a small price.

### IDEAFISHER
Fisher Idea Systems, Inc.
2222 Martin Street, #10
Irvine, CA 92715
800-289-4332
Fax: 714-757-2896
E-mail: **74104.57@compuserve.com**

Like other brainstorming software, *IdeaFisher* is designed to expand your mind's thought processes and create opportunities for problem-solving by mimicking the creative thought processes of the human mind. The program's strength is an exhaustive database of more than 61,000 words, ideas, and phrases (organized by major categories) that you navigate in a massive exercise of free association. This is "top-of-the-line" in brainstorming packages.

### INSPIRATION
Inspiration Software, Inc.
7412 SW Beaverton Hillsdale Highway, Suite 102
Portland, OR 97225-2167
800-877-4292
Fax: 503-297-4676
E-mail: **Sales@inspiration.com**
Web address: **http://www.inspiration.com**

This visual idea-development tool for planning and developing ideas helps you organize and present your ideas, thereby leaving you free to focus on the ideas themselves. *Inspiration* has two main features for generating ideas: an outliner and a diagram screen. Includes "Rapid Fire," a tool that allows you to type all your ideas at once, after which the program automatically organizes your ideas into separate boxes for diagramming. It is the ultimate tool for the visual thinker. An excellent collection of tools to brainstorm and map ideas, diagram information, and organize writing.

### MindLink Problem Solver

MindLink Software
247 Kings Highway
North Pomfret, VT 05063
800-253-1844
E-mail: **Mindlinker@aol.com**

This creative problem-solving and brainstorming tool helps you break down a problem and overcome mental blocks that might cloud your thoughts through the use of images, stories, and writing exercises that force you to think about something unrelated to your problem—and then connect your thoughts to the problem-solving process.


## Word processing—general

Various types and qualities of word-processing software are available. Some are household names, some are part of a larger integrated software package (that usually includes spreadsheet and database software programs), and some are specialized. It's a good idea to investigate the word-processing software your college uses in its computer labs since you probably will want to use the same software in your dorm room and at home.

Here are the top word-processing software titles:

### Claris Works

Claris Corporation
5201 Patrick Henry Drive
Santa Clara, CA 95052-8168
408-727-8227
Web address: **http://www.claris.com**

This award-winning integrated software offers powerful word-processing, database, spreadsheet, charting, and graphics capabilities. Claris can open seven documents simultaneously on screen and includes layout capabilities, flexible rulers, an editable preview mode, and mail merge. One of the layout capabilities is multiple column capability. You can also specify the point size for space between lines. When setting margins, you can specify in millimeters, centimeters, picas, and inches up to several decimal points.

### COREL WORDPERFECT FOR MACINTOSH

Corel Corporation
1600 Carling Avenue
Ottawa, Canada K1Z 8R7
800-772-6735
Fax: 613-761-9176
Web address: **http://www.corel.com/**

One of the best word-processing software programs, *Corel WordPerfect 3.5* for Macintosh allows you increased productivity and adds a personal touch to all documents. A "Smart Features" function in *WordPerfect* automatically corrects typos as you write as well as checks and corrects grammatical errors. Includes tools that let you read and publish information on the Internet. The "Make It Fit" feature will expand or contract text to fill the number of specified pages.

### MATHWRITER 2.0: THE SCIENTIFIC WORD PROCESSOR FOR THE MACINTOSH

Brooks/Cole Publishing Co.
511 Forest Lodge Road
Pacific Grove, CA 93950
800-354-9706
Fax: 408-375-6414
E-mail: **info@brookscole.com**
Web address: **http://www.thomson.com/brookscole.html**

This complete word-processing program allows you to enter mathematical expressions as text, not graphics, so both text and mathematics can be edited in the same document. In addition to a spell checker, thesaurus, and automatic hyphenation, the program also automatically sizes and centers mathematical symbols, italicizes variables, formats tables and matrices, and shows on-screen renumbering of both equations and references to equations. Includes a science-math-engineering supplemental dictionary.

### MICROSOFT WORD FOR THE MACINTOSH
Microsoft Corporation
One Microsoft Way
Redmond, WA 98052-6399
800-426-9400
Fax: 206-635-1049
E-mail: **www@microsoft.com**
Web address: **http://www.microsoft.com/**

This popular word-processing program gives you easy access to frequently used features such as columns, fonts, format changes, and a drawing tool. This version also includes a built-in grammar checker, a file find feature that can locate documents based on dates, keywords, or the author, and an auto-save reminder. Can be purchased separately or as part of a suite of programs.

### NISUS WRITER
Nisus Software, Inc.
107 South Cedros Avenue
Solona Beach, CA 92075
800-890-3030
Fax: 619-481-6154
E-mail: **info@nisus-soft.com**
Web address: **http://www.nisus-soft.com/**

This program includes menu keys, spell checker, mail merge, glossary, macros, unlimited undos, drag-and-drop, and multiple clipboards. You can create multimedia presentations and live reports using movies, sounds, and text-to-speech. You can also create, scale, and rotate graphics and wrap text automatically. Writes in more than eighteen languages including Arabic, Czech, Hebrew (right to left), Hungarian, Japanese, Korean, Polish, Russian, and many more. Foreign menus and dictionaries available.

### QUICKLETTER
Working Software, Inc.
P.O. Box 1884
Santa Cruz, CA 95061-1844
800-229-9675
Fax: 408-423-5699
E-mail: **info@working.com**
Web address: **http://www.webcom.com/~working/**

This word processor has special features for writing letters. You can use it as an application or as a desk accessory (under the Apple menu). Writing features include spell checker, address book, automatic envelope addressing, and page preview with automatic vertical centering of the letter on the page. You also have the ability to mix different fonts, styles, and sizes.

### Word processing—outliners

The outlining software included in this section offers the college writer powerful tools that can really help organize your papers. But before you go off spending more money, you should check your current word-processing software first to see if it has a built-in outliner. Many word processors—including *ClarisWorks*, *Corel WordPerfect*, and *Microsoft Word*—have built-in outliners that are often easier to use because you don't need to worry about shifting between programs or worrying about importing and exporting text.

The best stand-alone outliners:

*In Control*
Attain Corporation
48 Grove Street
Somerville, MA 02144
800-925-5615
Fax: 617-776-1626
E-mail: **sales@attain.com**
Web address: **http://www.attain.com**

This excellent time-management outliner—some say the premier outliner for Macs—lets you create a list of "to-do" items and then collapse, expand, indent, or move any item. It also features an electronic calendar with alarms and allows printing in six formats, including those that correspond to popular paper organizers, such as Day-Timers. With this software, you can link any activity in your outline to any document from any application, then launch it directly from *In Control*.

*INFODEPOT*

Chena Software, Inc.
640 Hamilton Mall, Suite 501
Allentown, PA 18101
800-245-4577
Fax: 610-770-9266
E-mail: **info@chena.com**
Web Address: **http://www.chena.com**

*InfoDepot* is a powerful outlining and project-management tool that allows you to build outline-based tables and time lines, making it an excellent tool for organizing and managing any project. It is designed as an all-in-one program for project planning, and includes tools for brainstorming and organizing ideas, for scheduling project steps, and for entering, calculating, and presenting data. *InfoDepot* is accelerated for the Power Macintosh.

*MAXTHINK*

MaxThink, Inc.
2425 B Channing, #592
Berkeley, CA 94704-2209
510-548-4686
E-mail: **neil@maxthink.com**
Web address: **http://maxthink.com/index1.html**

The purpose of this program is to quickly represent and organize ideas in your mind. It is designed around philosophies and practices leading to effective writing, thinking, and planning. *MaxThink* includes features such as an alarm and report generator.

*MORE*

Symantec
10201 Torre Avenue
Cupertino, CA 9514-2132
800-441-7234
Fax: 408-252-4694
E-mail: **info@symantec.com**
Web address: **http://www.symantec.com**

*More* has a rich set of features, but you should know up front that Symantec has decided against upgrading and supporting this product. Still, *More* is a powerful organizer/outliner that enables you to arrange ideas in an outline and then display them as a tree chart or as a series of bullet charts. *More* also provides tools for presenting your ideas after you've organized them.

## Word Processing—Spelling Checkers and Dictionaries

As is the case with outliners, many word-processing software packages now include both spell checkers and grammar checkers as standard; however, a niche still exists for specialized dictionaries and spell checkers. See chapter 2 for other "library reference" dictionaries.

The best follow:

*BRODY'S MEDICAL DICTIONARY*
Inductel, Inc.
5339 Prospect Road, Suite 321
San Jose, CA 95129
408-866-8016
Fax: 408-243-1762
Web address: **http://www.liberty.com/home/inductel**
Containing more than forty thousand entries, *Brody's* is the first and one of the largest electronic medical dictionaries with definitions. Medical abbreviations are shown, as well as diseases, drugs, and general medical terms. Allows major word-processing programs to use it to spell check documents.

*BOUVIER'S LAW DICTIONARY*
Inductel (refer to *Brody's Medical Dictionary*)
An excellent resource for writers involved in constitutional or common law writing, this is the law dictionary the manufacturer claims is preferred for use by the U. S. Supreme Court. Each entry in the dictionary contains a definition and citations referring to sources used for the definition.

*FUNK AND WAGNALL'S STANDARD DESK DICTIONARY*
Inductel (refer to *Brody's Medical Dictionary*)
This software includes definitions, tables, parts of speech, and etymologies for more than 100,000 words. Supplement contains a gazetteer, biographies, abbreviations, common computer terms, and secretarial handbook. Works with all major word-processing software.

### GEOGRAPHICAL DICTIONARY

Working Software, Inc. (refer to *QuickLetter*)

This is a supplemental dictionary for use with *Spellswell, Lookup, Microsoft Works, QuickLetter, Expert Writer, Expert Publisher,* and *Resume Maker.* Contains correct spellings of more than thirty thousand cities, states, countries, provinces, and bodies of water from all over the globe.

### LEGAL DICTIONARY

Working Software, Inc. (refer to *QuickLetter*)

For use with *SpellsWell,* this program contains more than twenty thousand words and abbreviations specific to work done by lawyers, legal secretaries, law enforcement professionals, and corporate legal departments.

### LOOKUP

Working Software, Inc. (refer to *QuickLetter*)

You can use this desk accessory for looking up the spelling of any word from any program. Includes a ninety-three-thousand-word dictionary. Also has "beep-while-you-type" spell checker.

### SPELLING COACH, SPELLING COACH PRO 4.1

Deneba Software

7400 SW 87th Avenue

Miami, FL 33173

800-733-6322

Fax: 305-273-9069

E-mail: **support@deneba.com**

Web address: **http://www.deneba.com**

This interactive spell checker and thesaurus desktop accessory eliminates the need for separate, application-specific dictionaries and spell checkers. Uses the largest dictionary of any Macintosh spell checker program: the ninety-five-thousand-word Proximity/Merriam-Webster dictionary, including geographical and biographical terms. Also includes a twenty-eight-thousand-word legal dictionary, a thirty-five-thousand-word medical dictionary, and a thirty-thousand-word technical and engineering dictionary.

*SPELLSWELL 7*
Working Software, Inc. (refer to *QuickLetter*)
This spell checker scans documents you create in *MacWrite, Microsoft Word*, and other programs. Provides the following features: accepts documents of unlimited size; includes ninety-three-thousand-word user-modifiable dictionary; checks for duplicate words; enforces abbreviation standards; checks homonyms; maintains capitalization; provides document dictionaries; and finds capitalization errors.

## Word processing—writing aids

The software programs in this category are designed to supplement word-processing software, often as an add-on that you can use while you are in the word processor. These software programs are designed to enhance your writing or your writing efficiency and include software that "coach" you through your writing and software that help you easily build and manage bibliographies for your papers.

Some of the best follow:

*BIBLIOGRAPHY BUILDER*
Master Software
20618 Cypress Way
Lynnwood, WA 98036
203-672-8708
This program formats raw data into bibliography, reference, or footnote lists with the appropriate order, italicization, and punctuation. Covers more than thirty of the most common formats from the fifth edition of Turabian's *A Manual for Writers. Microsoft Word* version allows users to enter and format bibliographies and then export the data to other word processors and database programs.

*BIG THESAURUS 2.1*
Deneba Software (refer to *Spelling Coach Pro*)
This electronic thesaurus is based on the world-renowned Merriam-Webster thesaurus and contains more than 1.4 million combinations of synonyms, antonyms, and related, compared, and contrasted words.

## BOOKENDS PRO

Westing Software, Inc.

134 Redwood Avenue

Corte Madera, CA 94925

800-325-1862

Fax: 415-945-3877

E-mail: **westing3@aol.com**

Web address: **http://www.westinginc.com/**

A reference management program specifically designed for the Macintosh, *Bookends Pro* is an essential tool for handling references, notes, and citations. It has a sophisticated database, reference formatting, and software linking capabilities. You can also import from CD-ROMs and on-line services.

## DRAMATICA

Screenplay Systems, Inc.

150 E. Olive Ave., Suite 203

Burbank, CA 91502

800-847-8679

Fax: 818-843-8364

E-Mail: **Dramatica-webmail@screenplay.com**

Web address: **http://www.well.com/user/dramatic/**

An invaluable story creation and analysis tool, *Dramatica* helps you make creative choices while keeping your character, plot, genre, and themes in sync with your plan. Especially valuable for beginning writers.

## ENDNOTE PLUS

Niles & Associates, Inc.

800 Jones Street

Berkeley, CA 94710

800-554-3049

Fax: 510-559-8683

E-mail: **info@niles.com**

Web address: **http://www.niles.com**

This is a complete bibliographic package that organizes your references and builds bibliographies in your word processor—in the proper style that you select (from hundreds, including the more standard MLA and APA styles). *EndNote Plus* has two exceptional functions. First, it's a database manager specializing in the storing, maintaining, and searching of bibliographic references in your private reference library. Second, it's a bibliography maker, building lists of cited works automatically.

### FICTIONMASTER

The WritePro Corporation
43 South Highland Avenue
Ossining, NY 10562
800-755-1124
E-mail: **WritePro@pipeline.com**
Web address: **http://www.writepro.com**

*FictionMaster* provides practical techniques for character and plot development that you will find in no other course or program. Contains four parts: creating memorable characters, developing page-turning plots, the dialogue doctor, and overcoming obstacles to publication. Deals with such matters as how to show a story instead of telling it, how to move flashbacks into the present, how to handle point of view, and fifty-four other subjects. Program is designed so that it can be used by talented beginners as well as professionals.

### INFOPEDIA

Softkey International
450 Franklin Road, Suite 100
Marietta, GA 30067
800-227-5609
Fax: 404-427-1150

This contains seven best-selling reference books—including *World Almanac and Book of Facts, Hammond World Atlas, Roget's 21st Century Thesaurus, Webster's Collegiate Dictionary of English Usage, Dictionary of Quotations,* and *Webster's New Biographical Dictionary*—plus a twenty-nine-volume encyclopedia allowing you to access more than 200,000 articles, videos, photos, animations, and recordings. Seamless cross-reference feature makes information even more accessible.

## MICROSOFT BOOKSHELF
Microsoft (Refer to Microsoft Word)

*Bookshelf* includes a dictionary with definitions and a biographical/geographical appendix, an almanac, a spell checker, and a zip code guide. Includes versions of *The American Heritage Dictionary, The Original Roget's Thesaurus, The Columbia Dictionary of Quotations, The Concise Columbia Encyclopedia, Hammond World Atlas, World Almanac, People's Chronology,* and *The Book of Facts.*

## PROCITE
Research Information Systems
Camino Corporate Center
2355 Camino Vida Roble
Carlsbad, CA 92009
800-722-1227
Fax: 619-438-5573
E-mail: **sales@ris.risinc.com**
Web address: **http://www.pbsinc.com/procite.html**

This powerful and full-featured reference management program makes it easy for you to store bibliographic information, notes, keywords, and full abstracts of your references. With this program, you can easily build and maintain a local library of references from on-line, CD-ROM, and library systems, and then search, sort, and print your citations in a variety of styles. *ProCite* comes with predefined bibliographic styles used by thousands of publications.

## WRITEPRO
The WritePro Corp. (refer to *FictionMaster*)

This program for professional and budding fiction writers shows you how to improve character development, plot, and other aspects of novels and stories through an eight-lesson process. *WritePro* has its own word processor and shows original and revised versions of what you have written on a split screen. Both versions can also be printed and/or exported to your own word processor.

## WRITEPRO FOR BUSINESS
The WritePro Corp. (refer to *FictionMaster*)

This *WritePro* is designed to improve business writing without the use of templates. Instead, an on-line editor asks questions and provides tips as you write, enabling you to overcome writer's block, catch mistakes, and enhance your effectiveness. You can transfer your perfected letter, memo, or report to any Windows word processor in seconds.

*WRITING COACH*
WritePlace Software
2852 Willamette Street, Suite 125
Eugene, OR 97405
800-264-7936
Fax: 503-686-3562
E-mail: **wcoach@writeplace.com**
Web address: **http://www.rio.com/~wplace**

An excellent tool for people who have trouble writing, *Writing Coach* is a set of worksheets, outlines, and techniques that help you write. It contains sixty worksheets designed to help you break down your writing task into "bite-sized" pieces and unlock your creativity, discover what you have to say, and express it effectively. Includes tools to help you brainstorm, organize, write, overcome writer's block, edit, and proofread. Works within *Word, Word-Perfect,* and *Claris.*

## DOS/WINDOWS

### Creativity and idea generation

As we mentioned earlier in the book, sometimes the hardest part of writing is thinking up ideas and then organizing those ideas. The products included in this section are designed to question you, challenge you, excite you, and to fire up your creativity.

Here are the best creativity generators, along with their main features:

*AXON IDEA PROCESSOR*
Axon Research
5, Lengkok Merak
Singapore 248860
65-7360422
Fax: 65-7379016
E-mail: **chanbok@pacific.net.sg**
Web address: **http://home.pacific.net.sg/~chanbok/axon_res.htm**

A program for visualizing and organizing ideas and solving complex problems,

*Axon's* sketchpad is designed to aid the thinking process and idea processing. Offers a visual workbench with a range of tools to record, process, and manipulate ideas. Based on cognitive principles, the system supports both top-down and bottom-up thinking styles, hierarchical, and network structures. Includes more than sixty checklists, including words of wisdom, noun triggers, interesting topics, problem-solving techniques, and more.

### BRAINSTORMER

Soft Path Systems
105 N. Adams
Eugene, OR 97402
503-342-3439

This no-frills problem-solving tool offers you the capability to run millions of ideas. *Brainstormer* is based on a problem-solving method called a Morphological Box, which is a matrix constructed of ten-by-ten dimensions that helps to visualize various combinations of ideas. Users go through three sessions in *Brainstormer:* Interest, Theme, and Probe.

### CREATIVE WHACK PACK

Creative Think Software
Box 7354
Menlo Park, CA 94026
415-321-6775

Based on the best-selling book, *A Whack on the Side of the Head,* and the resulting sixty-four-card Creative Whack Pack Card deck, this program takes you on a scavenger hunt into distant recesses of your imagination. The electronic cards are divided into four categories: Explorer, Artist, Judge, and Warrior. Each card asks a specific question or raises a specific issue related to the topic you're brainstorming about.

### CREATIVITY MACHINE

The Creativity Institute
1664 3rd Avenue
New York, NY 10128
212-289-8856

This program is designed to facilitate your creative production through a number of tools, including: "Paradigm Shift," which forces you to see and think differently; "Tao of Creativity," which contains eighty-one Tao poems as a way of attaining intuitive insights into almost any situation or problem; and "Alpha," which is a way of entering into a creative state of consciousness.

### GENIUS HANDBOOK

Sierota Systems
114 Parsippany Road
Whippany, NJ 07981-1126
201-560-9072
E-mail: **waxman@ix.netcom.com**

Using the *Genius Handbook* can make your days more productive and enjoyable by helping you expand and apply your creative abilities in both big and small ways. This product will help you save time and make breakthroughs—all for a small price.

### IDEAFISHER

Fisher Idea Systems, Inc.
2222 Martin Street, #10
Irvine, CA 92715
800-289-4332
Fax: 714-757-2896
E-mail: **74104.57@compuserve.com**

Like other brainstorming software, *IdeaFisher* is designed to expand your mind's thought processes and create opportunities for problem-solving by mimicking the creative thought processes of the human mind. The program's strength is an exhaustive database of more than sixty-one thousand words, ideas, and phrases that you navigate in a massive exercise of free association. *IdeaFisher* is structured around four windows: IdeaBank, Qbank, Notepad, and Question Notepad. This is "top-of-the-line" in brainstorming packages.

### THE IDEA GENERATOR PLUS

Experience in Software, Inc.
2000 Hearst Avenue
Berkeley, CA 94709-2176
800-678-7008
Fax: 510-644-0694
Web address: **www.experienceware.com**

This software is designed to help you come up with insights into your problems. It is divided into three major sections, each of which focuses on a particular aspect of the problem-solving process: problem statement, idea generation, and evaluation. After using *The Idea Generator Plus* to gain insights into your situation, you can easily transfer your idea to a word processor or outliner for further refinement. Designed by best-selling author of *The Art of Creative Thinking*, Gerard I. Neirenberg.

## INSPIRATION

Inspiration Software, Inc.
7412 SW Beaverton Hillsdale Highway, Suite 102
Portland, OR 97225-2167
800-877-4292
Fax: 503-297-4676
Web address: **http://www.inspiration.com**

This visual idea-development tool for planning and developing ideas helps you organize and present your ideas, thereby leaving you free to focus on the ideas themselves. *Inspiration* has two main features for generating ideas: an outliner and a diagram screen. Includes "Rapid Fire," a tool that allows you to type all your ideas at once, and then the program automatically organizes your ideas into separate boxes for diagramming. It is the ultimate tool for the visual thinker. An excellent collection of tools to brainstorm and map ideas, diagram information, and organize writing.

## MIND MAPPER

EGLE Magic
P.O. Box 27574
Mt. Roskill
Auckland
New Zealand
E-mail: **MMInfo@emagic.marc.cri.nz**

This allows the drawing of mind maps with textual content. The graphical components can be manipulated, the maps printed, and the content exported as either plain text or Rich Text Format (suitable for importing into a word processor or outline software). *Mind Mapper* is shareware, and the mindmap.zip file can be downloaded off the Internet from **ftp.cica.indiana. edu** in the directory **pub/pc/win3/pim**.

### MINDLINK PROBLEM SOLVER

MindLink Software Corporation
247 Kings Highway
North Pomfret, VT 05063
800-253-1844
E-mail: **MindLinker@aol.com**

A creative problem-solving and brainstorming tool, this program helps you break down a problem and overcome mental blocks that might cloud your thoughts through the use of images, stories, and writing exercises that force you to think about something unrelated to your problem—and then connects your thoughts to the problem-solving process. You can either brainstorm any part of a problem at will or let the program guide you through its procedure.

### PROJECT KICKSTART FOR WINDOWS

Experience in Software, Inc. (refer to *The Idea Generator Plus*)

This is a speedy project organizer (nicknamed the thirty-minute organizer) that will help you plan your projects in thirty minutes. But it doesn't stop there; the program also provides a wealth of strategic information, such as project goals and possible obstacles. You can also organize projects into phases, tasks, subtasks, and details.

### THOUGHTLINE

Experience in Software, Inc. (refer to *The Idea Generator Plus*)

*Thoughtline: The Intelligent Writer's Companion* is a conversational partner that helps you express, focus, and organize your thoughts as you write. *Thoughtline* deepens and expands your thinking, breaks through writer's block, and provides a logical, flexible framework for your ideas. Great for breaking writer's block!

## Word processing—general

Various types and qualities of word-processing software are available. Some are household names, some are part of a larger integrated software package (that usually includes spreadsheet and database programs), and some are specialized. It's a good idea to investigate the word-processing software your college uses in its computer labs since you probably will want to use the same software in your dorm room and at home.

Here are the top word-processing software titles:

### ACCENT, ACCENT PROFESSIONAL

Accent Worldwide, Inc.
1401 Dove Street, Suite 470
Newport Beach, CA 92660
800-535-5256
E-mail: info@accentsoft.com
Web address: http://www.accentsoft.com/

Multilingual word-processing software that offers you all the basic word-processing features—including a spell checker and thesaurus. Text can be entered in more than thirty languages based on any of the seven character sets for Western and Eastern Europe, as well as Cyrillic, Greek, Turkish, Arabic, and Hebrew. It supports bidirectional text in Hebrew and Arabic. On-line help is available in one of nine languages.

### COREL WORDPERFECT

Corel Corporation
1600 Carling Avenue
Ottawa, Canada K1Z 8R7
800-772-6735
Fax: 613-761-9176
Web address: http://www.corel.com/

One of the best and most widely used word-processing software programs, *WordPerfect* can print images anywhere on a page, rotate or scale graphics, and wrap text around an image. It comes with a utility that will capture images directly from the screen and convert formats it cannot read to its own format. Includes support for a wide range of fonts and print attributes and a feature for adjusting space between letters. Margins can be set in centimeters, inches, or points. You can electronically compare two versions of a document, and automatically update references to pages, footnotes, or figures when the length of document changes.

## DeScribe

DeScribe, Inc.
4820 Bayshore Drive
Naples, FL 33962
941-732-5500
Fax: 941-732-5414
E-mail: **dwpsupport@describe.com**
Web address: **http://www.describe.com/info.html**
This is designed for users who want professional-level word-processing capabilities at a rock-bottom price. Performs most of the usual word-processing functions including basic editing and formatting, mail merging, importing and exporting, macros, and tables. Includes an exceptional dictionary and thesaurus.

## EXP: The Scientific Word Processor 4.0

Brooks/Cole Publishing Co.
511 Forest Lodge Road
Pacific Grove, CA 93950
800-354-9706
Fax: 408-375-6414
E-mail: **info@brookscole.com**
Web address: **http://www.thomson.com/brookscole.html**
EXP is an advanced scientific word-processing system that knows the rules of mathematical typography: you get word-processed documents with automatically formatted mathematical equations and italicized variables. An integrated spell checker is included; symbols are sized automatically; long expressions are entered with only a few keystrokes; renumbering is eliminated; duplication is avoided; and columns set up easily. Contains four custom TrueType fonts with more than 500 special symbols.

## Microsoft Word

Microsoft Corporation
One Microsoft Way
Redmond, WA 98052-6399
800-426-9400
Fax: 206-635-1049
E-mail: **www@microsoft.com**
Web address: **http://www.microsoft.com/**

This popular word-processing program gives you easy access to frequently used features such as columns, fonts, format changes, and a drawing tool. This version also includes a built-in grammar checker, a file find feature that can locate documents based on dates, keywords, or the author, and an auto-save reminder. Can be purchased separately or as part of a suite of programs.

### MY WORD!

T.N.T. Software, Inc.
22170 Mitchell Lane
Antioch, IL 60002
847-838-4323

An inexpensive, small, but fast word processor, *My Word!* can do many of the functions found in powerful word processors, such as spell check your document. It also reads and writes plain ASCII files, which can then be transferred to any other word processor. Perfect for computers with limited memory.

### NOTA BENE

Nota Bene
285 West Broadway, Suite 460
New York, NY 10013
800-462-6733
Fax: 212-334-0845
E-mail: **notabene@soho.ios.com**
Web address: **http://soho.ios.com/~notabene/**

This presents itself as the word processor for ambitious scholars and is one of the fastest, most efficient software programs on the market for entering and editing text. *Nota Bene* offers exceptional power and speed and is especially useful for writing longer documents. The Lingua version adds full support for Eastern European, Greek, Hebrew, and Russian alphabets.

### PC-WRITE STANDARD, ADVANCED

Starlite Software Corp.
P.O. Box 370
Port Hadlock, WA 98339-0370
360-385-7125
E-mail: **starlite@waypt.com**

This DOS-based word processor works well in Windows and Windows 95 environments. In addition to an English spell checker dictionary, you can purchase

German, French, Spanish, and United Kingdom English dictionaries. The company also offers *Galaxy* and *Galaxy Pro*, ASCII text-editors.

### WordPro

Lotus Development Corporation
55 Cambridge Parkway
Cambridge, MA 02142
800-465-6887
E-mail: **info@lotus.com**
Web address: **http://www.lotus.com/wordpro/wordpro1.htm**
Provides all the tools you need to create powerful, persuasive documents with exceptional editing (includes both a thesaurus and grammar checker), formatting, and spell checker features (including SmartCorrect, which corrects mistakes as you type). Also includes SmartMasters—pre-formatted templates—that let you create documents automatically, from simple letters and memos to compound business documents.

## Word processing—outliners

The outlining software programs included in this section offer the college writer powerful tools that can really help organize your papers. But before you go off spending more money, you should check your current word-processing software first to see if it has a built-in outliner. Many word processors—including *Corel WordPerfect, DeScribe,* and *Microsoft Word*—have built-in outliners that are often easier to use because you don't need to worry about shifting between programs or worrying about importing and exporting text.

The best stand-alone outliner:

### In Control

Attain Corporation
48 Grove Street
Somerville, MA 02144
800-925-5615
Fax: 617-776-1626
E-mail: **sales@attain.com**
Web address: **http://www.attain.com**
This excellent time-management outliner—some say the premier outliner for Macs and now available for Windows—lets you create a list of "to-do" items

and then collapse, expand, indent, or move any item. It also features an electronic calendar with alarms and allows printing in six formats, including those that correspond to popular paper organizers, such as Day-Timers. With this software, you can link any activity in your outline to any document from any application, then launch it directly from *In Control.*

### Word processing—spelling checkers and dictionaries

As is the case with outliners, many word-processing software packages now include both spell checkers and grammar checkers as standard; however, a niche still exists for specialized dictionaries and spell checkers. See chapter 2 for other "library reference" dictionaries.

The best follow:

*BRODY'S MEDICAL DICTIONARY*
Inductel, Inc.
5339 Prospect Road, Suite 321
San Jose, CA 95129
408-866-8016
Fax: 408-243-1762
Web address: **http://www.liberty.com/home/inductel**
Containing more than forty thousand entries, this is the first and one of the largest electronic medical dictionaries with definitions. Medical abbreviations are shown, as well as diseases, drugs, and general medical terms. Allows major word-processing software to use it to spell check documents.

*BOUVIER'S LAW DICTIONARY*
Inductel (refer to *Brody's Medical Dictionary*)
An excellent resource for writers involved in constitutional or common law writing, this is the law dictionary the manufacturer claims is preferred for use by the U. S. Supreme Court. Each entry in the dictionary contains a definition and citations referring to sources used for the definition.

*FUNK AND WAGNALL'S STANDARD DESK DICTIONARY*
Inductel (refer to *Brody's Medical Dictionary*)
Definitions, tables, parts of speech, and etymologies are included for more than 100,000 words. Supplement contains a gazetteer, biographies, abbreviations, common computer terms, and secretarial handbook. Works with all major word-processing software.

*SPELL CHECK 3.3*

Next Generation Software, Inc.

2831 Gallows Rd., Suite 201

Falls Church, VA 22042

Fax: 703-560-1266

E-mail: **nextgensft@aol.com**

Web address: **http://www.xmission.com/~gastown/nextgensft/spell.html**

A high-performance spell checker designed for applications in the Windows environment that do not have spell checkers, such as *Eudora*, Netscape *Navigator*, and Windows *Notepad*. Can be downloaded by visiting its Web site.

## Word processing—writing aids

The software in this category are all designed to supplement word-processing software, often as an add-on that you can use while you are in the word processor. These software programs are designed to enhance your writing or your writing efficiency, and include software that "coach" you through your writing and software that help you easily build and manage bibliographies for your papers.

Some of the best follow:

*CITATION 7*

Nota Bene (refer to *Nota Bene*)

A powerful and easy-to-use bibliographic database system and notes organizer equipped with nearly 1,000 pre-defined academic press and scholarly journal reference style definitions. You can also concentrate on the substance of your writing and let *Citation* automatically generate your footnotes, endnotes, in-text citations, reference lists, and bibliographies. Compatible with most word processors, but as a special feature for *WordPerfect* and *Word* users, *Citation* installs directly onto the Tools menu so it is always available as you are writing. Also has pop-up "index cards" forms that allow you to enter notes about the references you are using.

*DRAMATICA*
Screenplay Systems, Inc.
150 E. Olive Ave., Suite 203
Burbank, CA 91502
800-847-8679
Fax: 818-843-8364
E-Mail: **Dramatica-webmail@screenplay.com**
Web address: **http://www.well.com/user/dramatic/**
An invaluable story creation and analysis tool, *Dramatica* helps you make creative choices while keeping your character, plot, genre, and themes in sync with your plan. Especially valuable for beginning writers.

*ENDNOTE PLUS FOR WINDOWS*
Niles & Associates, Inc.
800 Jones Street
Berkeley, CA 94710
800-554-3049
Fax: 510-559-8683
E-mail: **info@niles.com**
Web address: **http://www.niles.com**
This complete bibliographic package organizes your references and builds bibliographies in your word processor—in the proper style that you select (from hundreds, including the more standard MLA and APA styles). *End Note Plus* has two exceptional functions. First, it's a database manager specializing in storing, maintaining, and searching bibliographic references in your private reference library. Second, it's a bibliography maker, building lists of cited works automatically. The current version is compatible with ANSI text, *Ami Pro* (now *WordPro*), *Corel WordPerfect for Windows*, *Microsoft Word for Windows,* and *Rich Text Format* (RTF).

*FICTIONMASTER*
The WritePro Corporation
43 South Highland Avenue
Ossining, NY 10562
800-755-1124
Web address: **http://www.writepro.com**
Provides practical techniques for character and plot development that you will find in no other course or program. Comes in four parts: creating memorable

characters, developing page-turning plots, the dialogue doctor, and overcoming obstacles to publication. Deals with such matters as how to show a story instead of telling it, how to move flashbacks into the present, how to handle point of view, and fifty-four other subjects. The program is designed to be used by talented beginners as well as professionals.

### INFOPEDIA
Softkey International
450 Franklin Road, Suite 100
Marietta, GA 30067
800-227-5609
Fax: 404-427-1150
Contains seven best-selling reference books—including *World Almanac and Book of Facts, Hammond World Atlas, Roget's 21st Century Thesaurus, Webster's Collegiate Dictionary of English Usage, Dictionary of Quotations,* and *Webster's New Biographical Dictionary*—plus a twenty-nine-volume encyclopedia allowing you to access more than 200,000 articles, videos, photos, animations, and recordings. Seamless cross-reference feature makes information even more accessible.

### LIBRARY MASTER
Balboa Software
5846 Yonge Street
P.O. Box 69539
Willowdale, Ontario
Canada M2M 4K3
800-763-8542
Fax: 416-730-9715
E-mail: **Sales@balboa-software.com**
Web address: **http://www.balboa-software.com/**
A bibliographic and textual database manager that makes it easy for you to manage bibliographic information. The program automatically formats the bibliography, footnotes, and citations for your paper, thesis, or book to any style, making it easy to organize research notes and project records. You can download from on-line information services, CD-ROMs, on-line library catalogs, and other database programs.

### MAVIS BEACON TEACHES TYPING!

Mindscape
88 Rowland Way
Novato, CA 94945
800-234-3088
Fax: 415-897-5186
E-mail: **mscape@aol.com**
Web address: **http://www.mindscape.com/**

Designed to teach and improve typing dexterity—whether beginner or advanced typist—the program responds to your keyboard patterns and customizes each typing lesson to fit your specific needs. The program analyzes your typing strengths, weaknesses, and rhythms, and then develops a personalized learning program just for you.

### MICROSOFT BOOKSHELF

Microsoft (refer to *Microsoft Word*)

Includes a dictionary with definitions and a biographical/geographical appendix, an almanac, a spelling checker, and a zip code guide. Includes versions of *The American Heritage Dictionary, The Original Roget's Thesaurus, The Columbia Dictionary of Quotations, The Concise Columbia Encyclopedia, Hammond World Atlas, World Almanac, People's Chronology,* and *The Book of Facts.*

### OXFORD ENGLISH REFERENCE LIBRARY

Integrated Systems Solution
455 Park Place
Lexington, KY 40511
800-873-4772

This is an excellent writing aid that includes the *Concise Oxford Dictionary of Current English,* the *Oxford Thesaurus,* the *Oxford Dictionary for Writers and Editors, Oxford Guide to English Usage, Oxford Dictionary of New Words, Revised English Bible,* and the complete works of Shakespeare.

## PERFECT SCHOLAR
Perfect Scholar Software
1209 Stull Drive
Las Cruces, NM 88001
505-521-9261
E-mail: **Jerry@zianet.com**
Web address: **http://204.134.124.1/jerry/psfaq.html**
*Perfect Scholar APA* and *Perfect Scholar MLA* are auto-formatters and bibliography generators for *WordPerfect 5.1+* for DOS. These programs produce accurate bibliographies and auto-formatted papers in the proper style without your ever having to open the APA or MLA manuals and without your having to know a thing about *WordPerfect*.

## PROCITE
Research Information Systems
Camino Corporate Center
2355 Camino Vida Roble
Carlsbad, CA 92009
800-722-1227
Fax: 619-438-5573
E-mail: **sales@ris.risinc.com**
Web address: **http://www.pbsinc.com/procite.html**
This powerful and full-featured reference management program makes it easy for you to store bibliographic information, notes, keywords, and full abstracts of your references. With this program, you can easily build and maintain a local library of references from on-line, CD-ROM, and library systems, and then search, sort, and print your citations in a variety of styles. *ProCite* comes with predefined bibliographic styles used by thousands of publications.

## QUOTEMASTER LIBRARY
BookMaster, Inc.
1444 U.S. Route 42
Mansfield, OH 44903
800-247-6553
E-mail: **Order@bookmaster.com**
Web address: **http://www.quotemaster.com/**
Provides you with more than 15,000 of the best quotations ever recorded from all forums, including business, politics, sports, film, religion, and music.

It has a fully searchable quotation and anecdote database by topics, authors, quotes, and sources.

### SQUARENOTE

SQN, Inc.
60 East Chestnut St., #422
Chicago, IL 60611
312-266-2529
Fax: 312-440-0146
E-mail: **staff@sqn.com**
Web address: **http://sqn.com**

This software has four main uses: as a daily journal, in which you enter activities and business of the day; as an annotated list, where you can build a bibliography or any other kind of list; as a research notes organizer, where you can organize, index, store, and retrieve all your research notes and ideas; and as a contact manager, where you can keep and cross-reference notes about people (such as phone numbers, e-mail addresses, important dates, etc.).

### STORYCRAFT

StoryCraft Corp.
820 W. 21st Street
Norfolk, VA 23517
800-977-8679
E-mail: **story@exis.net**
Web address: **http://www.exis.net/story/**

This is an award-winning software program that guides writers through the entire process of writing a story. With *StoryCraft* you can write full-length novels and screenplays through a step-by-step process, starting with developing the story premise, designing the concept, identifying the category and type, and detailing the main characters.

### WRITEPRO

The WritePro Corp. (refer to *FictionMaster*)

This program for professional and budding fiction writers shows you how to improve character development, plot, and other aspects of novels and stories through an eight-lesson process. *WritePro* has its own word processor and shows original and revised versions of what you have written on a split screen. Both versions can also be printed and/or exported to your own word processor.

### WRITEPRO FOR BUSINESS

The WritePro Corp. (refer to *FictionMaster*)

Designed to improve business writing without the use of templates. Instead, an on-line editor asks questions and provides tips as you write, enabling you to overcome writer's block, catch mistakes, and enhance your effectiveness. You can transfer your perfected letter, memo, or report to any Windows word processor in seconds.

### WRITER'S BLOCKS FOR WINDOWS

Ashley Software
27758 Santa Margarita Pkwy., #302
Mission Viejo, CA 92691
714-583-9153
E-mail: **71064.1265@compuserve.com**

*Writer's Block*s is a story-development tool based on an index-card metaphor. Its features allow you to create a story outline, highlighting key scenes and ideas with various colors, fonts, etc. You can also link scenes together to form linear or nonlinear story lines.

### WRITING COACH

WritePlace Software
2852 Willamette Street, Suite 125
Eugene, OR 97405
800-264-7936
Fax: 503-686-3562
E-mail: **wcoach@writeplace.com**
Web address: **htttp://www.rio.com/~wplace**

An excellent tool for people who have trouble writing, *Writing Coach* is a set of worksheets, outlines, and techniques that help you write. It contains sixty worksheets designed to help you break down your writing task into "bite-sized" pieces and unlock your creativity, discover what you have to say, and express it effectively. Includes tools to help you with brainstorming, organizing, writing, overcoming writer's block, editing, and proofreading. Works within *Word*, *WordPerfect*, and *Claris*.

# **W**riting-related Internet sites

**As with our discussion** of on-line resources in chapter 2, what follows is the most current list of Web sites and Gopher addresses that relate to writing as of this book's publication date. For the updates to this list of Web sites, please go to the Write Your Way to a Higher GPA Web site at **http://www.stetson. edu/~hansen/gpa.html**.

We've categorized the Internet sites as follows:

On-line writing labs and centers on the Web
General writing and grammar resources on the Web
Subject-specific writing resources on the Web
Writing-related reference Web sites
Writing-related Gopher sites

For more information on searching the Internet and using the World Wide Web and Gopher resources, refer to chapter 2.

## ON-LINE WRITING LABS (OWLS) AND CENTERS ON THE WEB

As you can see, a number of writing labs are available on the Web—and this list is not all-inclusive; the writing labs listed here offer unique services or benefits to college writers. If your time is limited, however, visit the Purdue On-Line Writing Lab or the University of Missouri's On-Line Writery.

Bowling Green State University Writing Lab. Web address: **http://www.bgsu. edu/departments/writing-lab/Homepage.html**
Colgate University Writing Center. Web address: **http:www2.colgate.edu/diw/ center.html**
The Cyberspace Writing Center Consultation Project (a collaboration of Roane State Community College and the University of Arkansas at Little Rock). Web address: **http://fur.rscc.cc.tn.us/cyberproject.html**
Dakota State University Online Writing Lab. Web address: **http://www.dsu. edu/departments/liberal/owl/**
DeVry Online Writing Support Center. Web address: **http://www.devry-phx. edu/lrnresrc/dowsc/**

George Mason University Writing Center. Web address: **http://osf1.gmu.edu/ ~wcenter/**

Literacy Education Online (LEO): SCSU's Write Place. Web address: **http: //leo.stcloud.msus.edu/**

Michigan Technological University Writing Center. Web address: **http://www. hu.mtu.edu/wc/welcome.html**

The On-Line Writery. Web address: **http://www.missouri.edu/~wleric/ writery.html**

National Writing Centers Association: Links to Online Writing Labs and Centers. Web address: **http://www2.colgate.edu/diw/NWCAOWLS.html**

Oklahoma State University Writing Center. Web address: **http://opus.cislabs. okstate.edu**

Purdue On-Line Writing Lab Home Page. Web address: **http://owl.english. purdue.edu/**

Rensselaer Polytechnic Institute Writing Center. Web address: **http://www. rpi.edu/dept/llc/writecenter/web/home.html**

Syracuse University Writing Consultant Writing Program. Web address: **http://wrt.syr.edu/wrt/wc/wchomepage.html**

Trinity College Writing Center. Web address: **http://www.trincoll.edu/writcent/ aksmith.html**

University of Florida's Networked Writing Environment. Web address: **http: //www.ucet.ufl.edu/writing/nwe.html**

University of Maine Online Writing Center. Web address: **http://www.ume. maine.edu/~wcenter/others.html**

University of Michigan On-Line Writing Lab. Web address: **http://www.lsa. umich.edu/ecb/OWL/owl.html**

University of Missouri's Online Writery. Web address: **http://www.missouri. edu/~wleric/writery.html**

University of Richmond Writing Center and WAC Program. Web address: **http://www.urich.edu/~writing/**

University of Texas Undergraduate Writing Center. Web address: **http: //www.utexas.eduts/uwc/.html/main.html**

Virginia Tech's Online Writing Lab. Web address: **http://athena.english.vt.edu/ OW/_www/owl.html**

WORD: Writing Online Resource Directory. Web address: **http://darkwing. uoregon.edu/~jcross/word.html**

Writing Labs on the Net. Web address: **http://owl.english.purdue.edu/writing-labs.html**

Write Place Catalog. Web address: **http://leo.stcloud.msus.edu/catalogue.html**

Writing Resources & Labs on the Net. Web address: **http://owl.english.purdue.edu/resources.html**

## GENERAL WRITING AND GRAMMAR RESOURCES ON THE WEB

All the Web sites in this section are highly recommended for your use, but if we had to choose a few "must use" sites from the collection below, we would include Jack Lynch's Grammar and Style Notes, Hyper-Handouts from Texas A&M University, John Hewitt's Writer's Resource Center, The Research Paper, Inkspot's University Writing Resources, and the WritePlace.

Author, Author! Web address: **http://www.cloud9.net/~scharf/author.html**

The Bard's Notebook. Web address: **http://syndicate.com/Bard.html**

Basic Prose Style and Mechanics. Web address: **http://www.rpi.edu/dept/llc/writecenter/web/text/proseman.html**

BookWire. Web address: **http://www.bookwire.com**

Collected Advice on Research and Writing. Web address: **http://www.cs.cmu.edu/afs/cs.cmu.edu/user/mleone/web/how-to.html**

Cool Writing Resources. Web address: **http://www.mailboxes.com/~burrell/writing.html**

An Elementary Grammar. Web address: **http://www.hiway.co.uk/~ei/intro.html**

The Eleven Rules of Grammar. Web address: **http://ucsu.colorado.edu/~giaquint/grammar.html**

Essays and Articles for Writers. Web address: **http://www.inkspot.com/~ohi/inkspot/essays.html**

Essay Writing: Tips and Pitfalls. Web address: **http://shakti.trincoll.edu/~helton/syllabi/essayhlp.html**

Five Simple Ways to Make Your Writing Better. Web address: **http://www.wentworth.com/cyber/write.html**

Five Tools for Writing Timed Essays. Web address: **http://splavc.spjc.cc.fl.us/hooks/hooksessay.html**

Frequently Asked Questions about English. Web address: **http://snoopy.ling.lsa.umich.edu/jlawler/aue/**

Grammar and Style Guides for Writers. Web address: **http://www.inkspot.com/~ohi/inkspot/style.html**

Grammar and Style Notes. Web address: **http://www.english.upenn.edu/ ~jlynch/Grammar/**

Grammar Help Page. Web address: **http://www.hut.fi/~rvilmo/help/ grammar_help/**

Grammar Hotline Directory. Web address: **http://www.infinet/tcc/tcresourc/ hotline.html**

Hotlist: Composition & Writing. Web address: **http://sln.fi.edu/tfi/hotlists/ composition.html**

How to Write Good. Web address: **http://www.ccad.uiowa.edu/~sreinach/ WritGood.html**

Hyper-Handouts. Web address: **http://engserve.tamu.edu/files/writingcenter/ handouts.html**

Infinite Ink's Writing Page. Web address: **http://www.jazzie.com/ii/ writing.html**

Internet Resources for English Teachers and Students. Web address: **http: //www.umass.edu/english/resource.html**

Internet Resources for Writing, Research, and Documentation. Web address: **http://www.oac.uci.edu/faculty/strenki/internet.html**

John Hewitt's Writer's Resource Center. Web address: **http://www.azstarnet. com./~poewar/writer/writer.html**

Keith Ivey's English Usage Page. Web address: **http://206.2.192.66/~kcivey/ engusage/**

Library Research & Writing Tips. Web address: **http://www.chs.chico.k12.ca. us/libr/webres/ref.html**

On-Line English Grammar. Web address: **http://www.edunet.com/english/ grammar/**

Online Resources for Writers. Web address: **http://www.ume.maine.edu/ ~wcenter/resource.html**

On-Line Writing Guides and Labs. Web address: **http://bio444.beaumont. plattsburgh.edu/Students/Writing.html**

A Quick and Dirty Term Paper: The Twelve-Step Guide to Producing Literary Scholarship. Web address: **http://splavc.spjc.cc.fl.us/hooks/ hooksqd.html**

Reader's & Writer's Resource Page. Web address: **http://surf.rio.com/~drm/ webfeats/bookwriters.html**

References for Writing. Web address: **http://www.humberc.on.ca/~coleman/ cw-ref.html**

Rensselaer Writing Center Handouts. Web address: **http://www.rpi.edu/dept/ llc/writecenter/web/handouts.html**

The Research Paper. Web address: **http://www.wsu.edu:8080/~brians/general_ handouts_research_guide.html**

Resources for Writers and Writing Instructors. Web address: **http://dept. english.upenn.edu/~jlynch/writing.html**

Resources for Writers. Web address: **http://dept.english.upenn.edu/~wh/ resources/index.html**

Some General Advice on Academic Essay-Writing. Web address: **http://www. erin.utoronto.ca/academic/writing/essay.htm**

Standard Deviations of Writing. Web address: **http://www.greyware.com/ authors/Roger.Allen/mistakes.htm**

Tips for Writing Research Papers. Web address: **http://www.gmu.edu/gmu/ personal/paper.html**

Tips on Writing the Essay-Type Examination. Web address: **http://www. csbsju.edu/advising/help/essayexm.html**

Ultimate Book List and Writer's Page. Web address: **http://www.acpl.lib.in. us/information_resources/ultimate_book_list.html**

University of Texas Undergraduate Writer Center Handouts. Web address: **http://www.utexas.edu/depts/uwc/.html/handout.html**

University Writing Resources. Web address: **http://www.interlog.com/~ohi/ inkspot/university.html**

Vermont Portfolio Program Mini-Lesson in Writing. Web address: **http: //plainfield.bypass.com/~union/gum.html**

Way to Make Your Writing Better. Web address: **http://www.wentworth.com/ cyber/write.html**

The Word Detective. Web address: **http://www.users.interport.net/~wordsl/**

Wordmatters Virtual Writing Clinic. Web address: **http://www.negia.net/~cats/**

World Wide Web Resources for Rhetoric and Composition. Web address: **http://www.ind.net/internet/comp.html#handouts**

W.R.I.T.E. HomePage. Web address: **http://www.cstudies.ubc.ca/write/ write.html**

WritePlace. Web address: **http://www.rio.com/~wplace/**

Writers. Web address: **http://www.bocklabs.wisc.edu/ims/writers.html**

The Writer's Center. Web address: **http://www.writer.org/**

Writer's Depot. Web address: **http://members.aol.com/WritersD/index.html**

The Writer's Edge. Web address: **http://www.nashville.net/~edge**

The Writer's Resource. Web address: **http://www.cptcorp.com/**

Writer's Resources. Web address: **http://www.vmedia.com/shannon/writing.html**

Writers' Resources on the Web. Web address: **http://www.interlog.com/~ohi/ www/writesource.html**

Writer's (Stumbling) Block. Web address: **http://alf2.tcd.ie/~mmmchugh/ writer.html**

Writing Academic Essays and Mini-Dissertations. Web address: **http://www. aber.ac.uk/~ednwww/writess.html**

Writing an Essay. Web address: **http://josnet.jostens.com/kb/essay.html**

Writing Guidelines. Web address: **http://www.shss.montclair.edu/philrelg/ tomwrit2.html**

Writing Handouts by Subject. Web address: **http://www.english.purdue.edu/ by-topic-alternate.html**

Writing Project: Beyond the Theme. Web address: **http://cal.bemidji.msus. edu/English/Morgan/courses/EN220/Projects/BeyondTheme.html**

Writing a Research Report. Web address: **http://www.macarthur.uws.edu/au/ ssd/ldc/Research_report.html**

Writing Resources. Web address: **http://www.missouri.edu/~wleric/writehelp.html**

Writing Resources. Web address: **http://www.dfw.nte/~cnichols/writing/html**

Writing Tips. Web address: **http://www.trincoll.edu/writcent/writingtips.html**

Writer's Web. Web address: **http://www.urich.edu/~writing/wweb.html**

WWW Resources for Writing. Web address: **http://www.humberc.on.ca/ ~coleman/cw-res.html**

## SUBJECT-SPECIFIC WRITING RESOURCES ON THE WEB

### 1.   Literature Web sites

English and Humanities Sites. Web address: **http://odin.english.udel.edu/ humanities/humanities.html**

Literature Related Links. Web address: **http://elwing.ostago.ac.nz:889/dsouth/ links.html**

Literature Resources Page. Web address: **http://cal.bemidji.msus.edu/English/ Resources/Lit.html**

Tips on Analyzing and Interpreting Literature. Web address: **http://www. nhmccd.cc.tx.us/~ljc/lit/ritetips.html**

The Zuzu's Petals Literary Resource. Web address: **http://www.lehigh.net/ zuzu/index.htm**

## 2.  Business writing Web sites

Business Writing. Web address: **http://www.interlog.com/~ohi/www/biz.html**

Writing Standards (for Business Students). Web address: **http://www.bus.orst. edu/tools/writing.htm**

## 3.  Creative writing Web sites

Electronic Poetry Center. Web address: **http://wings.buffalo.edu/epc/**

Essays on the Craft of Dramatic Writing. Web address: **http://www.teleport. co.uk/~ei/intro.html**

Journal and Essay Writing. Web address: **http://www.azstarnet.com/~poewar/ writer/pg/essay.html**

The Journal Writer. Web address: **http://www.rio.com/~wplace/journal.html**

The Playwrights Project. Web address: **http://www.vnet.net/users/phisto/**

Poetry Portals for the World Wide Web. Web address: **http://www.infi.net/tcc/ tcresourc/faculty/dreiss/pomweb.html**

Poetry Writing Tips. Web address: **http://www.azstarnet.com/~poewar/writer/ Poet's_Notes.html**

Poets & Writers. Web address: **http://www.pw.org/**

Screenwriters and Playwrights Home Page. Web address: **http://elaine. teleport.com/~cdeemer/scrwriter.html**

Screenwriters Online. Web address: **http://screenwriter.com/insider/**

Script Tutor. Web address: **http://scripttutor.com/**

Ultimate Poetry Links. Web address: **http://www.kiosk.net/poetry/links.html**

## 4. Science/technical writing Web sites

Internet Technical Writing Course Guide: Contents. Web address: **http: //uu-gna.mit.edu:8001/uu-gna/text/wamt/acchtml/acctoc.html**

Science Writing Aids. Web address: **http://www.indiana.edu/~cheminfo/ ca_swa.html**

Technical Writing: Books and Reference Sources. Web address: **http://www.io. org/~ksoltys/twritres.html**

Technical Writing: Books and Resources. Web address: **http://rhetoric.agoff/ umn/edu/Rhetoric/misc/keithbook.html**

Writing the Formal Report. Web address: **http://library-www-scar.utoronto.ca/ Subject/Physical_Sciences/AA05.html**

## 5. Journalism and public relations writing Web sites

Columbia Journalism Review Home Page. Web address: **http://www.cjr.org/**

## 6. Other Writing Web Sites

Eye to I: Writing the Personal Essay. Web address: **http://www.nando.net/prof/ poynter/wrtper.html**

A Guide to Writing Philosophy Essays. Web address: **http://snaefell.tamu.edu/ ~colin/writing.html**

Online Medical Reference System. Web address: **http://www.kumc.edu/service/ dykes/refassist/oldhome.html**

Speech Writing Resources. Web address: **http://speeches.com/index.shtml**

Ultimate Book List and Writer's Page. Web address: **http://www.acpl.lib.in.us/ information_resources/ultimate_book_list.html**

The Writing Workshop. Web address: **http://www.writingshop.com/**

### WRITING REFERENCE SITES ON THE WEB

APA Publication Manual Crib Sheet: Contains some of the more commonly used rules and reference formats, but is not meant as a substitute for the 368-page *Publication Manual of the American Psychological Association* (4th ed., 1994). Web address: **http://www. gasou.ed/pscy-web/tipsheet/apacrib.htm**

APA Style of Citation: Offers numerous categories of bibliographic material, with good examples. Web address: **http://www.uvm.edu/~xli/reference/ apa.html**

Citing Electronic Materials with New MLA Guidelines: Provides information about citing electronic references in MLA format. Web address: **http://www-dept.usm.edu/~engdept/mla/rules.html**

Electronic Resources. Web address: **http://www-lib.iupui.edu/erefs/erefs.html**

Guide for Citing Electronic Information: Supplies some good general rules and basic formats of referencing, with examples. Web address: **http: //www.wilpaterson.edu/wpcpages/library/citing.htm**

The Human-Languages Page. Web address: **http://www.williamette.edu/ ~tjones/Language-Page.html**

List of Dictionaries. Web address: **http://math-www.uni.paderborn.de/html/ dictionaries.html**

Mind Mapping FAQ. Web address: **http://world.std.com/~emagic/mindmap.html**

MLA Style of Citation: Provides numerous categories of bibliographic material, with good examples. Web address: **http://www.uvm.edu/~xli/reference/mla.html**

NBNSOFT: Your Net Encyclopedia. Web address: **http://www.tricky.com/liz.html**

Research and Writing Guides: Maintains a bibliography of style guides in print. Web address: **http://weber.u.washington.edu/~krumme/readings/res+writ.html**

Quotations Page. Web address: **http://www.starlingtech.com/quotes**

Quotation Resources. Web address: **http://www.xmission.com/~mgm/quotes**

Reference and Interdisciplinary Information. Web address: **http://www.einet.net/galaxy/Reference-and-Interdisciplinary-Information.html**

Reference Page. Web address: **http://www.arts.cuhk.hk.Ref.html#dt**

Research Institute for Humanities. Web address: **http://www.arts.cuhk.hk/Ref.html#dt**

Research Links for Writers. Web address: **http://www.siu.edu/departments/cola/english/seraph9k/research.html**

Resources for Poets. Web address: **http://www.inkspot.com/~ohi/www/poetry.html**

Rhyming Dictionary. Web address: **http://www.cs.cmu.edu/~doughb/rhyme.html**

Strunk's Elements of Style. Web address: **http://www.cc.columbia.edu/acis/bartleby/strunk/**

University of Texas Undergraduate Writing Center Listing of Dictionaries and Thesauruses. Web address: **http://www.utexas.edu/depts/uwc/.html/dictionary.html**

Webster's Dictionary. Web address: **http://hpdce.stanford.edu/webster.html**

## GOPHER RESOURCES

Bowling Green State University's Online Writing Lab. Gopher address: **gopher.bgsu.edu:70/11/Departments/Write**

Lawrence University Writing Lab. Gopher address: **gopher.lawrence.edu/11gopher_root:{_campus._collegeplace}**

Temple University OWL. Gopher address: **astro.ocis.temple.edu:70/11/writing_ctr**

University of Delaware Writing Center. Gopher address: **gopher.udel.edu:70/ 11/.dept/wctr**

University of Georgia Writing Center. Gopher address: **parallel.park.uga.edu: 70/11/The%20Writing%20Center**

University of Oregon American English Dictionary. Gopher address: **gopher. uoregon.edu/77/Reference/.index/enquire.english**

University of Toledo Writing Center. Gopher address: **gopher.utoledo.edu: 70/11GOPHER_ROOT%#$%5B_CAMPUS-INFO.DEPARTMENTS-AND-DIVISIONS. uts-writing-center%5D**

University of Wisconsin Writing Lab. Gopher address: **gopher.adp.wise.edu: 70/11/.acad/.writing-lab**

# Index

For the most updated information on Internet resources for college writing and researching, visit the *Write Your Way to a Higher GPA Web* site at **http://www.stetson.edu/~hansen/gpa.html.**

The authors are always happy to talk with students about writing. Write to them as follows:

Randall and Katharine Hansen
1250 Valley View Lane
DeLand, FL 32720
**Khansen@tophat.stetson.edu**
**Rhansen@tophat.stetson.edu**